Grokking the
GIMP

by
Carey Bunks

New
Riders

201 West 103rd Street, Indianapolis, Indiana 46290

GROKKING THE GIMP

Copyright © 2000 by New Riders Publishing

International Standard Book Number: 0-7357-0924-6

Library of Congress Catalog Card Number: 99-067432

Printed in the United States of America

First Printing: February, 2000

03   02   01   00   7   6   5   4   3   2   1

Interpretation of the printing code: The rightmost double-digit number is the year of the book's printing; the rightmost single-digit number is the number of the book's printing. For example, the printing code 00-1 shows that the first printing of the book occurred in 2000.

TRADEMARKS

WARNING AND DISCLAIMER

Publisher
David Dwyer

Executive Editor
Laurie Petrycki

Product Marketing Manager
Stephanie Layton

Managing Editor
Sarah Kearns

Development Editor
Jim Chalex

Project Editor
Caroline Wise

Copy Editors
Kelli Brooks
Gayle Johnson

Technical Reviewers
Zach Beane
Guillermo Romero

Indexer
Cheryl Lenser

Proofreader
Debra Neel

Formatter
Daryl Kessler

Compositor
Wil Cruz

Cover Art
Tuomas Kuosmanen

Cover Designer
Aren Howell

Interior Designer
Louisa Klucznik

Dédié à mon amie, mon amour, ma femme Homaira.

TABLE OF CONTENTS

PREFACE

The title of this book, *Grokking the GIMP*, is drawn from Robert A. Heinlein's classic science-fiction novel *Stranger in a Strange Land*. His story is about Valentine Michael Smith, the only survivor of the first human expedition to Mars, raised from infancy by Martians. The rescue mission arrives twenty years later to bring a young man knowing nothing of his own kind back to earth. The story recounts his repatriation and his adventures as he comes to *grok* the human race and his place in it. Grok, a word he often uses, is the Martian word meaning "to drink," but which also serves as a quasi-religious metaphor in the Martian culture for having a profound appreciation and understanding for something.

Heinlein's book, published in 1961, drew immediate acclaim in the science-fiction world, and the story became a part of the iconoclastic cultural sentiment of the 60s in the United States. Today, the word grok is a part of the U.S. computer hacker vocabulary, and its definition can be found in *The New Hacker's Dictionary*.[1]

So, do you want to grok the GIMP? When I first came across it in 1996, I did. I was writing an article and had some photographs of poor quality I wanted to touch up and enhance before including them. I had heard about the GIMP, so I downloaded it from the Internet and compiled it. When I ran the program, it popped up a small toolbox. Without too much trouble, I discovered how to open image files and access the image menu containing all the GIMP functions and filters. Wow! It looked very cool…*and powerful!* But, I didn't have a clue how to use it to solve my photo problems.

I didn't know which functions to use and I didn't even really know what was wrong with my photos. I just knew they looked flat and washed out. I wanted them to look better, and that's what got me interested in the GIMP. I felt compelled to learn about it!

I started to look for help. I searched the Web, checked out books from the library, and little by little discovered useful things about the digital touchup and enhancement of photos. It was a slow and frustrating process, and it seemed like there was no unified, conceptual treatment of what I wanted to learn.

The most annoying thing was that almost every book I picked up was full of tips and tricks. Tips and tricks? I felt like I was getting advice on betting the ponies. I didn't want tricks; I wanted the ideas. What *is* photo touchup and enhancement? Where's the beef? How could I work on my photos if I didn't understand the basic concepts? Moreover, I wanted to learn the practical techniques used by the master artisans of digital image manipulation. Out of the hundreds of functions and filters in the GIMP, which were the right ones to use, and why?

After a lot of detective work and filling in the blanks myself, I finally felt I was beginning to grok what the touchup and enhancement of digital images was about. What's more, I was getting to know the GIMP tools more intimately. To share what I had learned, I wrote a tutorial called *Photo Touchup and Enhancement with the GIMP* and put it out on the Internet (see http://www.geocities.com/SiliconValley/Haven/5179).

That's the story of this book's beginnings and that explains the rationale for its underlying approach and philosophy. Working with digital images requires some understanding of what needs to be done. It's not a "choose the right tool, one click, and you're done" subject. Most books on digital image manipulation would have you believe the contrary…and perhaps they're right. However, that is not what this book is about. It is not about tips and tricks, and it's not a collection of recipes for solving someone's favorite image manipulation problems. It is first about understanding image manipulation concepts, second about knowing which GIMP tools are most effective, and third about the savvy use of these tools.

Many factors have contributed to the style and content of the material presented in this book: my educational training in signal processing, my professional work in various areas of imaging and image processing, the research I've done on colorspaces and image manipulation, and lots of experimentation with the GIMP. The result is a book that covers many areas of working with digital images, including touchup and enhancement, compositing, 3D rendering, and the presentation of graphics on the World Wide Web. This book also gives a unified and in-depth introduction to layers, selections, masks, colorspaces, and the use of blending modes.

Now, let's learn the GIMP, and, as Valentine Michael Smith might have said, "May you grok it in fullness!"

Carey Bunks
Senior Scientist
BBN Technologies
Cambridge, Massachusetts
October 26, 1999

ABOUT THE AUTHOR

Carey Bunks is a Senior Scientist at BBN Technologies in Cambridge, Massachusetts, where he currently works on a variety of research projects in underwater sonar, active noise and vibration control, and network security. He received a PhD in Electrical Engineering from the Massachusetts Institute of Technology in 1987, and has since specialized in the area of signal processing. Carey has worked on problems of seismic imaging, image artifact filtering, and motion estimation from image data. He has over twenty publications in scientific journals and holds several patents.

Carey is also a member of the development group for Scilab, an open-source scientific and engineering computation package. He developed the Scilab signal processing toolbox and is co-author of the book *Scientific and Engineering Computing with Scilab,* published with Birkhäuser in 1999.

In addition, Carey is a serious student of circus and vaudeville arts. He attended the Ringling Bros. & Barnum and Bailey Clown College in Venice, Florida, graduating in 1977. An accomplished magician and juggler, he has entertained hundreds of groups in the U.S. and Europe with his street-theater style show. He is an authority on trick roping and is the author of the online book entitled *The Lasso — A Rational Guide to Trick Roping*.

Carey and his wife, Homaira, live in Boston, Massachusetts. They enjoy sailing, skiing, and traveling in Europe.

Photo courtesy of Dan McCarthy.

ACKNOWLEDGMENTS

The GIMP began in the summer of 1995 as an enormously ambitious project of two undergraduates at the University of California, Berkeley. When they began, they probably didn't realize just how impossible it was, and yet they made it work. They created a beta version that captured the imagination of the open-source movement. Spencer Kimball and Peter Mattis were those students, and I would like to thank them as much for the creative inspiration they received as for that they created in others. This book, of course, would have never existed without them.

Spencer Kimball

Peter Mattis

The seed of inspiration planted by Peter and Spencer attracted a talented group of core developers who have grown the GIMP into the powerful digital image manipulation tool that it is today. They are a loose-knit collection of men and women from around the globe, connected only by the thin wires of cyberspace. Most of them have never met face to face, and nevertheless, they have collaborated and cooperated on a project of significant complexity and great value. What an amazing phenomenon the GIMP project is! I would like to thank each one of them. Their names, as of version 1.1.15 of the GIMP, are Lauri Alanko, Shawn Amundson, John Beale, Zach Beane, Tom Bech, Marc Bless, Edward Blevins, Roberto Boyd, Stanislav Brabec, Simon Budig, Seth Burgess, Brent Burton, Francisco Bustamante, Kenneth Christiansen, Ed Connel, Jay Cox, Andreas Dilger, Austin Donnelly, Scott Draves, Misha Dynin, Daniel Egger, Larry Ewing, Nick Fetchak, Valek Filippov, David Forsyth, Jim Geuther, Scott Goehring, Heiko Goller, Michael Hammel, Ville Häutamaki, James Henstridge, Christoph Hoegl, Wolfgang Hofer, Jan Hubicka, Simon Janes, Tim Janik, Peter Kirchgessner, Tuomas Kuosmanen, Karin Kylander, Olof S. Kylander, Chris Lahey, Nick Lamb, Karl LaRocca, Jens Lautenbacher, Laramie Leavitt, Elliot Lee, Marc Lehmann, Wing Tung Leung, Raph Levien, Adrian Likins, Tor Lillqvist, Ingo Luetkebohle, Josh MacDonald, Ed Mackey, Vidar Madsen, Marcelo Malheiros, Ian Main, Kjartan Maraas, Kelly Martin, Torsten Martinsen, Daniele Medri, Federico Mena, David Monniaux, Adam D. Moss, Sung-Hyun Nam, Balazs Nagy, Shuji Narazaki, Michael Natterer, Sven Neumann, Stephen Robert Norris, Erik Nygren, Tomas Ögren, Miles O'Neal, Jay Painter, Asbjorn Pettersen, Mike Phillips, Raphael Quinet, Vincent Renardias, James Robinson, Mike Schaeffer, Tracy Scott, Aaron Sherman, Manish Singh, Nathan Summers, Mike Sweet, Eiichi Takamori, Tristan Tarrant, Owen Taylor, Ian Tester, Andy Thomas, James Wang, Kris Wehner, Matthew Wilson, and Shirasaki Yasuhiro.

Of all those in the GIMP developers group, I would like to express an especially warm note of thanks to Karin and Olof Kylander. They are the authors of *The GIMP User Manual*, the first complete reference to the GIMP.[2,3] I personally found it to be invaluable in the drafting of my own book.

I would also like to thank the famous **tigert**, a.k.a. Tuomas Kuosmanen, GIMP developer and GIMP artist. He graciously accepted to create this book's cover art.

Editorially, there are many individuals that have directly helped me in the preparation of this book. I'd like to start by thanking Laurie Petrycki, executive editor at New Riders Publishing. Laurie is a genuine supporter of the open-source software community, and she has done a lot to change the editorial work flow at New Riders to accommodate authors, like me, using open-source tools. She was enthusiastic, open to ideas, and willing to change many boiler-plate business and design practices to make my book better. I would highly recommend her to anyone wanting to write an open-source software book.

I'd also like to thank Jim Chalex, my development editor. He encouraged me, gave good advice on improving this book's structure and content, displayed an uncommon mastery of the comma, and came up with a great book title. My hat's off to you, Jim!

The technical reviewers, Guillermo Romero and Zach Beane, deserve a lot of credit. They both read through a difficult first draft and, nevertheless, prepared excellent technical reviews making many useful comments and suggestions.

tigert

Laurie Petrycki

Jim Chalex

Zach Beane

Guillermo Romero

Louisa Klucznik

Aren Howell

Kelli Brooks

Caroline Wise

Gayle Johnson

I also greatly enjoyed interacting with both Louisa Klucznik and Aren Howell, responsible for the book's design. They taught me a lot about paper, spot glosses, type styles, and page layouts. My heartfelt thanks also go to Kelli Brooks and Gayle Johnson, who did a great job of copy editing. Finally, I'd like to thank the project editor, Caroline Wise, who smoothly orchestrated the entire editorial, layout, and printing process.

In addition to the list of individuals who have had an important influence on this book, there are also several organizations that merit acknowledgement here. The concepts and techniques presented in this book are greatly enhanced by a large collection of raw, digital-image materials used to illustrate them. The source for most of these images is from several United States governmental agency Web sites that generously allow their online photographic archives to be used without copyright assertion. These include the sites of the National Aeronautics and Space Administration (NASA), the National Oceanic and Atmospheric Administration (NOAA), and the U.S. Fish and Wildlife Service (FWS). These agencies provide a wonderful resource to the world, and I salute them. Many thanks to all, and Happy GIMPing!

TELL US WHAT YOU THINK!

As the reader of this book, *you* are our most important critic and commentator. We value your opinion and want to know what we're doing right, what we could do better, what areas you'd like to see us publish in, and any other words of wisdom you're willing to pass our way.

As the Executive Editor for the Linux team at New Riders Publishing, I welcome your comments. You can fax, email, or write me directly to let me know what you did or didn't like about this book—as well as what we can do to make our books stronger.

Please note that I cannot help you with technical problems related to the topic of this book, and that due to the high volume of mail I receive, I might not be able to reply to every message.

When you write, please be sure to include this book's title, author, and ISBN number, as well as your name and phone or fax number. I will carefully review your comments and share them with the author and editors who worked on the book.

Fax: 317-581-4663

Email: nrfeedback@newriders.com

Mail: Laurie Petrycki
          Executive Editor
          Linux/Open Source
          New Riders Publishing
          201 West 103rd Street
          Indianapolis, IN 46290 USA

README

The open-source software movement is like Lewis Carroll's *Alice in Wonderland*. It's a topsy-turvy world where up is down, down is up, and the normal laws of the universe no longer apply. Free software that's as powerful and useful as commercial software? Yes! It seems incredible, ludicrous, even outrageous...but it's absolutely true. The Internet could not operate without Bind, Sendmail, or Perl—all open-source, free software. Linux, a free and open-source operating system, is making powerful contributions to science, engineering, and business. And Apache, which has a dominant share of the Web server market, is also a free and open-source software package. There seems to be a mad rush from contributors around the globe to create the most useful, open, and free software, and one of the most remarkable examples of this phenomenon is the *GNU Image Manipulation Program*, a.k.a the GIMP.

In Lewis Carroll's story, objects marked "READ ME," "EAT ME," and "DRINK ME" were key to helping Alice during her adventures in Wonderland. As anyone who has installed open-source software knows, there is always a file in the top-level directory named README that serves exactly the same purpose. In the same spirit, this section, entitled README, provides a road map to this book and instructions on how to set up your computer to get the most out of the GIMP.

Welcome to Wonderland, and happy GIMPing!

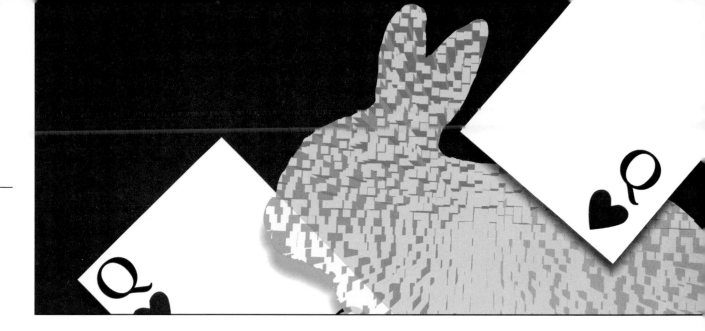

Book Overview

The first part of this book focuses on mastering core tools: layers, selections, masks, and colorspaces. The second part builds on the first by presenting an in-depth treatment of touchup, enhancement, compositing, rendering, and image creation for the Web. The following gives a synopsis of what you will find in each chapter.

Chapter 1 reviews the GIMP basics. It introduces the GIMP dialogs, reviews window features, and explains a host of functions that are basic but should not be taken for granted. An experienced GIMP user could quickly flip through this chapter of the book, especially if he or she is already familiar with the main features of version 1.2.

Chapter 2 covers layers. Layers are the fundamental building blocks of the GIMP. They are the image unit that plays the most important role in our work, and it is important to understand them and the functions that manipulate them. Even if you are already familiar with layers, this chapter will be worth reviewing because it contains many insights into how to use layers efficiently and effectively.

Chapters 3 and 4 give a unified and in-depth presentation of selections and masks. To the casual observer, selections and masks may seem like very different animals. However, they are really complementary implementations of the same thing. The goal of both is to isolate a part of an image. Selections do this by selecting a group of pixels in the image, and masks do it by masking some pixels, leaving the rest exposed. Thus, selections are masks, and masks are selections. These two chapters explain how selections and masks can be made to work efficiently and effectively together.

Because selections are often the most time-consuming part of any project, Chapter 3 compares the different selection tools and describes the applications for which each is best suited. Chapter 4 makes the conceptual link from selections to masks. This chapter describes a host of advanced mask techniques, including methods for refining selection edges and a super technique for finding natural masks you won't want to miss.

Chapter 5 adds the final component of our basic skill set by describing colorspaces and the tools used to get results with color. The first half of this chapter is conceptual, covering RGB and HSV colorspaces. The second half covers the GIMP's blending modes. These are often poorly understood and underutilized by beginning users. As will be seen in later chapters, the blending modes are valuable tools, without which many needed operations would be quite impossible. The material covered in this chapter is critical for color correction, compositing, rendering, and Web graphics…the entire second half of the book! The chapter's intuitive approach explains the aspects of color theory you'll need for your GIMP projects.

Chapter 6 presents techniques for photo touchup and enhancement. The main feature of this chapter is the use of `Curves`, a poorly understood but amazingly powerful tool. I think that the material covered in this chapter alone is worth the price of the book. In addition to the use of `Curves`, this chapter also covers the use of the `Clone` tool for the elimination of blemishes and the use of a sharpening filter, oddly named `Unsharp Mask`.

One of the most interesting, fun, and useful uses of the GIMP is compositing. Compositing is collage, photo montage, and all the techniques that go with these. Compositing is probably the premiere use of an image manipulation program such as the GIMP, and Chapter 7 covers this topic in detail. This chapter more than any other depends on using the methods and techniques presented in the earlier chapters and is strongly oriented around project work. The projects show how to effectively use selections, masks, and color correction techniques, among other tools, to achieve terrific compositing results.

Chapter 8 describes the tools and techniques for creating shadows, punchouts, and bevels. In addition, it gives an in-depth description of the `Emboss` and `Bump map` filters. These are powerful tools for creating 3D effects in images.

Chapter 9 is the final chapter of this book. It covers some of the most useful features in the GIMP for Internet Web applications. This chapter describes tools for creating animated GIFs and clickable image maps. It also covers several other topics that are required reading for anyone creating graphics for the Web.

MOUSE CLICKS

In this book *clicking*, *double-clicking*, and *clicking and dragging* refer to operations with the left mouse button. The terms *Shift-clicking*, *Control-clicking*, and *Alt-clicking* refer to the operations of clicking the left mouse button while also pressing the Shift, Control, or Alt key. When the right mouse button is used, the operation is referred to as *right-clicking*, and with the middle mouse button it is referred to as *middle-clicking*.

FUNCTION NAMES, MENUS, AND KEYBOARD SHORTCUTS

This book uses several conventions for describing keystrokes and for indicating the locations of menu items in the GIMP. This section describes these.

Figure 1(a) illustrates an image of a friendly looking fellow who is going to introduce us to the GIMP's Image menu. As described in the figure, the Image menu is obtained by either right-clicking in the image window or by clicking on the arrow icon in the window's upper-left corner. Either will display the Image menu, as shown in Figure 1(b).

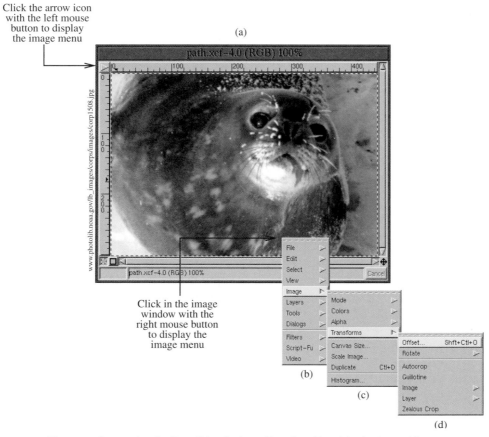

Figure 1: Convention for Describing Paths to Functions Found in the Image Menu

A menu item highlights when the mouse cursor is moved over it. When an entry in the Image menu has an arrow pointing to the right, this indicates that it is the title of a submenu. For example, moving the mouse cursor to the entry labeled `Image`, brings up the associated submenu, as shown in Figure 1(c). Moving the mouse cursor over the submenu entry labeled `Transforms` displays the subsubmenu, as shown in Figure 1(d). Finally, menu entries that do not have right-pointing arrows are functions that can be run by clicking on them. The `Offset` function is shown highlighted in Figure 1(d).

In order to compactly and efficiently describe where a function is located in a system of menus and submenus, the following notation is adopted for this book. For the example shown in Figure 1, the menu path to the function is denoted `Image:Image/Transforms/Offset`. This indicates that the `Offset` function is found in the `Colors` menu, which is in the `Image` menu, obtained by right-clicking in the `Image` window. The use of the typewriter typeface indicates that the text represents a GIMP function or tool.

Note that for certain menu entries in Figures 1(c) and (d), a keyboard shortcut is indicated. Learning these significantly accelerates access to GIMP functions. In the GIMP menus, the keyboard shortcuts are denoted by capital letters, perhaps with one or more modifier keys. In the menus the modifiers are indicated by `Ctl`, `Shft`, or `Alt`, which refer to the Control, Shift, and Alt keys on your keyboard. Thus, the keyboard shortcut for the `Offset` function, as shown in Figure 1(d), is `Shft+Ctl+o`. This is applied by moving the mouse cursor into the image window, simultaneously pressing the Shift and Control keys, and typing o. Note that although the key sequence is indicated with an uppercase `O`, the actual key required is lowercase, unless, of course, the Shift modifier is specifically indicated. Keyboard shortcut notation used in this book is slightly different from that seen in the GIMP menus. The Control, Shift, and Alt keys are denoted by uppercase `C`, `S`, and `A`. These modifier keys are followed by a dash and the keystroke in lowercase. Thus, the notation used in this book for applying the `Offset` function is `C-S-o`. As another example, the notation `C-S-l` indicates that the Control and Shift keys are pressed simultaneously, followed by typing the letter `l`. This corresponds to the `Float` function found in the `Image:Select` menu (but not shown in Figure 1).

Appendix B lists all the default keyboard shortcuts. It also describes how to customize the shortcuts to your personal tastes.

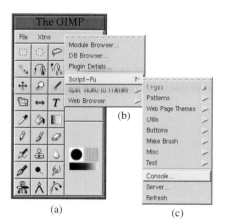

(a)   (b)   (c)

Figure 2: Conventions for Describing Paths for Functions Found in the Toolbox

The convention just described for specifying the menu location of a function is also used for items found in the Toolbox window. Figure 2(a) shows the Toolbox window, which contains the two menus File and Xtns, seen at the top of the window. Here the reference Toolbox:Xtns/Script-Fu/Console is the path to the submenu Script-Fu, shown in Figure 2(b), and then to the function named Console, as shown in Figure 2(c).

In this book, the functions represented by the icons in the Toolbox are referred to by name. Figure 3 illustrates an exploded view of the Toolbox, giving the name used for each icon.

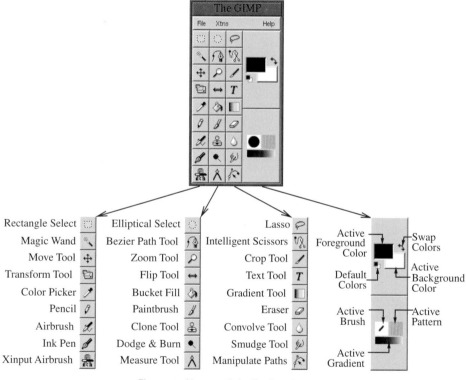

Figure 3: Names of the Toolbox Icons

Setting Up Your Computer to Get the Most from the GIMP

This section describes how to optimize the hardware and software configuration of your computer to optimize the performance of the GIMP.

Notes on RAM

The GIMP executable is about 7MB; however, depending on the size of the GIMP data directories (patterns, palettes, brushes, and so on), the memory footprint can grow another 2–10MB. In addition, the script-fu program that runs concurrently with the GIMP occupies about 2.5MB. Thus, the GIMP requires a minimum of about 11.5–19.5MB of RAM.

This is not all, though, because every image loaded into the GIMP also requires memory. For example, loading an RGB format image will require at least three times the number of pixels in the image (one byte per RGB channel and perhaps a byte for the alpha channel) per layer. Thus, an image with dimensions 640×480 pixels containing three equal-sized layers requires from 2.8 to 3.7MB of memory.

In addition to the memory required to display the image, there is also the memory required for the undo cache. This is what allows the GIMP to undo operations to an image being worked on.

The conclusion is that to work comfortably in the GIMP—to be able to open images, composite, touchup, and apply filters—32MB of memory should be considered a minimum. Of course, the RAM required will be proportionally more for large images containing multiple layers.

Notes on Video RAM

The ability to display large images on a video monitor depends on the amount of video RAM available on the video card. For example, if the display resolution is 1024×768 with only 8 bits (1 byte) of color per pixel, the minimum required amount of video RAM is 0.79MB. However, working with only 8 bits per pixel is paltry, because it only allows for 256 simultaneous colors on the screen at one time.

Increasing the color depth to 16 bits (2 bytes) at a resolution of 1024×768 doubles the required video RAM to 1.57MB. This is really the minimum video RAM required to get reasonable performance from the GIMP, and a higher-performance system might have a resolution of 1600×1200 with 24 bits (3 bytes) of color per pixel, requiring at least 5.76MB of video RAM.

Notes on Swap and GIMP Memory Management

The GIMP uses memory as specified by the `Toolbox:File/Preferences` dialog. Figure 4 shows the Environment Settings branch of the `Preferences` dialog.

As seen in the figure, the associated entry box for the tile cache size has the default value of 10MB. The cache is a piece of RAM that the GIMP reserves for caching the images you are working on. If you are working with large images or with many medium-sized ones, you can easily exceed this cache size. Under these circumstances, the additional required memory is obtained by creating a GIMP swap file in the user's .gimp directory. Since this memory is not necessarily located in RAM, this can significantly diminish the performance of the GIMP. Thus, if the user has good RAM resources and is working with large images, it makes sense to increase the 10MB value of the cache.

For example, with 128MB of RAM and with the GIMP running as the primary application, perhaps a reasonable size for the cache is 50 to 75MB. This number can be tuned to the user's needs. A useful tool for determining how much memory is required by your applications is the Linux/UNIX command top. This command dynamically shows many of the characteristics of running processes on your machine. In particular, the column %MEM gives the percentage memory used by each process. Typing s-m (i.e., an uppercase M) makes top display the processes sorted by memory use. The following is a truncated output from top on my Linux machine after sorting by memory use:

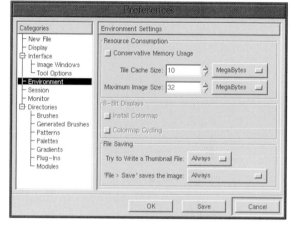

Figure 4: Specifying GIMP Memory Usage

```
11:51am  up  2:31,   2 users,   load average: 0.00, 0.02, 0.05
63 processes: 62 sleeping, 1 running, 0 zombie, 0 stopped
CPU states:  1.3% user,  0.9% system,  0.0% nice, 97.6% idle
Mem:  128012K av, 124096K used,   3916K free,  31492K shrd,   21908K buff
Swap: 136040K av,   2612K used, 133428K free                 47028K cached

  PID USER     PRI  NI  SIZE  RSS SHARE STAT  LIB %CPU %MEM   TIME COMMAND
 6253 cbunks     0   0 14888  14M  2908 S       0  0.0 11.6   0:01 gimp
  653 root      14   0 14324  13M  1304 S       0  1.1 11.1   4:50 X
  679 cbunks     0   0 13172  12M  4024 S       0  0.0 10.2   0:17 netscape
  663 cbunks     3   0  5236 5236  2088 S       0  0.0  4.0   0:05 emacs
 6234 cbunks     0   0  5072 5072  1784 S       0  0.0  3.9   0:00 knews
 6269 cbunks     0   0  3252 3252  1964 S       0  0.0  2.5   0:00 xfig
 6254 cbunks     0   0  2360 2360   928 S       0  0.0  1.8   0:00 script-fu
  555 xfs        0   0  2280 2280   244 S       0  0.0  1.7   0:00 xfs
  673 cbunks     0   0  1532 1532   976 S       0  0.0  1.1   6:14 Xquote
  607 news       0   0  1216 1216    76 S       0  0.0  0.9   0:00 innd
  662 cbunks     3   0  1088 1088   676 S       0  0.3  0.8   0:00 xterm
 6287 cbunks    16   0  1056 1056   848 R       0  0.7  0.8   0:01 top
```

As can be seen from the display, there is 128MB of RAM, of which GIMP is occupying 11.6%. In conjunction with the other processes, including X,

Netscape, and Emacs, about 50% of the RAM is being used. The remaining 50% equals 64MB of RAM. Thus, for my machine, it might be reasonable to set the GIMP cache to 50MB. Of course, your mileage will vary.

LOADING FONTS

The `Text` tool in the GIMP requires fonts served up by the X Window System. Unfortunately, not every X Window System is delivered with all the cool fonts you'll want to have. It is possible, though, to download a nice set of fonts from the Internet and to install them on your system. This section describes how to do that. Note that although the advice given here will work on many Linux and UNIX systems, it is not guaranteed to work on all of them. The goal of this section is to be helpful, but due to the variability of different systems, it would be impossible to cover all cases.

There are two widely used font collections for computers running the X Window System. These collections are called `freefonts` and `sharefonts`. They can be found at many places around the Web, but two places you might try are

```
ftp://ftp.gimp.org/pub/gimp/fonts/

ftp://metalab.unc.edu/pub/linux/X11/fonts/
```

The files to download will be named something like `freefonts-0.10.tar.gz` and `sharefonts-0.10.tar.gz`. The names may change to reflect updated version numbers.

Once downloaded, they must be installed in a font directory. For RedHat Linux systems, fonts are typically installed in `/usr/X11R6/lib/X11/fonts/`. However, this may be different for other systems running the X Window System. It is not necessary to install the fonts in the system directory. They can be installed anywhere that is convenient—even in the user's home directory. This last option may be necessary for a user who wants to use great fonts but doesn't have root privilege.

The following instructions assume that the installation is being made to the user's directory called `~/FONTS`. After downloading the two font packages and moving them to this directory, the instructions for installing the `freefonts` package are as follows:

```
% cd ~/FONTS
% gzip -dc freefonts-0.10.tar.gz | tar xvf -
```

This uncompresses and unpacks the font collection archive. This is followed by the commands that tell the X Window System where the new fonts live:

```
% xset fp+ ~/FONTS/freefont
% xset fp rehash
```

Follow the same instructions to install the `sharefonts` package and that's all there is to it! The `freefonts` package contains 79 fonts and the `sharefonts` package 22. The next time the GIMP is run, these new fonts will be available to the `Text` tool.

If these fonts were not pre-installed in the usual system directory, you'll need to tell the X Window System where to find them each time you start up a new X session. This can be automated by putting the last two commands above in your `.xinitrc` file.

SETTING THE X WINDOW SYSTEM TO RUN MORE THAN 8 BPP

Using the GIMP is greatly enhanced by having a display with sufficient color depth to display subtle color variations. A display with only 8 bits per pixel (bpp) can represent only 256 colors simultaneously, which is insufficient for many photographs. The result, as explained in Section 9.5.1, is a type of color distortion called dithering.

If your video adapter has sufficient RAM, it is possible to display at 16 or 24 bits per pixel, which will greatly enhance your viewing pleasure and your ability to work effectively with color. For example, to run at 16 bits per pixel at a 1024×768 screen resolution, you'll need about 1.6MB of video RAM. However, at a resolution of 800×600, you'll need less than 1MB. Whether it is reasonable to use the lower resolution to get better color depth is up to the individual user to decide.

The X Window System on Linux machines typically defaults to only 8 bpp. If you are using XFree86, the following command can be used to run a higher color depth (for other X Window Systems, consult your man pages):

```
% startx -- -bpp 16
```

This command will run X at 16 bpp only if there is an appropriate section in the XF86Config file. For Redhat Linux systems, this file is typically found in the directory `/etc` or `/etc/X11`. More details on how to configure the X Window System using XF86Config can be found in the XF86Config man page.

SOURCES OF RAW IMAGE MATERIALS

Part of the GIMP is about digital image creation, but much more is about digital image manipulation. One of the primary problems in any project, then, is finding the necessary raw materials: the digital images to be manipulated.

There are many sources for digital images. A scanner is one possibility. However, some care must be exercised, because fair use rules can be a little tricky concerning copyrights. It is particularly recommended that caution be used when using an image of a recognizable person or any trademarks or company logos. These sorts of images are often aggressively protected, even for non-commercial use.

Of course, scanning one's own photographs is an excellent source of material. If you don't have ready access to a scanner, photo-CDs are a relatively inexpensive way of having your photographs professionally scanned and saved in a convenient storage medium. Digital cameras are also excellent tools for getting the pictures you need. Many good-quality, low-priced digital cameras are now available. A major advantage of a digital camera is that photos can be taken and immediately evaluated. Thus, if the photo doesn't quite have the desired qualities, it can be taken again, until the right subject matter is created. Several of the images used in this book were obtained this way.

Nevertheless, it is often inconvenient or just impossible to personally take photos of some subjects—pictures of frosty icebergs at the South Pole, a Bengal tiger in its natural habitat, the space shuttle in orbit. Most of us just can't go there to get the shot. Let's not despair, though. There is a treasure-trove of free photographic material on the Internet, and all of the above and much more can be found with a little effort. The secret is that many United States government Web sites have no-copyright-assertion policies. This means that most of the photos on these sites can be freely used both commercially and non-commercially.

Examples of excellent sources of large, free image archives can be found at Web sites for the National Aeronautics and Space Administration (NASA), the National Oceanic and Atmospheric Administration (NOAA), and the U.S. Fish and Wildlife Service (FWS). These all have terrific image libraries containing tens of thousands of images of animals, plants, underwater life, space, planes, ships, and so on. The following is a list of Web sites that are the starting points for exploring some of these image collections. Just remember that there are some restrictions, and the responsibility of ascertaining the copyright of each image remains with you. Make sure you read the copyright claims on each site before using images found there.

Much of the raw photographic image material used in this book comes from three main sources. NASA has several excellent sites housing image collections. Here are the three I made the most use of:

```
http://www.nasa.gov/gallery/photo
http://images.jsc.nasa.gov
http://nix.nasa.gov
```

I have also made heavy use of the NOAA's main photo site, which can be found at

```
http://www.photolib.noaa.gov
```

The U.S. FWS also has a terrific photo library located at

```
http://www.fws.gov/images.htm
```

The convention used in this book for crediting photos taken from these sites is to give the complete URL of the image the first time it appears in the book. This not only credits the image source, but can also be used by the reader to directly access the photo from the Internet.

There are many more U.S. government services that provide some or all of their imagery free to the public. The U.S. Navy and Air Force, the Library of Congress, the U.S. Geological Service, and many more have Web sites with images free for public use. Although these sites offer large, useful collections of images, it is sometimes frustrating browsing their sites, trying to find the right image for a special project. A solution is to download the entire site using Web-mirroring software. The images can then be extracted and placed in a separate directory. This creates a personal image library that is much easier to browse than it would be online.

There are several free Web-mirroring programs available. The one I use is called GetWeb, and its homepage is at `http://www.enfin.com/getweb/index.html`. Figure 5 shows what the graphical user interface for GetWeb looks like. It is fairly self-explanatory, with fields allowing the entry of the root page's URL, descriptions of the types of files to be downloaded, file-filtering mechanisms, and the directory where to save the files.

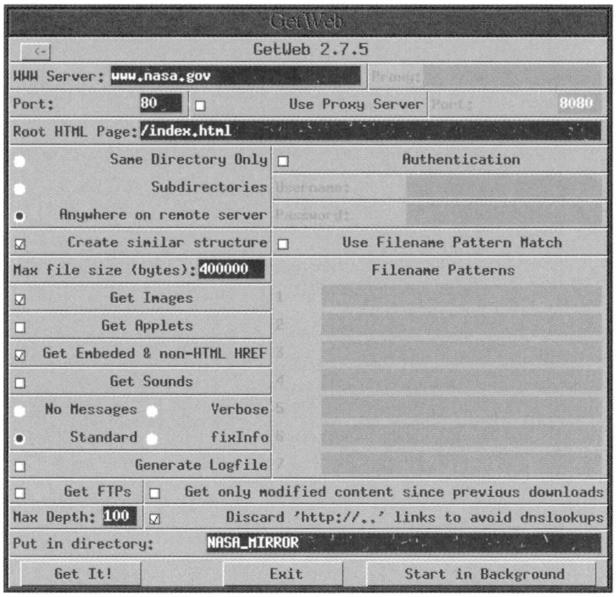

GetWeb downloads a Web site to the specified local directory, while maintaining the relative directory structure of the mirrored site. If the root of the local directory is called MIRROR, a bash shell script that can be used to cull all the JPEG image files might be

```
#!/bin/bash

mkdir IMAGES
find MIRROR -name "*.jpg" -exec mv {} IMAGES \;
```

You would use the script by moving it to the directory containing MIRROR and running it there (it might be necessary to make the script executable with the UNIX chmod command). This would produce the new directory named IMAGES containing all the JPEG files.

Figure 5: Graphic Interface for Web Mirroring Software: GetWeb

THE HISTORY OF THE GIMP

It would be difficult to write a book such as this one without recounting the history of the GIMP...so here it is.

The original GIMP was created of necessity by Spencer Kimball and Peter Mattis in August, 1995. They were working on a project for a computer science class at the University of California, Berkeley, and their project was dumping core. They decided, in extremis, to try something different—a pixel-based image manipulation program.

Six months later, in February of 1996, an early beta version of the GIMP was released onto the Internet, and the adventure had commenced. This early GIMP, version 0.54, relied on the Motif widget library for the core windowing capabilities. The use of this commercial software product went contrary to the currents of the open-source movement, which were beginning to gather momentum around the growing base of Linux users. A decision was made to generate an independent, open widget set based on an equally open core drawing library. The GIMP toolkit (GTK) was born. The first version of the toolkit was released in July of 1996.

At this point there were already many developers around the world working with Kimball and Mattis on debugging and improving the GIMP. The GIMP had several major weaknesses as a pixel-based image-manipulation program because it had an inefficient memory management system and did not have layers. After a long wait, version 0.99 was released in February of 1997. This version of the GIMP contained the main features and architecture of the GIMP as it is distributed today. It was layer-based, with a tiled memory management scheme built in, and a large number of plug-in filters had been written for it.

Finally, on May 19, 1998, the GIMP passed from beta development to its first stable release. The GIMP version 1.0 was delivered to the Internet community. Since then, development of the GIMP has continued at a rapid pace.

1

GIMP BASICS

This chapter reviews the features of the GIMP Toolbox and image windows, introduces the major dialogs, and presents important functions not covered elsewhere in this book.

1.1 INTRODUCING THE GIMP WINDOWS AND DIALOGS

This section gives an overview of the the main features of the GIMP windows and dialogs. The GIMP windows fall into four main categories. They are the Toolbox window; the image window; the Layers, Channels, and Paths dialogs; and the dialogs for selecting colors, brushes, patterns, gradients, and palettes. Each of these is briefly introduced in the following sections.

1.1.1 THE TOOLBOX

Figure 1.1(a) illustrates the Toolbox window. This window is the first to appear when the GIMP is run. It consists of 27 Toolbox function icons; the `File` and `Xtns` pull-down menus; and the `Active Foreground Color`, `Active Background Color`, `Default Colors`, `Switch Colors`, `Active Brush`, `Active Pattern`, and `Active Gradient` icons. The function icons are each named in the figure shown on page 7, and their uses are discussed in various places in this book.

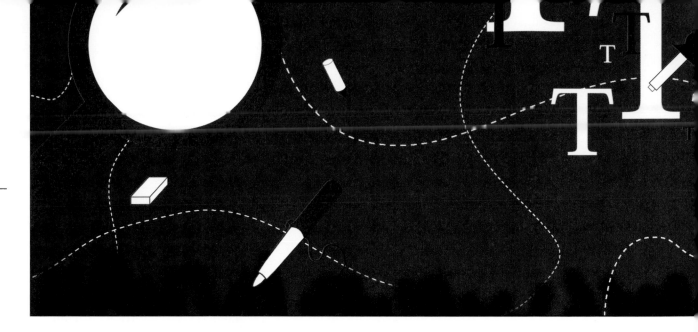

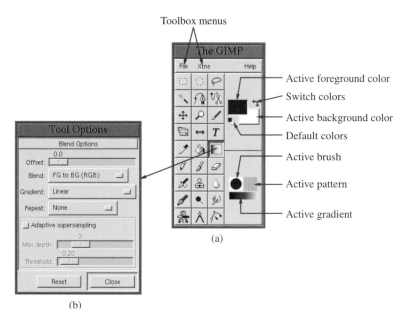

Toolbox menus

Active foreground color

Switch colors

Active background color

Default colors

Active brush

Active pattern

Active gradient

(a)

Tool Options

Blend Options

Offset: 0.0

Blend: FG to BG (RGB)

Gradient: Linear

Repeat: None

Adaptive supersampling

Max depth: 3

Threshold: 0.20

Reset   Close

(b)

Figure 1.1: The Toolbox Window

Almost all the tools in the Toolbox have options. Double-clicking on a tool brings up its Tool Options dialog. Once opened, the dialog remains open until it is explicitly closed, supplying the interface for the tool options in use at the moment. Changing tools automatically changes the Tool Options dialog, if its window is open. This dialog can also be invoked with Toolbox: File/Dialogs/Tool Options or by typing C-S-t in the Toolbox window. Figure 1.1(b) shows the Tool Options dialog for the Gradient tool.

1.1.2 The Image Window

The image window is the most important window in the GIMP. It is also the most feature-rich. Figure 1.2(a) illustrates a typical image window. Note that the window title bar is marked

```
*image-window.xcf-16.0 (RGB) 200%
```

which gives quite a bit of information about this image. The string `image-window.xcf` is the name of the file on disk which contains the original version of this image, and the `*` indicates that the image in the window has been modified with respect to the version on the disk. Thus, to avoid losing the changes made to the image it must be saved (see Section 1.2). The string `16.0` gives the window number, 16, and the view number, 0. Every time a new image window is opened, the window number is incremented, except when the new window is created using `New View` and then the view number is incremented (see Section 1.8.2 for more on view numbers). The string in parentheses, `(RGB)`, gives the image type (see Section 1.4), which can be RGB, Grayscale, or Indexed. Finally, the string `200%` indicates that the image is zoomed and is displayed in its window at twice its true size.

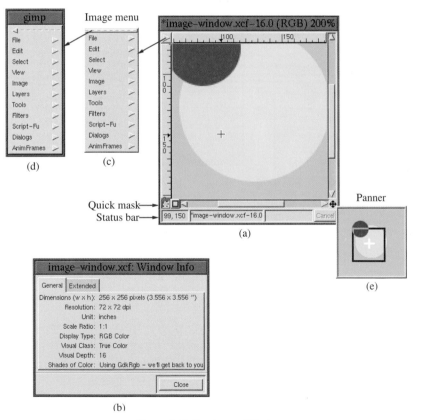

Figure 1.2: The Image Window

Additional information about the image can be had from the `Window Info` dialog, which is shown in Figure 1.2(b), and which is found in the `Image:View` menu, or can be displayed by typing `C-S-i` in the image window. This dialog gives the image type, its dimensions in pixels, and its resolution in dots per inch. The units of the rulers at the left and upper sides of the image window correspond to the dimensions shown in the `Window Info` dialog. Moving the mouse cursor into the image window makes an arrow appear on each ruler, indicating the cursor's position. The cursor position is also precisely shown in the status bar. In Figure 1.2(a), the status bar indicates that the mouse cursor is located at the position (99,150). Both the rulers and the status bar can be toggled off, which is done with `Toggle Rulers` and `Toggle Statusbar`, both found in the `Image:View` menu.

The most important feature of the image window is the Image menu, shown in Figure 1.2(c). This menu is displayed by right-clicking in the image window and can also be displayed by clicking the arrow icon found in the upper-left corner of the window (see Figure 1.2(a)). The Image menu and its submenus stay open until one of its items has been selected by the mouse. However, these menus can be opened as separate windows and, in so doing, be made to remain on the screen. This is done by clicking on the dashed line at the top of the menu. This is illustrated in Figure 1.2(d). The menu window can be eliminated from the screen by again clicking on the dashed line at the top of the menu.

When an image is larger than can be displayed by the image window, the scroll bars seen in Figure 1.2(a) allow the image to be panned inside the window. However, there is also a special panner window that can be displayed by clicking and holding the left mouse button on the four-way arrow icon found at the lower-right corner of the image window. The panner window is shown in Figure 1.2(e). Dragging the mouse in this window pans the image in the image window. Alternatively, the image can also be panned by middle-button-clicking and dragging with the mouse in the image window.

Finally, there are a pair of buttons found at the lower-left corner of the image window that are used for the `Quick Mask` function. This function is covered in Section 4.5.2.

1.1.3 THE LAYERS, CHANNELS, AND PATHS DIALOGS

The Layers, Channels, and Paths dialogs are very important tools in the GIMP. These dialogs can be displayed by selecting `Layers & Channels` from the `Image:Dialogs` menu or by typing `C-l` in the image window and selecting the appropriate tab. The three dialogs are shown in Figures 1.3(a), (b), and (c). The Layers dialog is discussed in detail in Section 2.1.1, the Paths dialog in Section 3.4, and the Channels dialog in Section 4.1.1.

Layers dialog   Channels dialog   Paths dialog

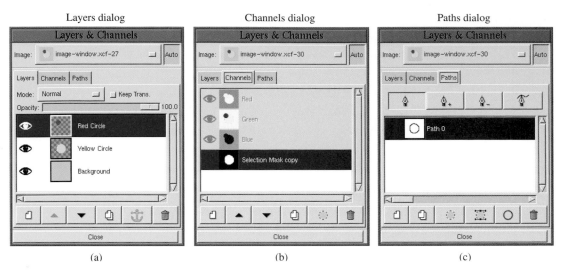

(a)   (b)   (c)

Figure 1.3: The Layers, Channels, and Paths Dialogs

1.1.4 THE DIALOGS FOR COLOR, BRUSHES, PATTERNS, GRADIENTS, AND PALETTES

Clicking on the `Active Foreground Color` or `Active Background Color` patches in the Toolbox window (see Figure 1.1(a)), brings up the `Color Selection` dialog shown in Figure 1.4(a). The rainbow-colored vertical bar is for choosing hue, and the large colored square is for choosing saturation and value. A color choice is made by clicking and dragging with the mouse to select the desired hue, saturation, and value. Numerical values can also be entered for R (red), G (green), B (blue), H (hue), S (saturation), and V (value) in the data entry boxes. More on these color space components is discussed in Chapter 5. Several other color-choosing dialogs can be used by clicking on the tabs located in the upper part of the window.

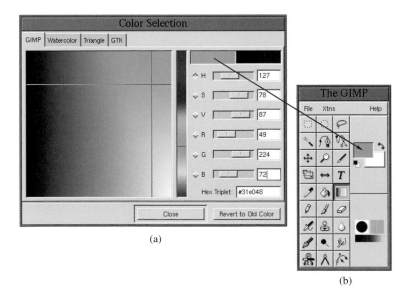

(a)

(b)

Figure 1.4: The Color Selection Dialog

Choosing a color in the Color Selection dialog makes that color appear in the Active Foreground Color or Active Background Color patch (see Figure 1.1(a)), depending on which patch was clicked to invoke the Color Selection tool. Clicking the Swap Colors icon (the two-headed arrow next to the active color patches) switches the foreground and background colors. This can also be accomplished by typing x in the image window. Clicking the Default Colors icon (the small black and white rectangles below the color patches) reverts the foreground and background colors to their defaults of black and white. This can also be accomplished by typing d in the image window.

Figure 1.5(a) shows the Brush Selection dialog. This dialog can be displayed by clicking on the Active Brush icon in the Toolbox window. Clicking on a brush from the dialog makes it appear as the new active brush in the Toolbox window, as shown in Figure 1.5(b).

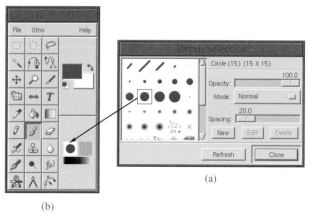

Figure 1.5: The Brush Selection Dialog

Figure 1.6(a) shows the Pattern Selection dialog. This dialog can be displayed by clicking on the Active Pattern icon in the Toolbox window. Clicking on a pattern from the dialog makes it appear as the new active pattern in the Toolbox window, as shown in Figure 1.6(b).

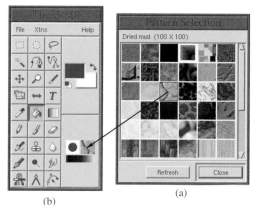

Figure 1.6: The Pattern Selection Dialog

Figure 1.7(a) shows the Gradients dialog. This dialog can be displayed by clicking on the Active Gradient icon in the Toolbox window. Clicking on a gradient from the dialog makes it appear as the new active gradient in the Toolbox window, as shown in Figure 1.7(b). Furthermore, custom gradients can be created by clicking on the Gradients dialog's Edit button. This produces the Gradient Editor, shown in Figure 1.7(c).

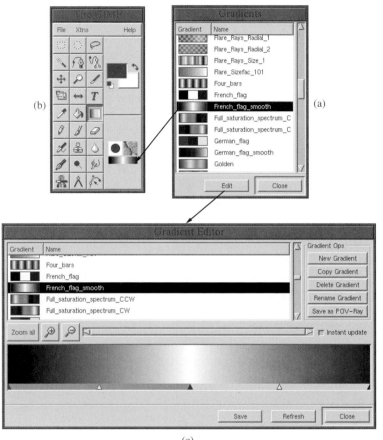

(b)   (a)

(c)

Figure 1.7: The Gradients Dialog

Figure 1.8(a) shows the Color Palette dialog. This dialog can be displayed from the Image:Dialogs menu or by typing C-p in the Toolbox window. The dialog consists of the Palette tab, which displays the active palette. Clicking on the Select tab allows you to choose from a large number of predefined palettes, as shown in Figure 1.8(b). In addition, you can create custom palettes by clicking on the Edit button. This produces the Color Palette Edit dialog, shown in Figure 1.8(c).

(a)   (b)

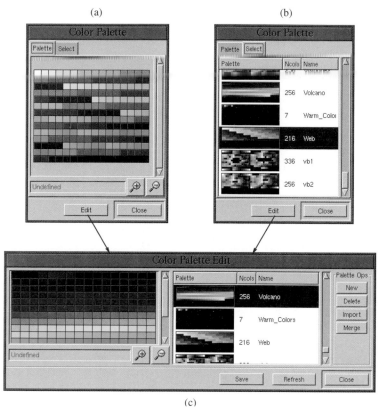

(c)

Figure 1.8: The Color Palette Dialog

1.2   LOADING AND SAVING IMAGES

The two most fundamental operations that can be performed in the GIMP are that of loading and saving
images. There are a few subtleties about these operations
worth noting. Figure 1.9 illustrates the `Load Image` dialog. This function can be called in several ways. It lives
in the `Image:File/Open` menu and the `Toolbox:Image/Open`
menu, and it can be obtained by simply typing `C-o` in
either the image or Toolbox windows.

You can navigate your file structure's directory tree
using the Load Image dialog. The directories are shown
to the left, and files to the right. Clicking on a file highlights it, and if a preview image for this file exists, it is
displayed in the preview box near the bottom of the
dialog. If no preview exists one can be created by

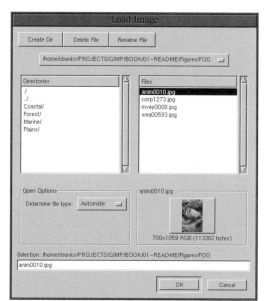

Figure 1.9: Loading Images into
the GIMP

clicking on the Generate Preview button (the button displaying the thumbnail in Figure 1.9). Clicking the OK button at the bottom of the dialog loads the highlighted image. Figure 1.9 shows a highlighted file, and the preview box shows the associated thumbnail for this image.

Clicking the OK button loads the image. A file can also be loaded by double-clicking on its name. Double-clicking on directory names navigates the Load Image dialog to that directory. It is possible to load multiple images into the GIMP by highlighting multiple files before clicking the OK button. Multiple files are highlighted by pressing the Shift key while clicking on the desired filenames. Dragging the mouse with the Shift key pressed highlights all the files that come under the mouse cursor.

Another very useful feature of the Load Image dialog is that file (and directory) name completion is enabled in the selection box. Typing a few letters of a filename followed by pressing the Tab key will automatically complete as much of the name as is uniquely defined by what has already been typed. The right side of the dialog then displays all the files that match the letters in the selection box. Adding a letter followed by pressing the Tab key will further complete as much as possible, and so on. For a good typist, this is an agreeable and rapid way to find the file to be loaded.

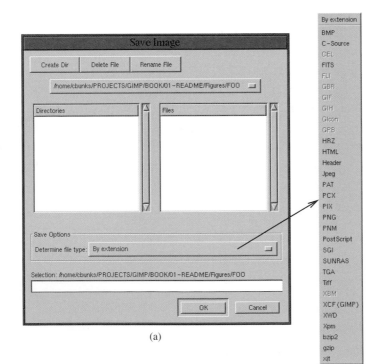

An image can be saved with the Save As function found in the Image:File menu. This brings up the Save Image dialog, shown in Figure 1.10(a). This dialog is similar to the Load Image dialog. The image can be saved to a new or existing file. Navigation of the file structure directory tree is the same as for the Load Image dialog. Entering a name in the selection box at the bottom of the dialog followed by clicking the OK button saves the image to the specified filename.

A convenient feature of the Save Image dialog is that the file is automatically saved in the format specified by the extension of the typed filename. As an example, if foo.jpg is typed, the file will be saved in JPEG format.

Figure 1.10: Saving Images

The GIMP can load and save in many file formats. The set of all formats can be seen by looking in the Save Options menu, shown in Figure 1.10(b). There are three file formats which are unique to the GIMP. The first is XCF, which is the native GIMP format. This is the only format that can save all the GIMP features and states when working on a project. If your image contains multiple layers, channels, selections, or paths, you must save using the XCF format to avoid losing parts of your work. Because the GIMP is the only program that can load XCF format files, you will also want to eventually save to other formats. See Sections 2.7.1 and 2.7.2 for precautions that should be used before saving to a different file format.

The two other file formats native to the GIMP are PAT and GBR. PAT is for saving image patterns such as those available in the Pattern Selection dialog. Placing a file saved with the PAT extension in your ~/.gimp/patterns directory will make it available in the Pattern Selection dialog the next time you run the GIMP. The GBR file format is used for creating GIMP brushes. This works like for pattern files, except GBR files must be placed in the ~/.gimp/brushes directory to be made available in the Brush Selection dialog.

1.3 CREATING NEW IMAGES

Figure 1.11 shows the New Image dialog. This is invoked with the New function, found in the Toolbox:File menu, or the Image:File menu, or by typing C-n in the Toolbox or image windows. The most important aspect of creating a new image is the specification of the Image Type, which can be RGB or Grayscale, and the image resolution. The image resolution is set by entering values into the Resolution X and Y entry boxes. The default values are 72 pixels per inch, which corresponds, approximately, to your computer monitor's screen resolution. If the final version of your image is to be output to a high-resolution printer, you should choose values corresponding to that output device's capabilities.

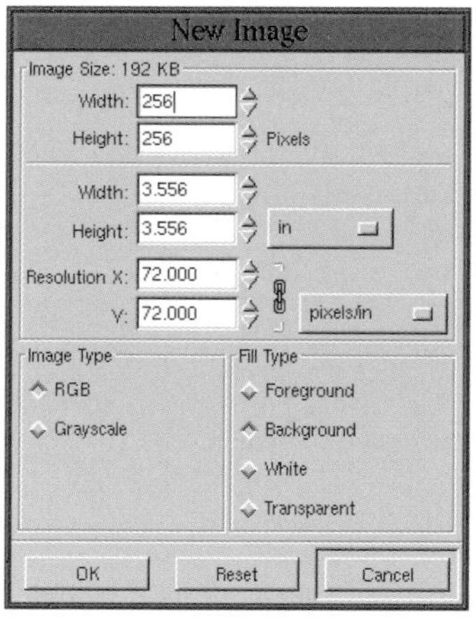

Figure 1.11: Creating New Images

1.4 RGB, GRAYSCALE, AND INDEXED IMAGES

The GIMP uses three formats for displaying and working with images. These are the RGB, Grayscale, and Indexed formats. Although Grayscale is discussed briefly in Chapter 5 and Indexed format in Chapter 9, the primary format used in this book is RGB.

Because most GIMP plug-ins do not work on Indexed image formats, it makes sense to immediately convert an indexed format image to RGB when it is first loaded into the GIMP. Conversion to RGB is performed with the RGB function found in the Image:Image/Mode menu.

1.5 UNDOING AND REDOING

An extremely useful feature of the GIMP is its ability to perform multiple undos and redos. The Undo function is found in the Image:Edit menu, as is the Redo function. These two functions are so useful and are employed so often that you will want to immediately memorize their keyboard shortcuts. These are C-z for undo and C-r for redo.

The number of undos that can be performed in the GIMP is controlled by the Interface branch of the Preferences dialog, and the Preferences dialog is found in the Toolbox:File menu. Figure 1.12 illustrates the dialog with the Interface branch highlighted. The default value for the number of undos is 5, but for the size of images I work with and the amount of RAM I have available on my computer, I like to have 25 levels of undo. If I were working with large images with many layers, this would not be possible, and I would change the number of undos to a lower value. See page 8 in README for more on how to budget your RAM.

An amazing feature of the GIMP is the Undo History function found in the Image:View menu. When invoked, this function displays a palette of thumbnails, each representing an image state in the sequence of operations performed on your image. Figure 1.13 illustrates such a sequence. Figures 1.13(a), (b), and (c) show the successive application of a selection, followed by a color fill. Figures 1.13(d), (e), and (f) show the respective entries in the Undo History dialog as the operations are performed.

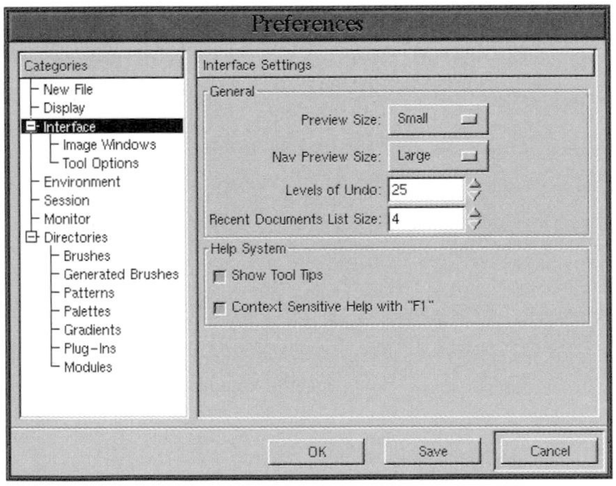

Figure 1.12: Setting the Number of Undo Levels

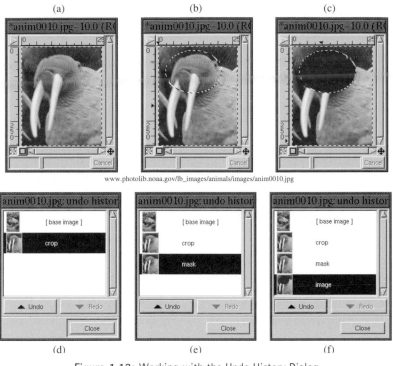

www.photolib.noaa.gov/lb_images/animals/images/anim0010.jpg

Figure 1.13: Working with the Undo History Dialog

In Figure 1.13, note how the highlighted thumbnail in the Undo History dialog indicates the current status of the image displayed in the image window. Performing an undo by typing C-z in the image window moves the highlighted thumbnail to a layer higher in the thumbnail stack, and performing redo with a C-r moves the highlighted thumbnail a layer lower. Furthermore, you can select any layer in the Undo History dialog at any time by clicking on it.

In this way, you have access to any prior version of the image available in the Undo History by one of two separate methods. The first is by repeatedly pressing C-z in the image window until arriving at the desired state. The second is by directly clicking on the corresponding thumbnail in the Undo History dialog.

1.6 RECALLING THE LAST FILTER DIALOG

Most GIMP filters are doted with a variety of parameters which control the filter effect. Because it is often difficult to know in advance how much of a certain filter parameter you want to apply to an image, a little experimentation is usually necessary. Unfortunately, the GIMP filters are three menus deep in the Image menu. Thus, experimenting with a filter means finding it in the appropriate submenu, evaluating its effect on the image, undoing the effect if it is unsatisfactory, and reapplying the filter with new settings. Repeatedly searching for the same filter in the system of image submenus can become annoying. One way to limit the annoyance is by tearing off the filter submenu, making access to it more rapid (see Section 1.1.2 for more on tear-off menus). A more direct method, however, is by using the keyboard shortcut for the Reshow Last function. The shortcut is A-S-f. This function recalls the dialog of the last filter applied to the image, along with the previously used dialog values. Thus, with two keystrokes, C-z followed by A-S-f, a filter effect can be undone and redone with new parameter values.

1.7 COPY, CUT, AND PASTE BUFFERS

Copying, cutting, and pasting of layers and selections are among the most common operations in the GIMP. In this book, these operations are used extensively in Chapter 4, where they are needed for building masks; in Chapter 8, where they are used for image rendering; and in Chapter 7, where they are essential for compositing.

The commands for copying, cutting, and pasting are found in the Image:Edit menu, but they are so useful that memorizing their keyboard shortcuts is indispensable. The Copy command can be performed by typing C-c in the image window, cutting by typing C-x, and pasting by typing C-v. As will be seen in Chapters 2, 3, and 4, copying, cutting, and pasting are the most expeditious methods of moving layers and selections between image windows and between layer and channel masks.

The GIMP manages copying, cutting, and pasting using buffers. Whenever a generic copy or cut is performed, it is placed into the default buffer, replacing whatever was there. A generic paste uses the contents of the default buffer without clearing it, so the contents can be reused until they are replaced by another copy or cut operation. A copy or cut places the *active* layer, channel mask, or layer mask into the buffer. If a selection is active in the image window, only the part of the active layer contained in the selection is placed in the buffer.

Several special paste functions are available in the Image:Edit menu. If an image contains an active selection, the Paste Into function places the contents of the default buffer into the selection, clipping the pasted image to the selection's boundaries. The pasted image can be repositioned using the Move tool. The Paste As New function places the contents of the default buffer into a new image window that has dimensions just large enough to accommodate the pasted image.

There is also a special copy function called Copy Visible. Instead of copying the active layer to the default buffer, this function copies all the visible layers or, if a selection is active, the parts of the visible layers within the selection boundaries. If the image consists of more than one layer, the copied contents are flattened, removing the layered structure before being placed into the default buffer.

In addition to the generic, default buffer, the GIMP also has named buffers. If a large number of copy, cut, or paste operations is required, the named buffers can be useful for organizing and distributing the pieces. Figure 1.14 illustrates the use of named buffers. Figure 1.14(a) illustrates a circular selection that is placed into a named buffer using Copy Named, found in the Image:Edit menu. Using this function displays the dialog shown in Figure 1.14(b), where the name of the buffer is entered. Figure 1.14(c) and (d) illustrate using Copy Named, repeated for a square selection.

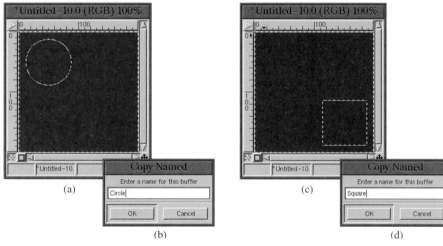

Figure 1.14: Using the Copy Named Buffer

Pasting from a named buffer is performed using the Paste Named command, found in the Image:Edit menu. Figure 1.15 illustrates the dialog that appears when using this command. The contents of any named buffer can be pasted by clicking on the name in the dialog, followed by clicking on the Paste button. Buffers can be removed from the list by highlighting them and clicking on the Delete button.

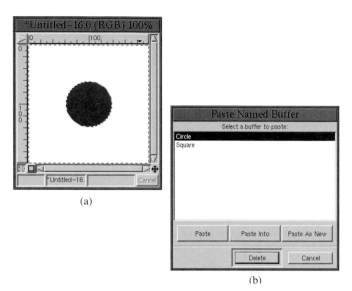

(a)

(b)

Figure 1.15: Using the `Paste Named Buffer`

1.8 ZOOM AND NEW VIEW

The functions `Zoom` and `New View` are for doing precision, pixel-scale work on an image. This section describes these particularly useful functions.

1.8.1 ZOOM

Figure 1.16 illustrates the use of `Zoom`. The `Zoom` function, enabled by clicking on the magnifying glass icon in the Toolbox, has two modes of operation. The first mode is used by clicking and dragging in the image window to frame a part of the image. When the mouse button is released, the delineated region is zoomed. Figure 1.16(a) shows a zoom selection area created with the mouse, and Figure 1.16(b) shows how this region is zoomed to fill the entire image window. This is a convenient way to zoom into a specific region of your image.

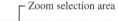

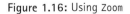

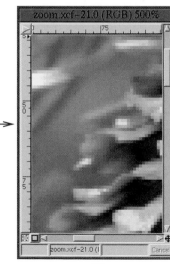

(a)

(b)

Figure 1.16: Using Zoom

The second mode of operation for the Zoom tool is accessed by simply clicking or Shift-clicking in the image window. Each click zooms in a step and each Shift-click zooms out a step. The image window can also be zoomed in or out with keyboard shortcuts. Zooming in is performed by typing = in the image window, and zooming out is performed by typing - (that is, the minus key). Notice that the = is on the same key as the +, which should remind you that it adds or increases zoom. By contrast, the - key subtracts or decreases zoom. An advantage of the keyboard shortcuts is that they function without having to first click on the Zoom icon in the Toolbox.

The function Shrink Wrap, found in the Image:View menu, can be used to resize the window to encompass the entire image, but only within the limits of your monitor's screen. Shrink Wrap can also be invoked by typing C-e in the image window.

Whenever a part of a zoomed image cannot be seen in the image window, the image panner, described in Section 1.1.2, can be used to pan to a desired image area. There are also three other possibilities for panning in a zoomed image. There are the window's scroll bars, however, these probably aren't the most convenient method. The second choice is to middle-click and drag in the image window. This can work reasonably well if the image needs to be adjusted only incrementally. If it is necessary to pan back and forth between many different regions of a zoomed image, the Navigation Window is probably the most convenient.

The use of the Navigation Window, found in the Image:View menu, is shown in Figure 1.17. Figure 1.17(a) illustrates an image zoomed to 200%, and Figure 1.17(b) shows the Navigation Window. This dialog allows the image to be panned in the image window by clicking and dragging on the view rectangle. You can also use the Navigation Window to control the degree of zoom by clicking on the + and - buttons.

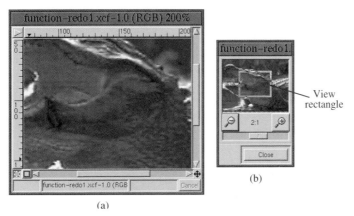

Figure 1.17: Using Zoom with the Navigation Window

1.8.2 New View

When performing detailed, pixel-scale operations on a zoomed image, it is useful to see what effect this is having on the image at normal scale, but it is inconvenient to zoom in and out after each operation. To solve this problem, there is the New View function, found in the Image:View menu. This function creates a new image window, which is a dependent view of the exact same image. Thus, operations performed in one window are also shown in the other. The Zoom function is the only exception to this and can affect one window without affecting the other. New View allows pixel-scale operations to be performed in one zoomed-in window while the same operations can be viewed in the other view window at normal scale.

Figure 1.18 illustrates how the New View function works. Figure 1.18(a) shows a zoomed view of a pinecone, while Figure 1.18(b) shows a view of the same image with no zoom. As shown in Figure 1.18(a), red paint is being applied to a leaf of the pinecone with the Paintbrush tool. Figure 1.18(b) shows that the red paint is also visible in the unzoomed window. Note that the image and view numbers shown in the window title bars of Figures 1.18(a) and (b) are, respectively, 26.0 and 26.1. This indicates that these windows show views 0 and 1 of image 26.

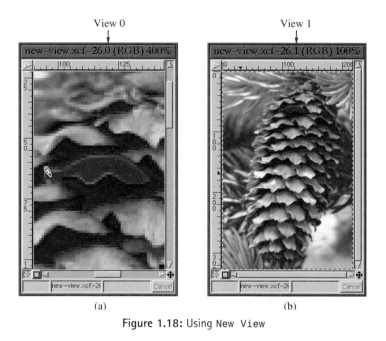

Figure 1.18: Using New View

1.9 THE HELP SYSTEM

The GIMP has an online help browser. The browser can be displayed with Toolbox:Help/Help or by pressing the F1 function key while the mouse cursor is in any GIMP window.

Figure 1.19 illustrates the help browser window. Pressing the F1 key when the mouse cursor is over a specific GIMP tool brings up the help page relevant to that tool. The Contents and Index tabs provide access to the general contents of the help database.

Figure 1.19: The Help System Browser

1.10 COMMON PROBLEMS AND FREQUENTLY ASKED QUESTIONS

Sometimes the GIMP displays what seems like inexplicable behavior. This is usually not a bug but a misunderstanding on how to properly use the GIMP. For this reason, Chapters 1 through 5 each have a final section that addresses common problems. These are presented in the format of an FAQ (frequently asked questions); here they are for this chapter:

- **I've opened an image in the GIMP and I want to run some plug-in filters on it, but hardly any are available. They all seem to be grayed out. What's wrong with my GIMP?**

  Nothing is wrong. You've probably loaded an indexed image (for example, a GIF format file), and most GIMP plug-ins don't work with indexed images. The solution is to convert your image to RGB format with the RGB function found in the Image:Image/Mode menu.

- **After hours of exhausting work during which I built an image with multiple layers, masks, and paths, I saved my image to a file. However, the next time I opened my image, much of what I did on the image was missing. What happened?**

  The GIMP XCF format should be used to save images with layers, masks, or paths (see Section 1.2). This is the only format that can save the state of your GIMP image projects. Once a project has been completed you may want to save it in another format such as JPEG, GIF, PNG, and so on. For this you will need to convert the image after merging it (see Section 2.7.1) or flattening it (see Section 2.7.2).

2

REVIEW OF LAYERS

The GIMP is a pixel-based image manipulation tool, but from the perspective of creative composition with digital images, pixels are neither the most convenient nor the most important component to work with. This honor is reserved for layers. Pixels are the basic stuff of layers, and layers are stacked to make images. This constitutes a hierarchy of scale. Pixels are small, which makes them too hard to work with. It would be difficult to build an image if it had to be done pixel-by-pixel. On the other hand, whole images are too unwieldy to work with comfortably. There are conceptual parts or particular components of images we want to work with without disturbing the rest. By constructing an image out of layers, it is possible to work with each component independently of the rest of the image. This makes layers the happy medium between pixels and images. They are "right-sized" for what we want to accomplish in the GIMP.

The images we want to make are usually constructed of conceptual pieces from other images: a part from here and there that we stitch together into a single whole. Layers allow us to combine all the pieces yet keep them separate. This collage view of working with digital images is extremely powerful. We can work on individual image pieces without affecting the others. Having the parts on separate layers allows for their separate processing. Layers can be positioned, repositioned, color-adjusted, and filtered independently. It is difficult to over-emphasize the utility of layers. Compositing, animation, selections, effects, and enhancements are all made easier because of layers.

The objective of this chapter is to develop a firm foundation for layer mechanics. You will learn how to use them effectively while avoiding common pitfalls. The material covered here will be referred to often in later chapters.

2.1 LAYERS AND THE ROLE THEY PLAY IN IMAGES

Figure 2.1 will be used to describe some of the fundamental features of layers. Although this image is constructed of three layers, this is not evident from looking at it in the image window. To understand and work with the layer structure of an image you must use the Layers dialog. However, before describing this important tool, let's look at Figure 2.2, which is a useful illustration of how layers are used to make up images.

Figure 2.1: A Three-Layer Image

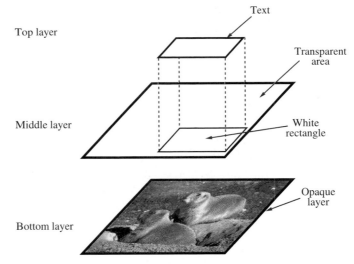

Figure 2.2: Visualizing the Layer Stack in 3D

Figure 2.2 shows a 3D break-out of how the three-layer stack relates to the 2D image shown in Figure 2.1. The bottom layer is a picture of a gopher couple; this layer is fully opaque. The middle layer has the same dimensions as the bottom layer and is completely transparent except for a small white rectangular region. The white rectangle itself is partially transparent (thus, the bottom layer can be perceived through it). Finally, the top layer's dimensions are smaller than either the bottom or middle layers. The top layer is also transparent except for the text "Prairie Pranks." The vertical red dashed lines in Figure 2.2 show that the text in the top layer is positioned directly over the white rectangle in the middle layer. The black frames shown in the figure have been drawn in to show the positions of the text and the white rectangle, but are not actually part of the image (refer to Figure 2.1).

The 3D layer stack shown in Figure 2.2 is a useful mental model for understanding how layers work in an image. It also underscores the utility of having image components on layers. Because the text is on a layer, it can be positioned independently of the lowest layer. Because the white rectangle is on a layer, its partial transparency can be adjusted without affecting the text.

2.1.1 THE LAYERS DIALOG

It is impossible to work with images without knowing their layer structure. This information is provided by the Layers dialog, which is part of the `Layers & Channels` window. The `Layers & Channels` window can be found in the `Image:Layers` menu, the `Image:Dialogs` menu, or can be invoked by simply typing `C-l` in the image window. Figure 2.3(a) shows the multilayer image from Figure 2.1, and Figure 2.3(b) shows the associated Layers dialog.

(a)

(b)

Figure 2.3: Layers Dialog

The Layers dialog has many components. Let's take a moment to briefly describe each one. Figure 2.4 illustrates the dialog's various components. The most important feature of the Layers dialog is the Layers Palette. This region of the dialog consists of horizontal strips, each representing a single layer in the image. It can be seen from Figure 2.4 that this is the Layers dialog for an image with three layers. Note that each strip displays a thumbnail image of its layer's contents. The strips are organized vertically in a stack, and this stack shows the 3D relationship of the layers in a 2D manner. The top, middle, and bottom layers of the stack represent the layers analogously to the conceptual 3D view shown in Figure 2.2.

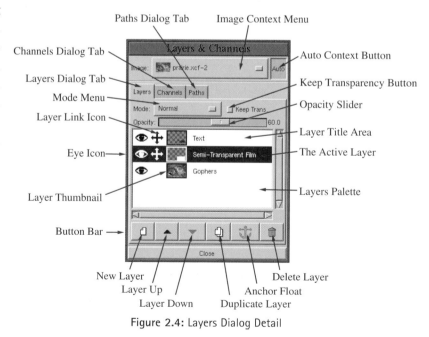

Figure 2.4: Layers Dialog Detail

In addition to showing the layer ordering structure of an image, the Layers Palette provides useful information and tools for working with the image. As shown in Figure 2.4, the area to the far left of the Layer Thumbnail contains the Eye icon. If this icon is visible, the corresponding layer is visible in the image window. The Eye icon can be toggled off by clicking on it. This makes the corresponding layer invisible in the image window. Toggling it again brings the layer back.

The region of the strip just to the left of the thumbnail and to the right of the Eye icon is the position of the Layer Link icon. Clicking in this area makes a four-way arrow appear, as shown in two of Figure 2.4's layer strips. When this icon is activated for several layers at once, they are linked together with respect to the Move tool. These layers will now move together as a single unit (the Move tool is covered in Section 2.6.1).

To the right of the thumbnail is the Layer Title Area, which, for a new image, is named Background by default. The title can be changed by double-clicking in the Layer Title Area. This brings up a dialog box where the new title can be entered.

The middle layer strip in Figure 2.4 is highlighted in blue, indicating that it is the active layer. GIMP tools applied to the image window are applied to this layer. This is very important, so read these last two sentences again! The GIMP tools and filters are applied to the *active* layer. Not knowing which layer is active is a formula for confusion and frustration. The identity of the active layer can only be reliably determined by having the Layers dialog open. Any layer can be made active by clicking on its thumbnail or Title Area. Only one layer can be active at a time.

Outside of the Layers Palette area are several other important features of the Layers dialog. First, there are two pull-down menus labeled Image and Mode. The Image menu is used to specify the context of the Layers dialog. The GIMP can have many image windows open simultaneously. When there is more than one image window open, this menu is used to select the one whose layers are displayed in the Layers Palette area. If the Auto Context button is toggled on (which it is by default), any keystroke in an image window will change the Layers Palette context auto-magically to that window. I like to use the space bar for this.

The Mode menu selects how the pixels of the active layer are visually blended with those beneath it. Each layer has a blending mode context that is specified using this menu. Blending modes are described in more detail in Chapter 5.

The remaining features of the Layers dialog consist of the Opacity slider, the Keep Transparency toggle button, and, at the bottom of the dialog, a row of function buttons that I call the button bar. These are all discussed in more detail later. However, of these features, the Opacity slider is of immediate interest because it is used in the example shown in Figure 2.3. Figure 2.3(b) shows that the middle layer strip is highlighted, indicating that this layer, containing the small white rectangle, is active. Careful examination of the Layers dialog shows that the Opacity slider is set to 60.0% for this layer. This means that the layer below can be seen through the white rectangle because the rectangle's layer is only partially opaque. Just like the blending modes, opacity can be independently set for each layer.

2.1.2 THE LAYERS MENU

In addition to the features described in the previous section, the Layers dialog has a hidden menu. This menu is displayed by right-clicking on the highlighted active layer in the Layers Palette. This is called the Layers menu. Figure 2.5(a) illustrates the Layers dialog, and the Layers menu is shown in Figure 2.5(b) and (c). The functions provided by the Layers menu are described shortly, but before covering them we need to take a slight detour to discuss another element of images: channels.

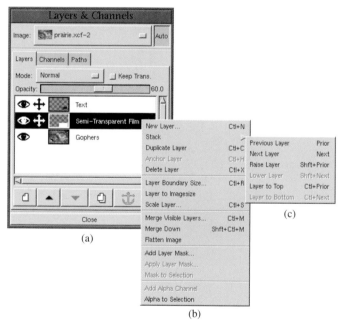

Figure 2.5: Layers Menu

2.2 CHANNELS AND THEIR RELATIONSHIP TO LAYERS

Recall that images are constructed from layers, and layers from pixels. However, there is another important component in the image structure hierarchy. Layers can be decomposed into sublayers called channels. Layers are constructed of one to four channels. In this book almost all our work is performed on RGB images. For these types of images each layer consists of four channels known as R, G, B, and A. These are the red, green, blue, and alpha components of a layer, respectively. The R, G, and B channels contain the color information about the layer, and the A channel describes how opaque the layer is to what is behind it. An exception to this rule is that the default background layer of a newly created or freshly opened RGB image contains no alpha channel.

A complete diagram of the image component hierarchy is illustrated in Figure 2.6. In the standard distribution of the GIMP, channels are 8 bits deep, meaning that each pixel in a layer is represented by up to 32 bits. However, there is a special development version of the GIMP that uses channels that are 16 bits deep, making for layers with pixels represented by up to 64 bits. This is known as the Hollywood branch of the GIMP because it is useful for film and high-quality studio production imagery. More on Hollywood can be found at `http://film.gimp.org`.

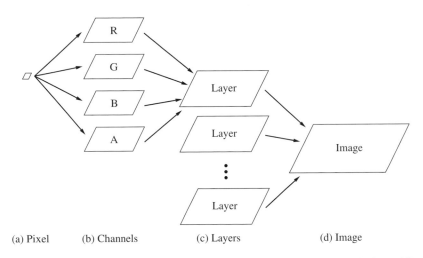

| (a) Pixel | (b) Channels | (c) Layers | (d) Image |

Figure 2.6: Image Component Hierarchy: Each Layer Consists of a Matrix of Pixels, and Each Pixel is Constructed of an R, G, B, and A Channel

2.2.1 THE CHANNELS DIALOG

Similar to layers, there is a dialog for viewing channels called the Channels dialog. This is accessed by clicking on the Channels tab in the `Layers & Channels` window (see Figure 2.4). The Channels dialog is shown in Figure 2.7. Here the Red, Green, and Blue channels are labeled. They can be seen in the Channels Palette area, which is analogous to the Layers Palette discussed in the previous section. Note that unlike the Layers palette, more than one channel can be active at a time. In fact, all three channels are active at once, meaning that all operations performed in the image window are applied to all three channels.

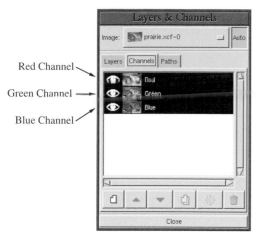

Red Channel

Green Channel

Blue Channel

Figure 2.7: Channels Dialog

Also note that there are just three channels in this dialog, not three channels for each layer. These channels represent the global red, green, and blue of the image. For multilayer images, the R, G, and B channels of each individual layer are not accessible in the Channels dialog. They can be extracted for an individual layer by deleting the other layers or by copying and pasting the layer to a separate image window. Another possibility for accessing the individual color channels of a layer is to use the Decompose function, which is discussed in Section 4.5.3.

Any of the R, G, and B channels can be made inactive by clicking on the channel title. Doing so means that subsequent operations in the image window affect only the remaining active channels. The visibility of the channels, similar to layers, can be toggled using the Eye icons.

The Channels dialog can be used to create additional channels for an image. These are called Channel Masks, and a discussion of these is deferred to Section 4.1. As a final note, Figure 2.6 suggests that the alpha component of a layer should be found somewhere in the Layers or Channels dialogs. This is indeed correct, but this topic is deferred to Section 4.2.

2.3 LAYER CREATION, DELETION, DUPLICATION, AND ORGANIZATION

We now return to the functions contained in the Layers menu shown in Figure 2.5. The most basic layer operations are those of creation, deletion, duplication, and organization. These functions are controlled with the menu entries shown in Figures 2.5(b) and (c) but are more easily accessed using the button bar located at the bottom of the Layers dialog.

2.3.1 CREATING NEW LAYERS

The first entry in the Layers menu is New Layer. Clicking on this function brings up a dialog that allows the user to name the new layer and choose its dimensions. The default dimensions are those of the existing image. Also, the user can choose whether the created layer is white, the foreground or background colors, or transparent. The foreground and background colors are those displayed in the Active Foreground Color and Active Background Color patches in the Toolbox window. The new layer is inserted just above the active layer, becoming immediately apparent in the Layers Palette. The New Layer function is also provided by the button depicting the single sheet of paper.

2.3.2 RAISING LAYERS

The order of layers in the Layers Palette controls how the layers are perceived in the image. The Raise Layer entry, shown in Figure 2.5(c), shifts the active layer up by one, if possible, in the layer stack. The function Layer to Top puts the active layer at the top of the stack.

Raise Layer and Layer to Top are also available from the button bar. The upward-pointing arrow icon provides these functions. Clicking on this button raises the active layer, and Shift-clicking raises the layer to the top of the stack. Note that if the lowest layer of the stack does not have an alpha channel, it cannot be raised.

2.3.3 LOWERING LAYERS

The Lower Layer entry in the Layers menu shifts the active layer down by one in the layer stack, and Layer to Bottom moves it to the bottom of the stack. The same functions are provided by the downward-pointing arrow icon in the button bar. Clicking on the icon lowers the active layer once, and Shift-clicking puts it to the bottom of the stack. Note that if the lowest layer of the stack does not have an alpha channel, another layer cannot be made lower than it.

2.3.4 DUPLICATING LAYERS

The active layer can be duplicated by clicking on the Duplicate Layer entry in the Layers menu. The duplicated layer is positioned just above the active layer. This function is also provided by the button depicting the two sheets of paper in the button bar.

2.3.5 DELETING LAYERS

The active layer can be deleted by selecting the Delete Layer entry from the Layers menu. This function is also provided by the button depicting a Trash Can.

2.4 LAYER EXPORT AND IMPORT

Collecting separate, raw image elements into a single image window is one of the most-used layer operations in this book. This is a fundamental component of compositing, a subject discussed in great depth in Chapter 7. However, it is also useful for a wide range of core and advanced techniques in the GIMP.

The importation of layers into an image is accomplished using the `Copy`, `Cut`, and `Paste` editing functions (see Section 1.7). The technique for importing a layer is so important that this section develops an example in detail to illustrate the methodology. Study it well, because this technique is used often in this book.

To illustrate the process, we begin with the two images shown in Figure 2.8. Each image consists of a single layer, and each will be imported into a third image that, on completion of the procedure, will contain three layers.

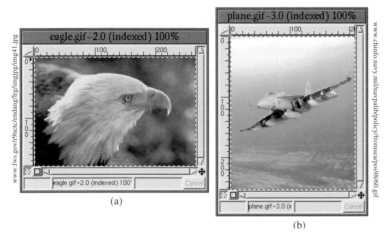

Figure 2.8: Two Images to Illustrate the Use of `Copy` and `Paste`

To begin, a new image is created that has width and height sufficient to accommodate the two single-layer images. Once open, the eagle image in Figure 2.8(a) is copied and pasted into it. This is accomplished by moving the mouse cursor into the eagle image window and selecting the `Copy` function from the `Image:Edit` menu. This can also be accomplished by simply typing `C-c` in the image window. This copies the active layer of the eagle image into the default buffer. Note that for multiple-layer images, it is the active layer that is copied into the buffer. Thus, it would be prudent to verify which layer is active by inspecting the Layers dialog before copying. The whole procedure could also be performed by cutting the image instead of copying. Cutting puts a copy of the layer in the buffer and then deletes it from the image window. To cut the image, use the `Cut` function from the `Image:Edit` menu. This function can be more easily employed by typing `C-x` in the image window.

Now that the eagle image is in the buffer, it can be pasted into the new image. This is done by moving the mouse cursor into the new image window and using the `Paste` function found in the `Image:Edit` menu, which can be more expeditiously accomplished by typing `C-v` in the image window. The result of the paste is shown in Figure 2.9(a). The Layers dialog for this image is shown in Figure 2.9(b), and it shows that the pasted layer appears as a floating selection. The Background layer, the only other layer in the dialog, is grayed out, meaning that it cannot be selected as the active layer.

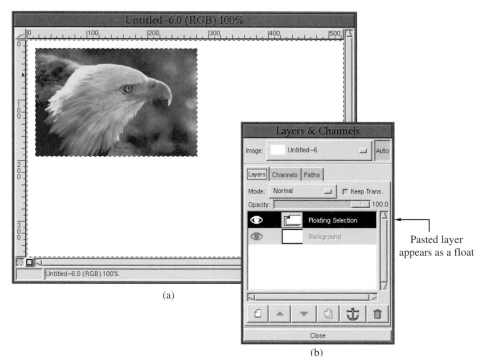

(a)

(b)

Figure 2.9: Importing the First Pasted Image

The pasted layer appears in Figure 2.9(a) as a selection with a moving dashed line around it. (Recall that these moving dashes are referred to as the *Marching Ants*.) This floating selection can be positioned in the new image with the Move tool from the Toolbox.

Once the layer is positioned, it can be anchored to the underlying layer by bringing up the Layers menu and selecting the Anchor Layer function from the Layers menu or by typing C-h in either the Layers & Channels or image windows. It is also possible to simply click on the Anchor button in the Layers dialog. For this example, however, the layer is not anchored to the layer below it. Rather, it is converted into a new layer. This is done by using the New Layer function found in the Layers menu. Figure 2.10 illustrates the result of the conversion. Figure 2.10(a) shows how the converted layer is smaller than the image window. Figure 2.10(b) illustrates the corresponding Layers dialog showing that the float was converted to a layer. A floating selection can also be converted to a new layer by typing C-n in the Layers & Channels window or by clicking on the New Layer icon in the button bar.

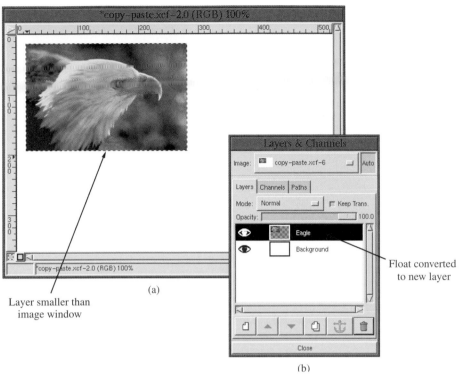

Layer smaller than
image window

(a)

Float converted
to new layer

(b)

Figure 2.10: Creation of a New Layer

The sequence just described for importing the eagle image is used so
often that it deserves to be memorized. Let's concisely recap the steps
required...then bookmark this page! The following list slightly
generalizes the procedure by assuming that there is a multilayer source
image window containing a layer to be exported and another multilayered
destination image that will import it:

1. In the source image window, type C-l to bring up the Layers dialog.
2. In the Layers dialog, make the source layer active by clicking on its
   thumbnail in the Layers Palette.
3. Back in the source image window, type C-c to copy the active layer to
   the default buffer.
4. In the destination image window, type C-v to paste the buffer contents
   into a floating selection. (Note that the context of the Layers dialog
   automatically changes to the destination image window when C-v is
   typed there.)
5. Position the floating selection as desired with the Move tool.
6. Type C-n in the Layers dialog (or click on the New Layer button) to
   anchor the float to a new layer. Otherwise, type C-h or click the
   Anchor button to anchor it to the last active layer of the destination
   image.

By the way, when the floating selection is converted to a new layer, the resulting dimensions of the layer are just large enough to contain the contents of the pasted layer. As shown in Figure 2.10(a), the resulting pasted eagle image layer is smaller than the image window. It is easy to put the pasted image into a separate layer having the same dimensions as the destination image window. Just create a new layer in the destination image before pasting from the buffer. After pasting, anchor the floating selection to this new layer by clicking the Anchor icon in the button bar.

Repeating the import procedure for the airplane in Figure 2.8(b) produces the result shown in Figure 2.11.

Figure 2.11: Importing the Second Pasted Image

Note that the boundary of the active layer in Figure 2.11(a) is visible as a black-and-yellow dashed line. Typically we are not aware of layer boundaries because often all the layers have the same dimensions. When this is the case, the layer boundary is coincident with the window edge. However, for the case illustrated in Figure 2.11(a), the layer boundary is apparent because the pasted layer is smaller than the image window.

The visible boundary of a layer can be a problem, especially when you're trying to adjust the relative position of two layers or when you're trying to carefully match colors at layer edges (for a particularly good example of this problem, see Section 7.5). When it is desirable to suppress the layer boundary, its visibility can be turned off with the function `Toggle Selection`, found in the `Image:View` menu or by typing `C-t` in the image window.

2.5 FLOATS

In the previous section, we came across a special layer called a floating selection, often simply referred to as a float. A float is a temporary layer that gets created automatically under certain circumstances and that can be explicitly created if needed. A float is a special type of layer. All other layers are disabled when a float is created, and nothing can be done with the other layers until the float is anchored. Although the other layers are disabled, almost all GIMP operations can still be performed on the floating layer.

Floats are sort of a throwback, a vestige of prehistoric times when the GIMP had not yet evolved into a layer-based tool. Back then, it was necessary to have floats because that was the only way to selectively process parts of an image. Now it is more effective to separate various image components into different layers, allowing you to more conveniently and effectively process and combine them. Nevertheless, as already noted, they are created automatically, so it is important to know how they work and what to do with them. There are basically three things about floats that you need to know: when they are automatically created, how they can be explicitly created, and how they are anchored.

2.5.1 AUTOMATIC CREATION OF FLOATS

There are two circumstances under which floats are created. The first occurs after you make a selection. After the selection is made, it becomes immediately possible to move it (even without selecting the `Move` tool). This is done by placing the mouse cursor inside the selection (the cursor becomes a four-way arrow) and by clicking and dragging. After you release the selection, it automatically becomes a floating selection. Figure 2.12(a) illustrates a selection that has been moved. The corresponding Layers dialog, shown in Figure 2.12(b), shows the new layer, entitled

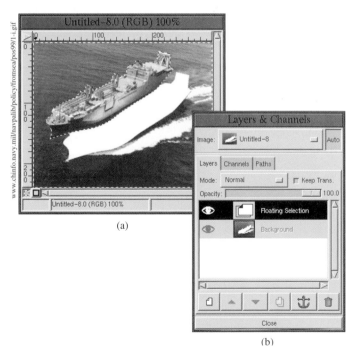

(a)

(b)

Figure 2.12: A Moved Selection Becomes a Float

Floating Selection. Also note that the original layer is grayed out, indicating that it has been disabled from other GIMP operations.

The second way that a floating layer is automatically created is after a copy and paste, or a cut and paste operation. Whether the default buffer contains a selection or an entire layer, pasting from the buffer produces a float.

2.5.2 EXPLICIT CREATION OF FLOATS

A selection can be explicitly made into a float without moving it. This is done by using the `Float` function found in the `Image:Select` menu or by simply typing `C-S-l` in the image window. A good use for the explicit creation of a float is described in Section 2.6.2.

2.5.3 ANCHORING FLOATS

After a float has been created, normal operations cannot continue in the GIMP until the float is anchored. Anchoring is just the operation of depositing the float into a normal layer. Once this is done, the other layers become available for GIMP operations again. A layer can be anchored either to a new layer or to the last active layer before the float was created. A float is anchored to a new layer by selecting `New Layer` from the `Layers` menu or by clicking on the `New Layer` button in the Layers dialog. A float is anchored to the previously active layer by using the `Anchor Layer` function from the `Layers` menu, by typing `C-h` in the image window, or by clicking on the `Anchor` button in the Layers dialog.

2.6 MANIPULATING LAYERS

As already discussed, layers are the most important image components for image manipulation. They are the basic raw materials you want to work with and combine. In most every GIMP project, layers need to be moved, resized, positioned, transformed, cut, pasted, and so on. These types of layer operations are discussed in this section.

2.6.1 POSITIONING LAYERS

One of the most basic layer operations is positioning. Compositing from a set of raw image materials requires that the various components, each on a separate layer, be appropriately positioned. This section describes several techniques for layer positioning.

MOVING LAYERS

Moving a layer is accomplished using the `Move` tool. This tool is invoked by clicking on the Toolbox button displaying the four-way arrow icon. Clicking on this tool changes the mouse cursor to a four-way arrow when it is in the image window. Clicking and dragging while the cursor is in the image window causes the layer underneath the mouse cursor to move. The layer affected is the one that is highest in the layer stack and has pixels more than 50% opaque under the mouse cursor (see Section 5.7 for more on opacity and transparency). This means that if the top layer is transparent at the mouse cursor position, it is not moved. This also means that if the active layer is transparent at the mouse cursor position, it is not moved. Rather, it is the first layer from the top that has more than 50% opaque pixels under the mouse cursor that is moved. Alternatively, the active layer can be forced to move by Shift-clicking and dragging. This moves the active layer regardless of its visibility, degree of transparency, or position with respect to the cursor.

ALIGNING LAYERS WITH GUIDES

Sometimes a layer needs to be positioned more carefully than can be easily judged by eye. Under these circumstances, it is often convenient to use guides to facilitate their placement. Guides are useful because they have a snapping property. A layer released sufficiently near a guide will jump to the guide position. The snapping property of guides is controlled by the Snap to Guides checkbox in the Image:View menu. The checkbox must be toggled on for the snapping property to work.

To illustrate how guides are useful for layer positioning, the three planet images shown in Figures 2.13(a), (b), and (c) were each copied and pasted to new layers in a larger image window with a black background. This is shown in Figure 2.14.

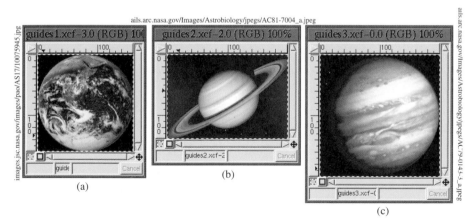

Figure 2.13: Images to be Aligned with Guides

Figure 2.14: Images Aligned with Guides

The objective is to organize the planets on a diagonal, but with a uniform black border between them and the window edge. This was done by placing two horizontal and two vertical guides in the image window, each positioned exactly three ruler tick marks from the edge. Where do the guides come from? Well, they are hidden inside the rulers at the left and top edges of the image window. Clicking on a ruler and then dragging the mouse into the image window drags a guide along with it. Releasing the mouse button positions the guide. Any number of guides can be created in this way. Once the guides are positioned, their visibility can be toggled on or off with the `Toggle Guides` function, found in the `Image:View` menu, or by typing `C-S-t` in the image window.

The guides can be seen in Figure 2.14 as blue dashed lines. The Jupiter and Earth layers were positioned with the `Move` tool so that their corners were aligned at the cross-hairs of the guides. It can be seen that the active layer, designated by the yellow dashed boundaries shown in Figure 2.14, are perfectly aligned with the guides. That the layers snapped to the guides simplified the positioning operation. When no longer needed, the guides can be moved off the image by first activating the `Move` tool from the Toolbox and then using the mouse to drag the guides back into the rulers.

Toggling the Layer Boundary

Careful alignment or color matching between layers is often required for layer edges that are overlapping or abutting. The layer boundaries of the active layer can be seen in the image window, even when the layer contents cannot be seen. This boundary, consisting of a black–and–yellow dashed line, can impede the precision with which alignment and color matching work is performed. Under these circumstances it is useful to visually toggle off the layer boundaries, which is easily done with the `Toggle Selection` function, found in the `Image:View` menu. Alternatively, `C-t` can be typed in the image window. The visibility of the layer boundaries is restored by toggling a second time.

2.6.2 RESIZING AND SCALING

As was seen in Figures 2.2 and 2.10(a), the layers in an image need not all be the same size. Furthermore, changing a layer's dimensions can be quite useful. In the parlance of the GIMP, a layer can be *resized*, which means that its boundaries are shrunk or enlarged without changing the dimensions of the image's contents. Alternatively, a layer can be *scaled*, which means that the dimensions of the layer are changed and the image contents are stretched or squeezed to exactly fit within the new layer boundaries. Six functions in the GIMP resize or scale layers and images:

- `Layer Boundary Size`, found in the `Layers` menu
- `Scale Layer`, found in the `Layers` menu
- `Canvas Size`, found in the `Image:Image` menu
- `Scale Image`, found in the `Image:Image` menu
- The `Crop` tool from the Toolbox
- The `Transform` tool from the Toolbox

Each of these are discussed and compared in the following sections.

IMAGE SCALING

Scaling an image results in changing the dimensions of all the layers at once, while simultaneously stretching or squeezing the image contents to fit. The function `Scale Image`, found in the `Image:Image` menu, is the tool that accomplishes this. Figure 2.15(a) shows an example image, and Figure 2.15(b) shows the `Scale Image` dialog. The new width and height of the image can be specified in pixels or as a percentage of the current dimensions. The default is to scale the two dimensions proportionally, but this can be changed by toggling the chain icon next to the Ratio X and Y entry boxes. The result of scaling down the image shown in Figure 2.15(a) by 75% is shown in Figure 2.15(c). The result of scaling it up by 125% is shown in Figure 2.15(d).

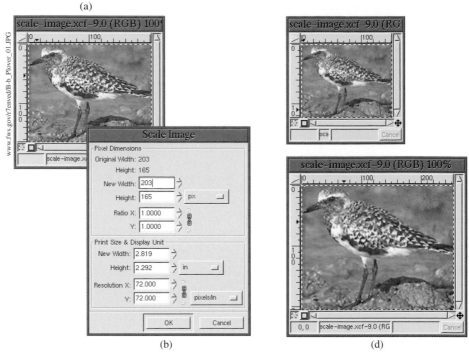

Figure 2.15: Image Scaling

Image Resizing

At first blush it would seem that the `Canvas Size` function found in the `Image:Image` menu should work in a similar fashion to `Scale Image`. However, there is an important difference between resizing an image and scaling it. Because the image contents do not change with the image boundaries, there is a non-unique choice in how they are positioned within the resized image window. Thus, when resizing to a smaller image window, the position of the image within the new window depends on the values for the new width, height, and X and Y offsets.

Figure 2.16 illustrates how using `Canvas Size` can give rise to an inconvenient problem. Figure 2.16(a) shows the original image, and Figure 2.16(b) shows the `Set Canvas Size` dialog. In the dialog the X and Y ratios have been set to 50% of the original image size. The result is shown in Figure 2.16(c). As can be seen, the image is poorly positioned within the new window. This can be compensated for by using the `Move` tool to reposition the image inside the window. The result of doing this is shown in Figure 2.16(d). However, the result still leaves the image subject, the wolf's head, poorly framed. The problem is that there is no easy way to enter numbers into the `Set Canvas Size` dialog to obtain an aesthetically pleasing result.

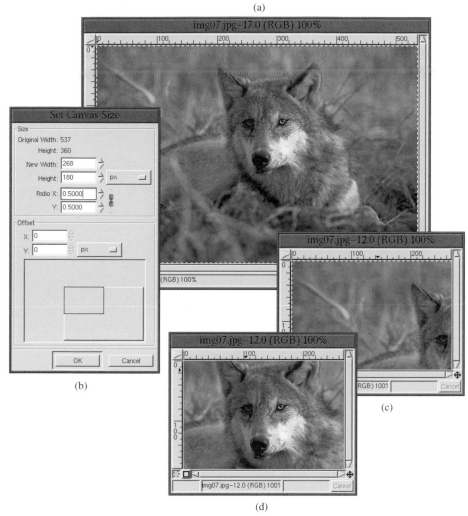

(a)

(b)

(c)

(d)

Figure 2.16: Image Resizing (Original Becomes Smaller)

A better solution is to resize the image interactively using the Crop tool. Figure 2.17 illustrates how the original image can be resized smaller this way. The tool is applied by clicking on the Crop tool icon in the Toolbox and then clicking and dragging in the image window to create the crop rectangle. Once drawn, the dimensions of the crop rectangle can be adjusted by clicking and dragging either the upper-left or lower-right corners of the rectangle. The rectangle can also be repositioned by clicking and dragging the upper-right or lower-left corners.

Figure 2.17: Resizing Using the Crop Tool

The result of using the Crop tool to nicely frame the wolf's head is shown in Figure 2.17(a). When using this tool, the Crop dialog appears, as shown in Figure 2.17(b). It is possible to crop the image by clicking on the Crop button in the dialog or by simply clicking inside the crop rectangle in the image window. This makes the image smaller and simultaneously discards the image parts outside of the window. Alternatively, the image can be resized by clicking on the Resize button in the Crop dialog. This makes the image window smaller *without* discarding the image parts outside the resulting window.

Figure 2.17(c) shows the result of cropping the image to the crop rectangle seen in Figure 2.17(a). From the above discussion, it should be clear that there is really no reason to use Canvas Size to make an image window smaller. It is simply more convenient to do it with the Crop tool.

Although Canvas Size is not optimum for making an image smaller, it is quite useful for making it larger. This is especially valuable when compositing several raw images. Typically you discover, after positioning various imported layers, that the resulting image window is not large enough to adequately frame the composition. When this happens, Canvas Size is the tool that fixes the problem. Figure 2.18 illustrates the result of resizing an image.

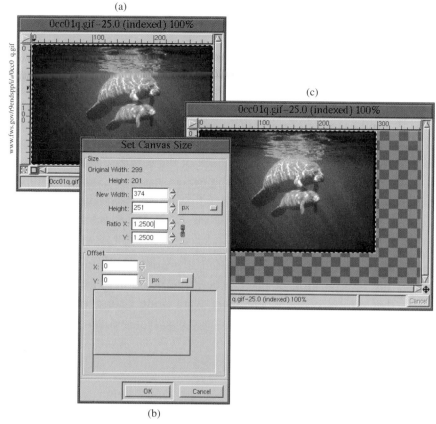

(a)

(b)

(c)

Figure 2.18: Image Resizing (Original Becomes Larger)

Figure 2.18(a) shows the original image, and Figure 2.18(b) shows the Set Canvas Size dialog box. This time the X and Y ratios are scaled to 125% of the original. The result is shown in Figure 2.18(c). Once the image window has been resized it is possible to reposition the image layer or layers using the Move tool.

LAYER SCALING

As has already been discussed in this section, it is possible to scale an entire image. However, it is also possible to scale a single layer within an image. There are two tools for doing this in the GIMP: the Scale Layer function, found in the Layers menu, and the Transform tool in the Toolbox.

As for entire images, a layer can be scaled either smaller or larger. The most typical use of layer scaling is to adjust the relative size of an image on one layer with respect to an image in another. This is needed for almost every compositing project (for examples, see Chapter 7). When it is necessary to scale a layer smaller, either the Scale Layer function or the scaling option of the Transform tool will do the trick. However, the Transform tool might be

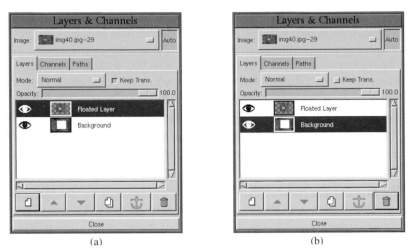

(a)   (b)

Figure 2.20: Resizing a Layer Smaller: Anchoring the Float to a New Layer and Deleting the Old Layer

The result of resizing the layer smaller is shown in Figure 2.21. In Figure 2.21(a), the layer has been resized smaller, which can be seen by the black-and-yellow dashed layer boundary. Figure 2.21(b) shows the resulting Layers dialog. The procedure, as described, allows the layer contents to be carefully positioned within the resized layer.

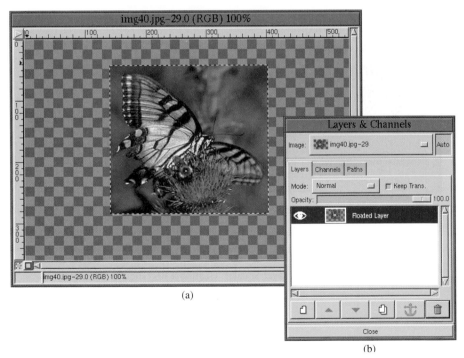

(a)

(b)

Figure 2.21: The Resulting Resized Layer

Although there are good reasons to resize an *image* larger, it is difficult to imagine a good reason for resizing a *layer* larger. However, due probably to a rationale of symmetry, a layer can be resized larger. It should be noted that, as for layer scaling, the GIMP does not allow a layer to be resized to dimensions larger than the window boundaries of an image. To resize a layer larger than the current image boundaries, the image must first be resized to accommodate it.

2.6.3 FLIPPING

The active layer can be flipped around its vertical or horizontal axes with the `Flip` tool from the Toolbox. A flip is performed by clicking on the `Flip` tool icon, represented by a two-way arrow in the Toolbox, and then clicking in the image window. When in the image window, the mouse cursor appears as a two-way arrow that is oriented horizontally for horizontal flips and vertically for vertical flips.

As an example of using the `Flip` tool, Figure 2.22(a) shows an image of a pelican and Figure 2.22(b) shows the result after flipping the image horizontally. Note that the Horizontal radio button is selected in the `Tool Options` dialog, as shown in Figure 2.22(c). Selecting the Vertical radio button, as shown in Figure 2.22(e), produces the result in Figure 2.22(d).

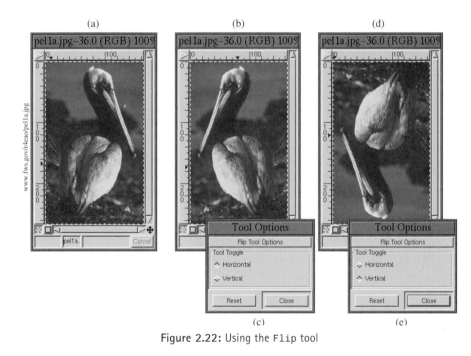

Figure 2.22: Using the `Flip` tool

Note that if the Horizontal radio button is selected in the `Tool Options` dialog, the flip option can be momentarily toggled to Vertical by Control-clicking in the image window. Similarly, if the Vertical radio button is selected in the dialog, the option can be toggled to Horizontal option by Control-clicking in the image window.

2.6.4 ROTATING BY 90° INCREMENTS

An image or layer can be rotated in 90° increments using the `Rotate` menus. For an image, use the `Image:Image/Transforms/Rotate` menu shown in Figure 2.23(a). For a layer, use the `Image:Layers/Rotate` menu shown in Figure 2.23(b). As you can see, these menus can be used to rotate either the entire image or the active layer by 90, 180, or 270°.

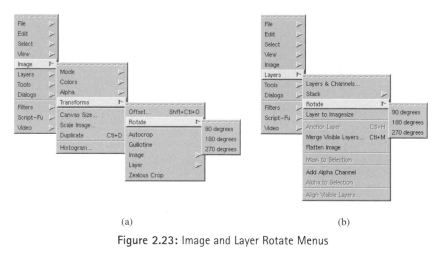

(a)   (b)

Figure 2.23: Image and Layer Rotate Menus

2.6.5 THE TRANSFORM TOOL

General transformations of a layer can be done using the `Transform` tool from the Toolbox. This tool can perform rotation, scaling, shearing, and perspective transformations of the active layer. As usual, care must be taken to specify the active layer before applying this tool.

Figure 2.24(a) illustrates an image layer contained in a somewhat larger window. Shown in Figure 2.24(b) is the `Tool Options` dialog, which is obtained by double-clicking the `Transform` tool icon in the Toolbox window. The four radio buttons in the Transform area of the dialog are used to select the desired transformation type, which are Rotation, Scaling, Shearing, or Perspective.

Transforming a layer requires interpolation of pixel values, and this can introduce some jagged-edge artifacts into the result. The toggle button labeled Smoothing diminishes this effect, which is why it is on by default. It does tend to make the image a little less sharp, though (see Section 6.4.1 for a discussion on how to recover some of the lost sharpness).

The Tool paradigm area of the dialog has two options. The default is Traditional, which maps the image to a transformed grid (see Figure 2.26). For those who like to go against the grain, the Corrective option maps the transformed grid to the image, thus producing an inverse transformation. For example, rotating the transform grid in one direction with the Corrective option maps the grid back to the image, making the image itself rotate in the opposite direction. Sound complicated? It isn't. Just try it yourself and you'll see.

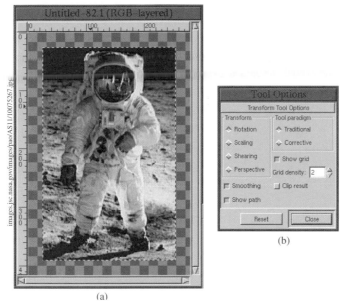

(a)

(b)

Figure 2.24: Transform Tool Dialog

Rotation   Figures 2.25 and 2.26 illustrate the use of the Rotation option of
the Transform tool. Figure 2.25(a) shows the image layer, and Figure 2.25(b)
shows the Rotation Information dialog that appears when the left mouse button is clicked in the image window. The Rotation Information dialog has entry
boxes that can be used to give a specific angle of rotation as well as the position of the point that will be the center of rotation. By default, the center of
rotation is the geometric center of the active layer.

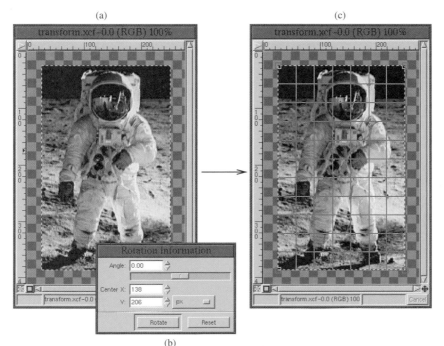

(a)   (c)

(b)

Figure 2.25: Initiating the Rotation Transformation

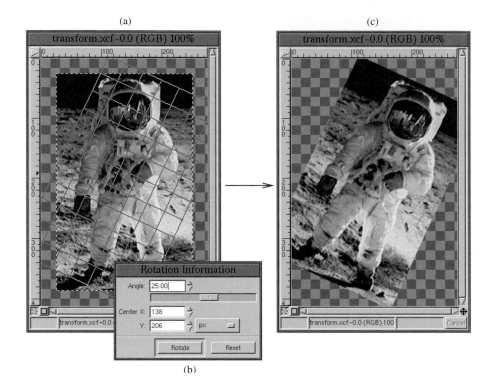

Figure 2.26: Finalizing the Rotation Transformation

For each of the Transform options, Rotation, Scaling, Shearing, or Perspective, the first mouse click on the image brings up a dialog specific to the chosen option. This mouse click also displays a grid superimposed on the active layer in the image window. The number of grid lines can be controlled from the `Tool Options` dialog (see Figure 2.24(b)). The grid lines can be seen in Figure 2.25(c). Placing the mouse cursor within the active layer in the image window changes the cursor in accordance with the type of transformation to be performed. The image outline and grid can then be transformed by clicking and dragging. The transformation of the *grid* can be adjusted as many times as desired because the transformation of the *image* is not initiated until the option transform button is clicked. For example, the Rotate button in Figure 2.26(b) must be clicked to cause the actual rotation of the image.

As the grid is rotated for the Rotate option of the `Transform` tool, the angle is interactively reported in the `Rotation Information` dialog. The rotated outline for an angle of 25° is shown in Figure 2.26(a). As already stated, once the desired angle of rotation is found, the image itself is rotated by clicking on the Rotate button, seen in the dialog shown in Figure 2.26(b). The resulting rotated layer is shown in Figure 2.26(c).

As an alternative to interactively rotating the grid with the mouse, the rotation can also be performed by entering a value into the Angle entry box or by using the slider in the Rotation dialog. Useful values of rotation can be determined with the Measure tool. An example of this is illustrated in Section 7.2.

Scaling Figure 2.27 illustrates the Scaling option of the Transform tool. Similar to rotation, scaling can be performed interactively with the mouse or by entering values into the Width and Height entry boxes in the Scaling dialog.

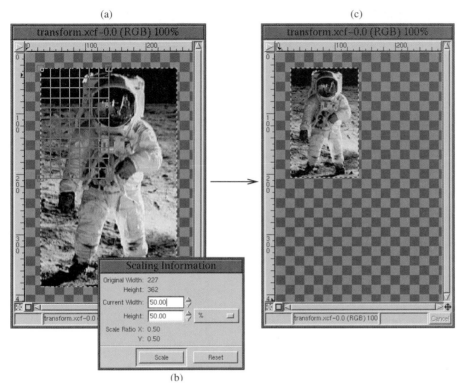

Figure 2.27: The Scaling Transformation

Values can be entered into the Scaling dialog in a number of units, the default being pixels. It is often convenient to perform scaling as a percentage of the original dimensions (which are shown at the top of the Scaling dialog as the Original Width and Height). This can be done by choosing the % option from the pull-down menu in the dialog. Figure 2.27(b) shows that this choice was used to scale the grid in Figure 2.27(a) by 50% in both dimensions. When the Scale button in the dialog is clicked, this produces the result shown in Figure 2.27(c).

It is useful to be able to constrain the X and Y scale ratio so as to maintain their aspect ratio when scaling a layer with the Transform tool. This is done by pressing both the Control and Alt keys while using the mouse to scale the transform grid. Useful values for scaling can be determined using the Measure tool. Section 7.5 illustrates an example of this.

Shearing Figure 2.28 shows the application of the Shearing option of the Transform tool. As with the other options, shearing can be applied interactively with the mouse or by entering values into the Shear Information dialog. Shearing can be applied either horizontally or vertically, but not in both directions simultaneously. If applied using the mouse, the direction of shear is determined by the mouse's initial direction of movement. Otherwise, it depends on the first entry box used in the dialog.

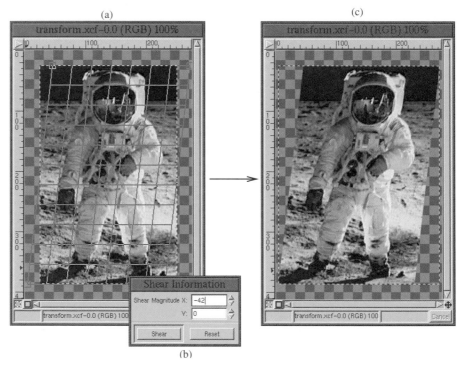

Figure 2.28: The Shear Transformation

Perspective Perspective is perhaps the most intriguing option of the Transform tool. This option is illustrated in Figure 2.29. This is the only transform option where values cannot be directly entered into a dialog. As shown in Figure 2.29(b), there is numerical feedback about how the Perspective transform option is applied to the image, but this is not particularly valuable because it is unclear how to reuse the information. The consequence is that the Perspective option may only be applied interactively with the mouse.

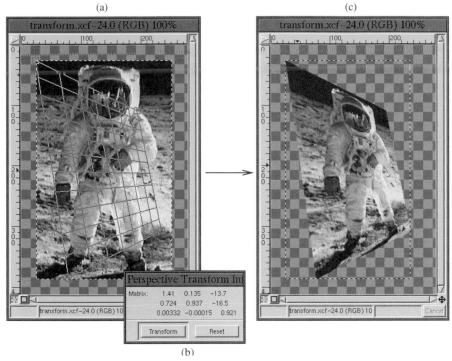

(a)

(c)

Perspective Transform In
Matrix: 1.41   0.135   −13.7
           0.724   0.937   −16.5
           0.00332 −0.00015 0.921

[Transform]   [Reset]

(b)

Figure 2.29: The Perspective Transformation

Figure 2.29(a) shows that the grid line feature provides very useful feedback for this particular tool. The lines help visualize the perspective warping that will take place once the Transform button is clicked in the `Perspective Transform` dialog. The perspective transform allows each of the four corners of the layer to be independently repositioned. The resulting image is warped to a general quadrilateral. Figure 2.29(c) shows the result of applying the perspective transform specified by the grid shown in Figure 2.29(a).

It should be noted that all the transforms can be used in conjunction with the Transform Lock option of the Paths dialog. This is extremely useful and is discussed in more detail in Section 3.4.1. A relevant example is shown in Section 7.2.

2.7 COMBINING LAYERS

It is often necessary to combine several layers into one. This is particularly useful prior to saving an image to a non-GIMP format such as JPEG or GIF. There are two ways of combining layers in the GIMP. The method to use depends on the final use of the resulting image.

2.7.1 MERGING

It is possible to merge a subset of layers from an image into a single layer. This is accomplished by choosing `Merge Visible Layers` from the `Layers` menu or by simply typing `C-m` in the image window. Alternatively, it is sometimes convenient to merge just two adjacent layers in the layer stack. This can be done with `Merge Down`, found in the `Layers` menu. The use of this function merges the active layer with the next *visible* layer down in the stack. `Merge Down` can be conveniently invoked by typing `C-S-m` in the Layers dialog. A nice use of `Merge Down` is illustrated in Section 9.1.4.

2.7.2 FLATTENING

The function `Flatten Image`, found in the `Layers` menu, is an alternative to `Merge Visible Layers`. This function merges all the layers regardless of their visibility in the image window. In addition, `Flatten Image` applies all the layer masks to their respective layers (for more on layer masks, see Section 4.2) and deletes any remaining alpha values in the image. In fact, `Flatten Image` is the only function in the GIMP that can remove the alpha channel from an image. Channel masks, however, are neither applied nor deleted (see Section 4.1 for more on channel masks). Typically an image is flattened in order to save it in an image format that does not support layers or transparency. The JPEG format is an example of this.

2.8 COMMON PROBLEMS AND FREQUENTLY ASKED QUESTIONS

Layers can be tricky, and it is sometimes possible to run into what seem like incomprehensible difficulties while using them. The following list of problems addresses some common difficulties with layers. In a nutshell, the information in the Layers dialog almost always contains the solutions to these problems.

- **I am trying to draw, paint, select, or apply some other operation on the image window, and repeated efforts just don't seem to produce any results. What's going on?**

  GIMP operations are applied to the active layer. A common problem with layers is that the active layer is not visible. It is possible that the active layer is blocked by layers above it or that the visibility of the active layer is not turned on. To solve the problem, make sure that the Eye icon of the active layer is on, and turn off the Eye icon of the layers above it.

- **I am trying to paint in a transparent part of a layer and am getting no results. Why?**

  If you are trying to draw or paint on a transparent part of a layer and nothing seems to leave a mark, the problem is that the Keep Transparency button is on in the Layers dialog. Toggle this button off and your problem will disappear.

- **I want to add a layer mask to my image, but it is grayed out in the Layers menu. Why isn't this option available?**

  Background layers and flattened images (see Section 2.7.2) have no alpha channels and thus cannot have a layer mask. This problem is easily solved, though, by applying the Add Alpha Channel function from the Layers menu.

- **The top layer of my image is labeled Floating Selection, all my other layers are grayed out, and I can't make any of my layers active except the top one. What's wrong?**

  A floating selection disables all the other layers until it is anchored to a new layer or to the last active layer. To anchor to a new layer, choose New Layer from the Layers menu or click on the New Layer button in the Layers dialog. To anchor to the previously active layer, choose Anchor Layer from the Layers menu, or type C-h in the image or dialog window, or click on the Anchor button in the Layers dialog.

- **I saved a finished project's image to disk, but when I try to view the saved image in another image display program, it's missing elements and it doesn't look like the one I saved. Why is this?**

  Not all image formats support layers or transparency (JPEG is one example). For finished projects that are saved to formats supporting alpha channels, use the Merge Visible Layers function from the Layers menu before saving. If alpha is not supported, use Flatten Image from the Layers menu instead. Also, read the next item.

- **I spent hours working on an image with multiple layers, channel masks, layer masks, and paths and then saved it. But when I tried to reload my image back into the GIMP, everything but a single layer was gone! What happened!?**

  Work in progress and finished projects should be saved in the GIMP's native XCF format. This is the only format that saves all the information about layers, masks, and paths.

3

SELECTIONS

Selections are extremely important tools for working with digital images. They are a means for partitioning an image into two groups of pixels: those we want to work on and those we do not. Selections allow the *selective* application of enhancements, functions, filters, and plug-ins to specific target regions of an image. Furthermore, selections are essential tools for compositing image material from several sources into a single image. This is core to collage and photo montage, two subjects developed in detail in Chapter 7.

This chapter covers the selection tools in the GIMP. However, the material presented here is really only half the story on the subject of selections. The other half is presented in Chapter 4, which covers masks. As described there, selections and masks are really just two implementations of the same principle. They both result in a separation of subject from background. They arrive at this result, however, using different and very complementary methods. You really need both to get the best selection results.

Selections are the scalpel of the image manipulator's toolbox, and you will use them a lot. Because selections can easily be the most time-consuming and frustrating part of a project, it is important to know how to use the selection tools artfully and effectively. This chapter explains how each selection tool works, and it presents the array of GIMP functions that are directly related to those selections. Furthermore, the conditions for which each selection tool is most effective are described, and each tool is rated against the others for its usefulness.

Before launching into the descriptions of the various selection tools, it is worthwhile to mention where selections fit into the structure of images. The relationship of pixels, channels, layers, and images was described in Section 2.2. Where, then, do selections fit in? A selection can be seen in the image

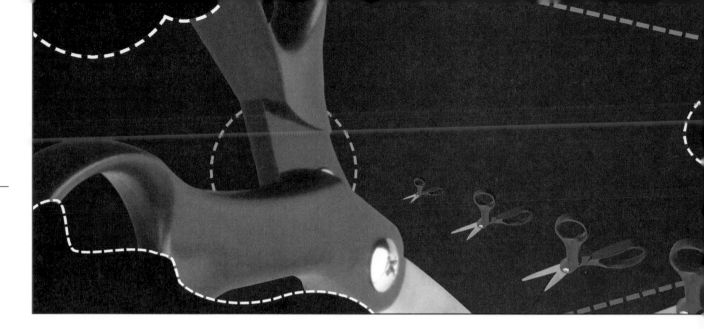

window—does that mean it is part of the image? The answer to these questions won't be fully given until Chapter 4, which covers masks. However, for now it suffices to know that selections are special channels, independent of the image layers, and whose selective effects apply only to the active layer.

3.1 The Basic Selection Tools

There are two types of selection tools. The first type works by drawing lines that separate the selection subject from its background. The second type makes a selection by specifying a representative *seed* pixel from the subject. The selection is then made automatically by including other pixels in the image that are sufficiently similar to the seed in color.

A goal of this chapter is to explain how to decide which type of selection tool should be applied. Often it is some combination that is the most effective. The decision is partially based on evaluating the characteristics of the subject that best differentiate it from the background. These could be a combination of its color, shape, value, or saturation (for more on the characteristics of color, value, and saturation, see Chapter 5). For difficult selections it is often necessary to experiment in order to discover the most effective approach.

3.1.1 The Six Selection Tools from the Toolbox

In this section, we start to develop our skills by reviewing the GIMP's basic selection tools and by exploring their underlying strengths and weaknesses. To begin, we discuss the six selection tools found in the GIMP Toolbox, shown in Figure 3.1. They consist of the `Rectangle Select`, the `Ellipse Select`, the `Free-Hand Select` (also known as the `Lasso`), the `Fuzzy Select` (known as the `Magic Wand`), the `Bezier Path` tool, and the `Intelligent Scissors`. Of these, the

`Bezier Path` and the Lasso are the most useful. `Rectangle Select` is also of some use. Of less use are the `Magic Wand` and `Ellipse Select` tools. Finally, although the `Intelligent Scissors` has an intriguing name, there is nothing this tool can do that can't be done better and more efficiently using other tools.

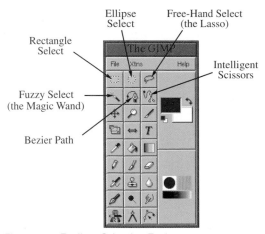

Figure 3.1: Toolbox Selection Tools

THE RECTANGLE SELECT AND ELLIPSE SELECT TOOLS

The `Rectangle Select` and `Ellipse Select` tools are used for selecting rectangular and elliptical regions in an image. A selection is initiated by clicking and dragging in the image window, and the selection is completed by releasing the mouse button. The selection process is interactively facilitated by an outline of the selection that can be seen while the mouse is being dragged.

Figure 3.2 shows examples of both the `Rectangle Select` and `Ellipse Select` tools. When completed, selections are displayed as moving dashed lines, traditionally referred to as the *Marching Ants*. In the figure, the arrows are just for illustrating where the selections begin and end. They don't actually appear when you use these tools. The arrows' tails show where the selections were initiated, and the heads show where they were terminated. Note that for the `Ellipse Select` tool the selection is inscribed in a rectangle defined by the arrow's head and tail.

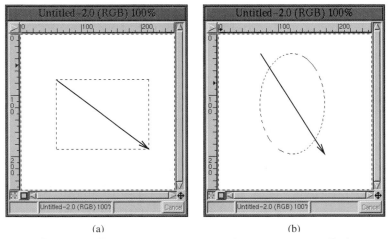

(a)   (b)

Figure 3.2: The `Rectangle Select` and `Ellipse Select` Tools

A perfectly square selection can be made with the `Rectangle Select` tool, and a perfectly circular selection can be made with the `Ellipse Select` tool. The trick is to use the Shift key, but read on carefully. Two other selection tricks are also performed with the Shift key (see Section 3.2 for the other). To avoid confusion, it is important to pay close attention to how this works.

To obtain a perfectly square or circular selection, begin the selection by clicking and dragging in the image window. While the mouse button is down, press the Shift key. In the image window, the resulting selection shape becomes a perfectly square or circular, depending on the tool you are using. The Shift key must remain pressed until the selection is finished and the mouse button has been released. Only then may the Shift key be released. If the Shift key is released before the left mouse button, the selection will revert to a normal rectangle or ellipse selection. The results of using the Shift key with the `Rectangle Select` and `Ellipse Select` tools are illustrated in Figure 3.3.

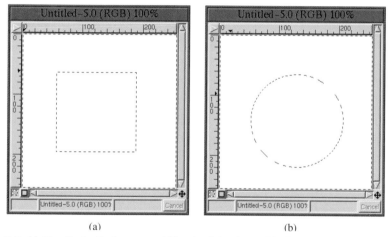

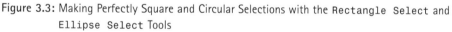

(a)   (b)

Figure 3.3: Making Perfectly Square and Circular Selections with the `Rectangle Select` and `Ellipse Select` Tools

Instead of initiating a rectangular or elliptical selection at one corner and terminating at the opposite one, it is also possible to initiate from the selection's center, terminating at a corner. The trick for this is similar to the technique just described for creating a perfectly square or circular selection. It is done by pressing the Control key after initiating the selection with the left mouse button. The Control key must remain pressed until after the mouse button is released. To combine perfectly square or circular selections in conjunction with center initiated ones, the Shift and Control keys must both be pressed after the left mouse button is clicked and remain so until after the mouse button is released.

THE LASSO (THE FREE-HAND SELECTION TOOL)

The Lasso is used to draw free-hand selections. Although its official name is the Free-Hand Selection tool, the Lasso will be preferred in this book because the tool's icon in the Toolbox resembles a lasso (and it's also a lot shorter to type).

The Lasso is used by clicking and dragging in the image window, tracing out the shape to be selected. Releasing the mouse button completes the selection. While tracing with the Lasso, the outline of the selection can be seen, and, when completed, the selection is shown by the Marching Ants. Figure 3.4 shows an example of a Lasso selection.

Figure 3.4: A Lasso Selection

The advantage of the Lasso is that it can be used to select arbitrarily complex objects. The disadvantage is that the work can be painstakingly slow, requiring extremely fine control of the mouse. Even the small selection shown in Figure 3.4 was difficult, because the tree's outline is so jagged and rough. Another aspect of the Lasso that makes it difficult for precision work is that the mouse button cannot be released while the selection is being made. This precludes using this tool for making large, complicated selections. For these reasons, the Lasso will not be our selection tool of choice for fine-grain work. Rather, it will mainly be used to rough-out selections around complicated shapes or for completing work on masks. A good example of the latter use of the Lasso is demonstrated in Sections 4.5.3 and 7.4.

THE MAGIC WAND (THE FUZZY SELECT TOOL)

Although its name is officially the Fuzzy Select tool, the Magic Wand will be preferred in this book because the tool's icon, as shown in the Toolbox, resembles a magic wand. The Magic Wand makes selections based on specifying a seed pixel in the image. The seed is the first selected pixel, and the pixels directly adjoining the seed are included in the selection if their colors are sufficiently close to the color of the seed. This creates a second set of selected pixels. This process is repeated with the neighboring pixels of the second selected set, and so on, until no more pixels can be added.

Figure 3.5 illustrates how the Magic Wand works. Figure 3.5(a) shows a smoothly-varying, radial gradient of pixel values going from black at the center to white at the edges. The location where the seed was chosen with the mouse is indicated. The resulting ring-like region selected by the Magic Wand is shown by the Marching Ants. The ring selection is equally thick on both sides of the seed because the Magic Wand includes pixels that have both higher and lower color values than the seed's.

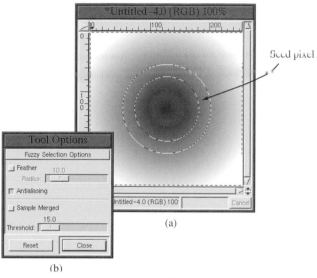

Figure 3.5: A Magic Wand Seed Pixel and Selection

So, how much lower and higher can adjoining pixel colors be and still be included in the selection? This is specified by the Magic Wand's selection threshold, which, as shown in Figure 3.5(b), can be set with the Threshold slider in the Tool Options dialog (see Section 3.1.2 for more on this). It can also be set interactively with the mouse. The threshold is set interactively by keeping the left mouse button pressed when selecting the seed pixel. When the outline of the selection appears, and with the left mouse button continually pressed, the mouse can be moved either to the right (or downward) to increase the threshold or to the left (or upward) to diminish it. Increasing the threshold results in a larger selection, and decreasing it, a smaller one. Changing the threshold should be done by moving the mouse in small increments so that the changes in the selected region can be carefully controlled.

The Magic Wand is a conceptually attractive tool. In principle, it automatically makes the selection by grouping pixels that are similar in color and that are spatially connected, being grown from a seed pixel. In practice, however, it is often difficult to get good results with the Magic Wand. This is because it is hard to find the seed pixel and threshold pair that will produce the selection we want. As an example, imagine a subject you want to select using the Magic Wand and that has pixel color values ranging from X to Y. To make the selection with the Magic Wand, a pixel whose value is exactly midway between X and Y must be selected as the seed. But how do we determine what X and Y are for our subject, and how do we find the pixel in the subject that has the midway value? These practical problems are not easily solved!

Fortunately there is another tool in the GIMP that allows you to more easily exploit the color-grouping selection concept. This tool is called Threshold and is found in the Image:Image/Colors menu. Its use is presented in Section 4.5.3.

Bezier Paths

The `Bezier Path` selection tool is very powerful. It is the only selection tool that allows the interactive adjustment of the selections it makes. The `Bezier Path` tool works by placing *control points* on an image. These are initially connected by straight-line *path segments*; however, using the *control handles* hidden inside each control point, the path segments can be made to curve in practically arbitrary manners. By using a Bezier path, an initial selection can be interactively corrected until the final result fits the desired selection like a glove.

Figure 3.6 illustrates the basic operations of a Bezier path. The initial Bezier path shown in Figure 3.6(a) was created by clicking in the image window five times. The upper-left corner was the first point, and the lower-left, lower-right, and upper-right corners were the second, third, and fourth points added to the path. The final click of the mouse was made on the initial point, thus closing the path. As each point was added, the straight-line segments seen in the figure appeared between the control points.

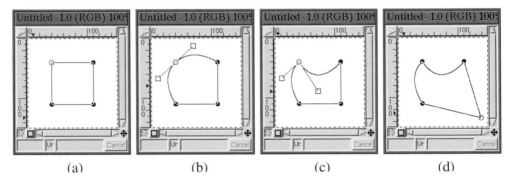

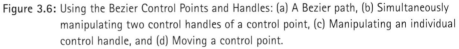

Figure 3.6: Using the Bezier Control Points and Handles: (a) A Bezier path, (b) Simultaneously manipulating two control handles of a control point, (c) Manipulating an individual control handle, and (d) Moving a control point.

While constructing a Bezier path, the mouse cursor appears as an arrow, with a filled circle just below and slightly to the arrow's right. This circle indicates that the path is not closed and that the next mouse click will create a new control point. Note that Bezier paths need not be closed. This is discussed in more detail in Section 3.4, which describes the Paths dialog.

The path segments between control points can be made to curve by manipulating the points' control handles. For a closed Bezier path, the control handles are made visible by clicking on a control point and dragging. Figure 3.6(b) shows how the control handles for the upper-left corner of the Bezier path have been pulled out of that control point. The dragging action of the mouse positions one of the control handles while the other moves in tandem with, but diametrically opposite, the first. As can be seen in Figure 3.6(b), the two path segments attached to the control point are made to curve by the action of the control handles.

Note that the control handles do not disappear once the mouse button has been released and that the handles can be readjusted at any time by clicking the mouse on either handle and dragging. However, only one set of handles may be visible at once. Clicking on another control point displays its handles while toggling off the visibility of the handles for any other point. Also note that when the mouse cursor is close enough to a control point or control handle to manipulate it, the cursor changes from an arrow with a filled circle below it to an arrow with the outline of square. Because control handles resemble squares, this special cursor is a useful way to indicate that the mouse cursor is close enough to the control point for the handles to be active.

The two control handles for a point can be moved independently of each other by using the Shift key. Pressing the Shift key while dragging a handle with the mouse makes that handle move while the other remains stationary. Moving a single control handle in this way allows the curvature of a single path segment to be manipulated. Figure 3.6(c) shows the result of using the Shift key to move one of the control handles independently of the other. Note how this changes the curve of the upper segment of the square while leaving the curve of the left segment as it was.

It is also possible to reposition a control point. This is done by pressing the Control key before clicking on a control point. Dragging the mouse while the mouse button and Control key are pressed moves the control point. The result of repositioning a control point is shown in Figure 3.6(d).

After creating a Bezier path with all the control points properly positioned and all the path segments appropriately curved, it may then be converted to a selection. This is done by clicking inside the closed path. Note that when the mouse cursor is moved inside the closed path, the cursor changes to an arrow with the outline of a dashed rectangle below it. The dashed rectangle resembles the Marching Ants, which will appear when the Bezier path is converted to a selection.

Figures 3.7 through 3.9 show the application of the `Bezier Path` tool in a practical example. Figure 3.7 shows that a closed Bezier path has been created by placing seven control points around the perimeter of a sea turtle's shell. Although the points are all positioned on the edge of the shell, the straight-line segments between points do not marry well to the shell's shape.

Figure 3.7: Creating a Bezier Path

As just described, the Bezier path can be adjusted to the shell's shape by manipulating the control handles. The first pair of handles are shown in Figure 3.8. The two handles had to be adjusted independently of each other to properly match the curve of the shell on either side of the control point. This can be seen in the figure by the different lengths of the control handles and by the slight angle between them.

Figure 3.8: Manipulating the Control Handles of a Bezier Control Point

After adjusting the control handles for each point in the Bezier path it is converted to a selection. The result, showing the Marching Ants, is illustrated in Figure 3.9. What is particularly interesting about this example is that the selection has been made with only a few control points. This is a strength of this tool. However, there are limitations to what can be accomplished with a Bezier path. A very irregular shape will need many control points and will require a lot of work to adjust the path to the shape.

Figure 3.9: Selection Created from the Bezier Path

A practical question is where should the control points be placed? Another is how many control points are necessary to adequately select a shape? For the placement of control points here are some rules of thumb:

- A control point must always be placed at a corner (like the one found at the rear-most point of the sea turtle's shell in Figures 3.7 through 3.9).

- A straight-edge region can only be created by placing a control point at each end of the edge, as shown in Figure 3.10(a).

- An inflection point on a curve can be created between a pair of control points, as shown in the bottom path segment of Figure 3.10(b). It can also be created with a single control point if this is placed exactly at the point of inflection.

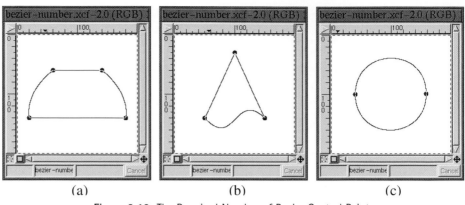

Figure 3.10: The Required Number of Bezier Control Points

The number of control points needed to adequately adjust a Bezier path to a shape is a more difficult question. Figure 3.10(c) shows that a pair of control points are all that is needed to create a circle. Thus, a single control point can cover up to 180 degrees of curve. However, this doesn't account for all curve characteristics. I personally like to place control points as the shape of my selection passes through 90 degrees of curve. This personal rule is borne out in the sea turtle selection shown in Figure 3.7.

In any case, the issue of the number of points required for a shape is not critical because it can be resolved using the Add Point and Delete Point functions available in the Paths dialog. These are discussed in detail in Section 3.4.

THE INTELLIGENT SCISSORS

In principle the Intelligent Scissors is supposed to work by following, as closely as possible, constant-valued color contours in the image between subsequent points clicked by the mouse. However, at the time of this writing, the Intelligent Scissors is a GIMP tool that seems to be broken. Much perplexed discussion has passed through the GIMP developers' mailing list on this tool and, unfortunately, it seems that for the present time this tool has little or no value. Even if the tool did work, I would still rank it as a tool of little utility.

3.1.2 SELECTION TOOL OPTIONS

Double-clicking on any of the Toolbox icons brings up the Tool Options dialog for that tool. For selection tools the important options are Antialiasing, Feather, Sample Merged, and Threshold. Each of these is discussed in this section.

ANTIALIASING

Antialiasing is an important edge treatment for selections. Figure 3.11 illustrates the antialiasing concept. Figure 3.11(a) shows an array of pixels that has been partitioned into two regions by a selection edge. However, due to the slope of the selection and the finite area of the pixels, some pixels are on both sides of the selection edge. That is, these pixels are only partially selected. What happens to this set of partially selected pixels is important for the aesthetic presentation of the selection's edge.

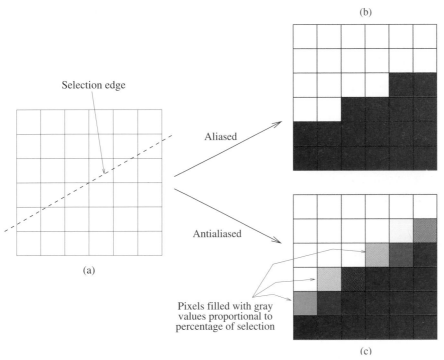

Figure 3.11: How Antialiasing Works

For example, let's assume that white represents a selected pixel and black an unselected one. Figure 3.11(b) shows what happens if pixels are included in the selection when more than 50% of the pixel is above the selection edge and unselected otherwise. This seems like a reasonable criterion; however, notice that the selection edge obtained by applying this rule produces a staircase effect on the edge. This staircase effect, known as *aliasing*, makes the edge look harsh. We'll see this in a more realistic example in a moment.

Alternatively, Figure 3.11(c) illustrates the concept of antialiasing. Here white represents a pixel which is fully selected, black one that is fully unselected, and gray represents partially selected pixels, where the level of gray indicates the percentage of the pixel that falls inside the selection. Thus, a lighter value of gray indicates a more fully selected pixel and a darker value a less selected one. Assigning gray values to partially selected pixels has the effect of visually smoothing the staircase effect illustrated in Figure 3.11(b), which is why this is called antialiasing.

The way antialiasing is actually implemented is by using the layer's alpha channel. Alpha channels were introduced in Section 2.2 and a more comprehensive presentation of them is given in Chapters 4 and 5. However, for the purposes of discussing antialiasing it is sufficient to know that the white pixels in Figure 3.11(c) represent pixels that are fully opaque, the black pixels those that are fully transparent, and the gray pixels those that are partially opaque (or transparent).

Figure 3.12 illustrates a more realistic example of aliased and antialiased pixels. Figures 3.12(a) and (b) each show a circle created using the `Ellipse Select` tool. For both, the selections were filled with black using the `Bucket Fill` tool. The selection made in part (a) of the figure was made without antialiasing, and that in part (b) with. From these two figures it can immediately be seen that the antialiased circle seems to have a much smoother edge.

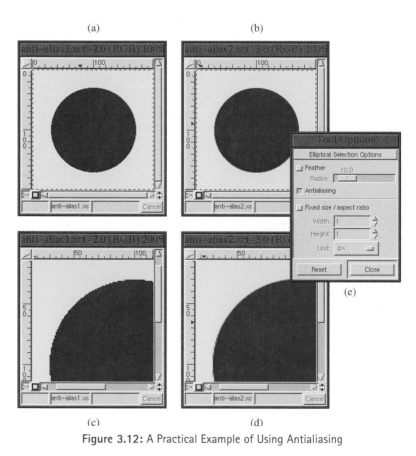

Figure 3.12: A Practical Example of Using Antialiasing

Figures 3.12(c) and (d) show zoomed versions of Figures 3.12(a) and (b). The staircase effect can be clearly seen in Figure 3.12(c). Alternatively, in Figure 3.12(d) there are black edge pixels that are partially transparent and that allow part of the yellow background to show through. Figures 3.12(b) and (d) demonstrate that antialiasing really does improve the aesthetic appearance of the selection edge. Figure 3.12(e) shows that the Antialiasing checkbox in the Tool Options dialog for the Ellipse Select tool is toggled on for Figures 3.12(b) and (d). For all the selection tools, Antialiasing is on by default.

As a final remark, note that the Rectangle Select tool does not have an antialiasing option. This is normal because this selection tool can never produce sloping edges. Consequently, the staircase problem illustrated in Figure 3.11 can never occur, and antialiasing is not needed.

FEATHERING

Feathering is a selection edge treatment similar to antialiasing. It works by changing the alpha value of pixels as a function of their radial distance from the selection edge. Figure 3.13 illustrates an example of a feathered selection. Figure 3.13(a) shows how two guides have been placed to aid in framing a selection using the Ellipse Select tool.

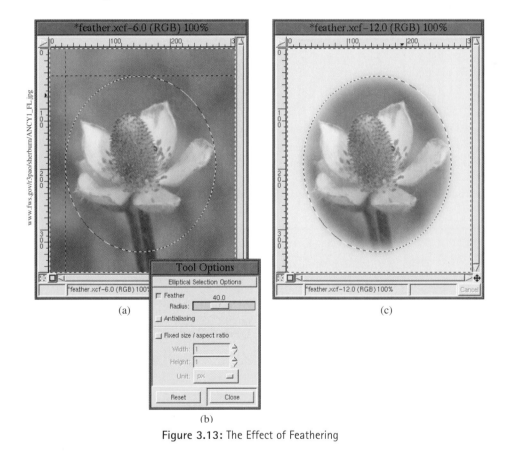

Figure 3.13: The Effect of Feathering

As shown in Figure 3.13(b), a value of 40 has been chosen for the Feather Radius in the `Tool Options` dialog for this selection tool. Furthermore, Antialiasing has been turned off. The result of inverting the selection and cutting away the background is shown in Figure 3.13(c). This result is actually displayed on a yellow background so that the transparency of the flower pixels can be better seen. Also, superimposed on Figure 3.13(c) is the original elliptical selection.

The transparency of the flower image shown in Figure 3.13(c) is 50% at the selection edge. The transparency increases moving outward from the edge and decreases moving inward from it. The rate at which the transparency changes while moving away from the selection edge is determined by the Feather Radius. For this example, the value chosen is 40, meaning that there is a feathering effect up to 40 pixels away in both directions from the selection edge. Note that for all the selection tools, feathering is off by default.

Partially selected pixels are discussed again in Section 4.1.7.

SAMPLE MERGED

Normally the `Magic Wand` selection tool only operates on the pixel values in the active layer. However, if this layer is not fully opaque, or if this layer is using a blending mode (see Chapter 5), some of the pixel values from lower layers affect the color in the active layer. The Sample Merged option in the `Tool Options` dialog for the `Magic Wand` takes this into account. When this option is on, it is the merged color values of pixels that are used in the comparison algorithm for the `Magic Wand`. Figure 3.14 shows the Sample Merged option toggled on in the `Magic Wand`'s `Tool Options` dialog.

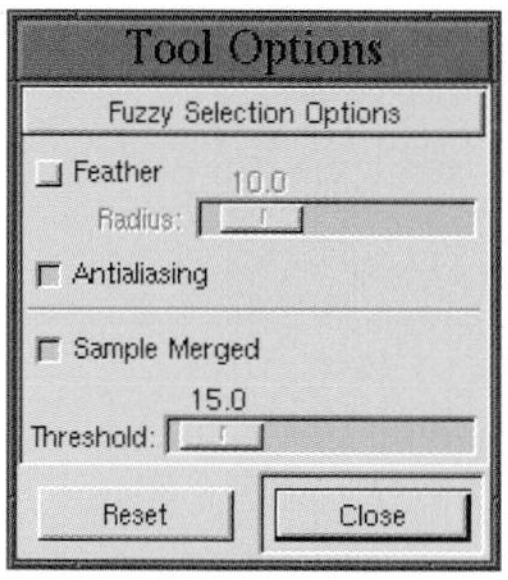

Figure 3.14: The Sample Merged Option

THRESHOLD

As described in Section 3.1.1, the `Magic Wand` uses a search algorithm based on the color of a seed pixel and a specified threshold value. All contiguous pixels that have color values that are less than the threshold from the seed are included in the selection. As already described, the Threshold can be set interactively. However, it can also be specified in the `Magic Wand`'s `Tool Options` dialog. Figure 3.14 illustrates the Threshold slider which can take values from 0 to 255.

3.2 COMBINING SELECTIONS

Selections can be combined in various ways. In particular, the GIMP provides the capability to add, subtract, and intersect selections.

3.2.1 ADDING

Adding a selection to an existing one means that the resulting selection is the union of the pixels from the two. Thus, if A is the set of pixels defined by the first selection and B the set for the second, then $A \cup B$ is the result of adding the second to the first, where $\cup$ is the set union operator.

If a selection already exists in the image window, the addition is made by pressing the Shift key *before* clicking to begin the new selection. Once the mouse button has been pressed, the Shift key should be released. Figure 3.15(a) shows an initial rectangular selection, and Figure 3.15(b) shows the result of adding an ellipse to this.

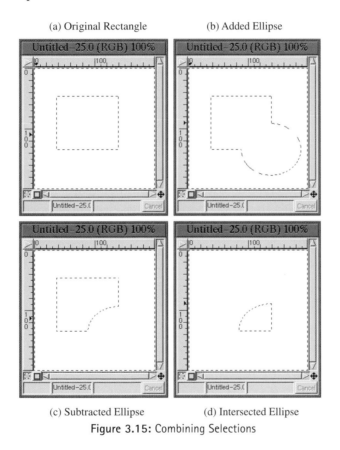

(a) Original Rectangle   (b) Added Ellipse

(c) Subtracted Ellipse   (d) Intersected Ellipse

Figure 3.15: Combining Selections

It is useful to note that pressing the Shift key while the mouse is in the image window has the effect of changing the mouse cursor to an arrow with a plus sign below it. This indicates that the next selection will be added to any selection already existing in the image window.

3.2.2 SUBTRACTING

Subtracting a new selection from an existing one means that the result is the first selection less the pixels contained in the intersection of the two. Thus, if A is the set of pixels defined by the first selection and B is the set for the second, $A-(A\cap B)$ is the result of subtracting the second from the first, where $\cap$ is the set intersection operator.

A subtraction is made by pressing the Control key *before* beginning the new selection. Once the new selection is begun, the Control key should be released. The result of subtracting an ellipse from the rectangular selection in Figure 3.15(a) is shown in Figure 3.15(c). Note that it is the new selection that is subtracted from the old selection, not vice versa.

It is useful to note that pressing the Control key while the mouse is in the image window has the effect of changing the mouse cursor to an arrow with a minus sign below it. This indicates that the next selection will be subtracted from any selection already existing in the image window. Because I always forget which key controls addition and which controls subtraction, I find the mouse cursor indicators are particularly useful.

3.2.3 INTERSECTING

Intersecting two selections means that the resulting selection is, you guessed it, the intersection of the two. Thus, if A is the set of pixels defined by the first selection and B the set for the second, $A\cap B$ is the result of intersecting the two. The intersection is made by pressing the Shift and Control keys together *before* pressing the left mouse button to begin the new selection. The Control and Shift keys should be released before releasing the mouse button. The result of intersecting an ellipse with the rectangular selection in Figure 3.15(a) is shown in Figure 3.15(d).

It is useful to note that pressing the Shift and Control keys together while the mouse is in the image window has the effect of changing the mouse cursor to an arrow with a $\cap$ sign below it. This indicates that the next selection will be intersected with any selection already existing in the image window.

3.2.4 USING ADD, SUBTRACT, AND INTERSECT WITH THE RECTANGLE AND ELLIPSE SELECTION TOOL FEATURES

As described in Section 3.1.1, the Shift key can be used to create perfectly square or circular selections, and the Control key can be used to perform selections centered at the position of the mouse click. In addition, Section 3.2 describes how the Shift key can be used for adding selections, the Control key for subtracting them, and the Shift and Control keys together for intersecting them.

The question you may be asking, then, is how can these features be used together? How can a perfect square be subtracted from a prior selection or a center–initiated ellipse added to one? The answer is quite simple. The trick is to remember that adding, subtracting, and intersecting selections is signaled by pressing the Shift key, the Control key, or both *before* clicking to initiate the selection. The sequence for creating a perfectly square or circular selection or for center-initiated selections is by pressing the Shift key, Control key, or both *after* clicking to initiate the selection. These features can be combined by applying the following steps:

1. Begin by pressing the appropriate combination of Shift and Control to specify whether the selection is to be added to, subtracted from, or intersected with an already existing selection.

2. While the keys are pressed, click and drag in the image window to initiate the new selection.

3. While the left mouse button is pressed, release the Shift and/or Control keys.

4. Apply the appropriate combination of Shift and Control keys to specify a perfectly square, circular, and/or center-initiated selection.

5. While keeping the last combination of Shift and Control keys pressed, release the mouse button, thus completing the selection.

3.2.5 MOVING A SELECTION BOUNDARY

Occasionally it is useful to be able to move a selection after it has been made. That is, it is useful moving the selection itself, not the selection contents. This can be done by Alt-clicking and dragging the selection boundary.

3.3 THE SELECT MENU AND FRIENDS

Complementary to the selection tools are the 12 functions in the `Image:Select` menu. In addition to these functions, there are five other important functions related to selections. These are `Toggle Selection`, found in the `Image:View` menu, and `Copy`, `Cut`, `Paste`, and `Stroke`, found in the `Image:Edit` menu. Each of these functions is described in this section.

3.3.1 THE INVERT FUNCTION

A selection partitions an image into two sets—the selected pixels and the unselected ones. It is often useful to invert a selection, which is just the swapping of these two sets. When inverting, the unselected pixels become selected pixels and vice versa. The command that does this is `Invert` from the `Image:Select` menu. The `Invert` function is used so often you'll want to remember the keyboard shortcut for it, which is `C-i`.

3.3.2 THE ALL FUNCTION

The function `All` in the `Image:Select` menu selects everything in an image. If the active layer in the image is smaller than the largest layer, the selection is clipped to the boundaries of the active layer. I personally don't find this to be a very useful command.

3.3.3 THE NONE FUNCTION

The function `None` in the `Image:Select` menu deselects everything in an image. This is very useful, as will be seen in the ensuing chapters. The keyboard shortcut for this command is `C-S-a`.

3.3.4 THE FLOAT FUNCTION

A selection can be made into a floating selection by choosing `Float` from the `Image:Select` menu. Floating selections were discussed in Section 2.5. A useful application of `Float` is described in Section 2.6.2.

3.3.5 THE FEATHER FUNCTION

Feathering was explained in Section 3.1.2. Normally a feather is applied by toggling on the Feather checkbox in the selection tool's `Tool Options` dialog before making the selection. However, it is possible to apply a feather after the selection has been made by choosing `Feather` from the `Image:Select` menu.

3.3.6 THE SHARPEN FUNCTION

The concept of a partially selected pixel was introduced in Section 3.1.2, in the discussion on antialiasing, and was extended in the discussion on feathering. The function `Sharpen`, from the `Image:Select` menu, removes partially selected pixels in an image by transforming those that are 50% or more selected into fully selected pixels, and by fully deselecting all the remaining pixels. Thus, this function sharpens the active selection (not the image).

3.3.7 THE SHRINK FUNCTION

It is sometimes useful to be able to shrink a selection a little. If a selection has been made with a tool like the `Magic Wand` or with the `By Color` selection function, it is possible that the resulting selection is a little too large. The `Shrink` function, found in the `Image:Select` menu, shrinks the boundary of the current selection by the amount specified in its dialog. The default unit is 1 pixel, but other values can be chosen.

3.3.8 THE GROW FUNCTION

In contrast to `Shrink`, the function `Grow`, from the `Image:Select` menu, grows the boundary of the current selection by the amount specified in its dialog. The default unit is 1 pixel.

3.3.9 THE BORDER FUNCTION

The `Border` command, found in the `Image:Select` menu, replaces a selection with just those pixels within a specified radius of the selection edge. Thus, this function creates a selection of the border around the previous selection's edge.

This command is a combination of the two functions `Shrink` and `Grow`. In particular, if A represents the set of selected pixels obtained by applying `Grow` to a selection and B represents the set obtained by applying `Shrink`, `Border` produces the set that could otherwise be obtained by doing $A-B$ (see Section 3.2 for more on combining selections). The width of the border is specified by the border dialog.

Figure 3.16(a) illustrates an image with a selection, and Figure 3.16(c) shows the result of applying `Border`. The value chosen for the border is shown in the associated dialog, illustrated in Figure 3.16(b). Note that the dialog contains a menu that allows the border width to be specified in a variety of different units. The default unit is pixels.

Figure 3.16: The Effect of `Border`

`Border` is particularly useful for refining selection edges. An example of using `Border` is presented in Section 7.4.

3.3.10 THE SAVE TO CHANNEL FUNCTION

Channels were introduced in Section 2.2. As will be discussed in greater detail in Section 4.1, channels can be used to store selections. This is an extremely useful feature of the GIMP because it allows you to save your selections, to reuse them in the current image or in others, and to edit them with the masking utilities (more on this in Chapter 4). The operation of saving a selection to a channel is performed with the `Save to Channel` function, found in the `Image:Select` menu.

Figure 3.17(a) illustrates an image with a selection, and Figure 3.17(b) shows the Channels dialog after applying the function `Save to Channel`. The Channels dialog for an image is displayed by typing `C-1` in the image window to bring up the `Layers & Channels` window and clicking on the Channels tab.

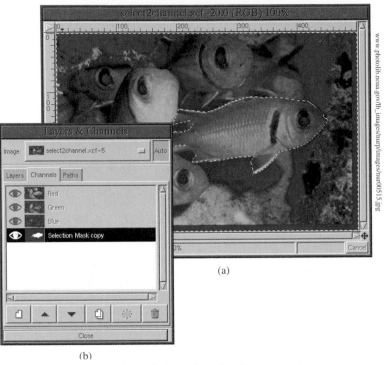

(a)

(b)

Figure 3.17: Saving a Selection to a Channel

It can be seen in Figure 3.17(b) that, other than the usual Red, Green, and Blue channels usually found in the Channels dialog, there is a channel named Selection Mask Copy. This channel shows a thumbnail of the mask representing the selection. Much more on the subject of masks and selections is discussed in Chapter 4. This is a very powerful feature of the GIMP. Check it out!

3.3.11 THE BY COLOR FUNCTION

The By Color selection tool, found in the Image:Select menu, is similar to the Magic Wand in that it automatically selects pixels in the active layer that are close in color to a seed pixel value. The difference, however, is that the selected pixels are not obtained by growing a contiguous region around the seed. The By Color selection tool selects *all* the pixels in the layer that are within a specified threshold of the seed pixel's color. This is a subtle but important difference. It means that if two regions of similar pixel colors are separated by one of very different values, the By Color selection tool will get both regions, and the Magic Wand will not.

Choosing By Color brings up the dialog pictured in Figure 3.18(a). This dialog box allows a Fuzziness Threshold to be chosen. The default is normally 15, but here it has been set to 30. This number determines how far a pixel can vary in color from the seed pixel's and still be selected. The seed is chosen by clicking in the image window.

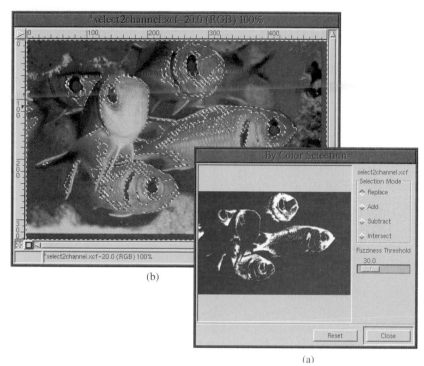

Figure 3.18: The By Color Selection Tool

Clicking in the image window produces a black and white mask in the thumbnail area of Figure 3.18(a). This mask corresponds to a selection in the image window, as can be seen in Figure 3.18(b). The selection can be removed by clicking on the Reset button in the By Color Selection dialog.

When the dialog's Replace radio button is selected, clicking a second time in the image window replaces the selection that was there with one based on the new seed pixel's color. The three other radio buttons in the dialog can be used to add, subtract, or intersect the selection created with the By Color function with an existing selection in the image window. Adding, subtracting, and intersecting selections was explained in Section 3.2.

3.3.12 THE TO PATH FUNCTION

Selections can be converted to Bezier paths. As was described in Section 3.1.1, Bezier paths are extremely useful tools because they allow selections to be interactively modified. The To Path function, found in the Image:Select menu, converts a selection to a Bezier path by automatically finding the control points and the control handle settings to re-create the selection.

Figure 3.19(a) illustrates a selection created with the Ellipse Select tool, and Figure 3.19(b) shows the result of applying To Path to it. Applying this function removes the selection from the image window and replaces it with a

Bezier path. The path can now be used to interactively modify the selection, as described in Section 3.1.1. To recover the selection, click inside the closed path.

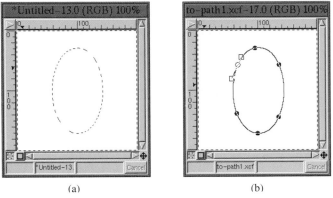

Figure 3.19: Converting a Selection to a Bezier Path

Note that clicking inside a path to convert it to a selection might not toggle off the path's visibility. If this happens, the path can be toggled off by clicking on any icon (other than the `Bezier Path`'s) in the Toolbox. Much more on Bezier paths is covered in Section 3.4.

3.3.13 The Toggle Selection Function

Unlike the other selection functions discussed in this section, `Toggle Selection` is found in the `Image:View` menu. This command is very useful when trying to carefully position layers or selections (for examples, see any project in Chapter 7), or when trying to color-match a layer or selection edge (for an example, see Section 7.5).

The `Toggle Selection` command toggles on and off the visibility of a selection's Marching Ants. However, this function *does not* eliminate the selection. The selection is still there, it is just not visible in the image window. The `Toggle Selection` feature also toggles on and off the visibility of the black-and-yellow layer boundaries in an image. This feature is also used extensively in Chapter 7.

There is a pitfall when using `Toggle Selection`. It is easy to forget that selection boundaries have been toggled off. This can lead to confusion, especially when a subsequent selection is made. Because selection visibility has been toggled off, the Marching Ants do not appear. I've scratched my head many times trying to figure out why all of a sudden the GIMP no longer seemed to be working! The GIMP, of course, was working just fine. The selection is there; it just can't be seen until its visibility is toggled back on.

The `Toggle Selection` function is so useful that you might want to memorize its keyboard shortcut, which is `C-t`.

3.3.14 THE COPY, CUT, AND PASTE FUNCTIONS

Copy, Cut, and Paste are probably the most frequent operations performed on selections. These three functions are found in the Image:Edit menu. However, they are used so frequently that it would be worth your while to memorize their keyboard shortcuts. The keyboard shortcut for Copy is C-c, Cut is C-x, and Paste is C-v. More on these functions can be found in Section 2.4.

3.3.15 THE STROKE FUNCTION

The Stroke function is found in the Image:Edit menu. This command paints a selection edge's outline with the active foreground color using the active brush. Figure 3.20(a) illustrates an image with a selection, and Figure 3.20(c) shows the effect of applying Stroke to it using black as the foreground color. As indicated in Figure 3.20(b), a soft round brush was used to stroke the selection.

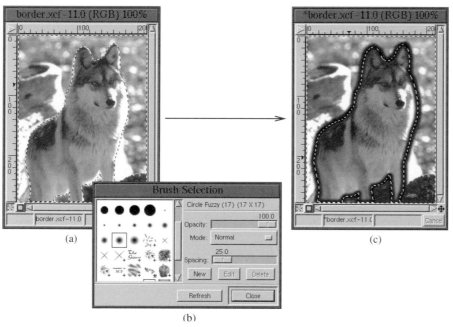

Figure 3.20: The Effect of Stroke

3.4 THE PATHS DIALOG

Because Bezier paths are so useful, there is a special Paths dialog that allows multiple Bezier paths to be edited, managed, and saved. The Paths dialog, shown in Figure 3.21, is displayed by typing C-l in the image window to produce the Layers & Channels window, then clicking on the Paths tab. The elements of the Paths dialog are described in this section.

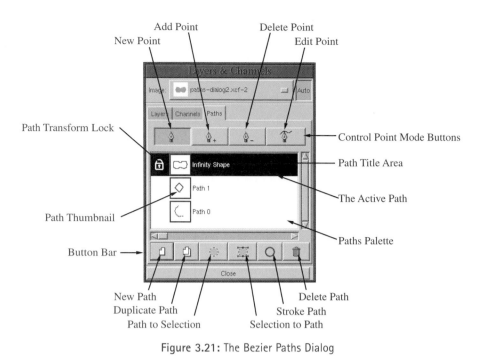

Figure 3.21: The Bezier Paths Dialog

3.4.1 THE PATHS PALETTE

The most important part of the Paths dialog is the Paths Palette. The palette contains horizontal strips, where each strip represents a single path for the image. Each strip contains a Path Thumbnail, a Path Title, and a Path Transform Lock.

Figure 3.21 illustrates a Paths Palette containing three strips. The top strip is highlighted in blue, indicating that it represents the active path. Only the active path can be seen and manipulated in the image window. Clicking on a path strip in the Paths Palette makes that path active and also makes it visible in the image window. Figure 3.22(a) illustrates an image window where the path visibility has been toggled on by clicking on its strip in the Paths Palette. Figure 3.22(b) shows the associated Paths dialog. To toggle off the path's visibility, it is necessary to click on a tool icon (other than the one for the `Bezier Path`) in the Toolbox window.

A path's title can be changed by double-clicking in the title area. This brings up a dialog where the text of the new title can be entered. Figure 3.22(c) illustrates the dialog for changing the Path Title.

Finally, the Path Transform Lock can be toggled on and off by clicking to the left of the Path Thumbnail. When the icon is toggled on, the path's shape is locked to the active layer with respect to the `Transform` tool. This means that any transform applied to the active layer is also applied to the path.

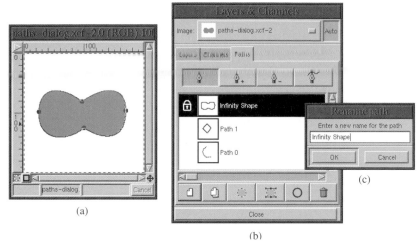

(a)

(b)

(c)

Figure 3.22: Making a Path Visible in the Image Window and Changing a Path Title

Figure 3.23 illustrates an example of using the Path Transform Lock. Figure 3.23(a) shows the Path Transform Lock has been toggled on for the path in the top path strip. This path corresponds to the outline of the blue shape in the image window shown in Figure 3.23(b). The image window consists of two layers: a white background and the blue shape, the latter being the active layer. Because of the Path Transform Lock, applying the `Transform` tool will affect the blue shape and the path defining the shape's boundary.

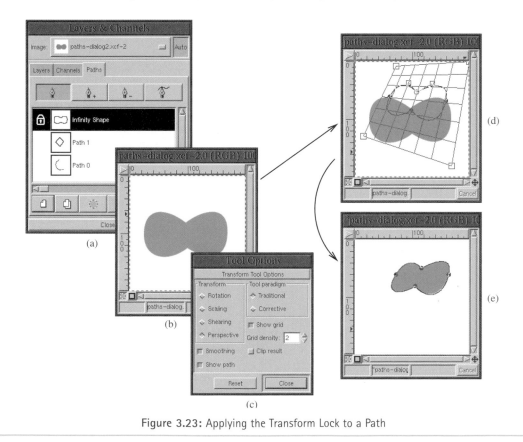

(a)

(b)

(c)

(d)

(e)

Figure 3.23: Applying the Transform Lock to a Path

Figure 3.23(c) shows the dialog for the Transform tool. The Perspective radio button has been selected, and the Show path checkbox has been toggled on. This last button makes the active path visible in the image window while it is being transformed. Figure 3.23(d) shows the perspective transform of the grid and the active path. When the transform is actually performed by clicking on the Transform button in the Perspective Transform dialog, the result is as shown in Figure 3.23(e). The active layer containing the shape is transformed and the path associated with this shape is transformed along with it.

The ability to see a path superimposed on the transform grid while performing a transformation of a layer is a particularly useful capability. There is no more precise way of warping one image to another than with this feature. A concrete example of using the Path Transform Lock is illustrated in Section 7.2.

3.4.2 THE CONTROL POINT MODE BUTTONS

The Control Point Mode Buttons are shown in Figure 3.21. These consist of the New Point, Add Point, Delete Point, and Edit Point buttons. These control the behavior, or mode, of mouse clicks in the image window when you're using the Bezier Path tool.

When using the Bezier Path tool with the New Point mode button selected in the Paths dialog, there are two behaviors for a mouse click in the image window. The first behavior is associated with working on an open path. In this case, clicking in the image window creates a new control point that is immediately connected to the last control point on the path by a path segment. The last new control point on an open path is displayed as a circle outline. All the other points on the path are displayed as solid circles.

The second behavior of the New Point mode button is when there is no open path. Then, a mouse click in the image window initializes a new path.

When the Bezier path is in New Point mode, the mouse cursor appears in the image window as an arrow with a filled circle below it. This indicates that the next mouse click will create a new control point.

The Add Point mode button is for adding a point to a path segment between two existing control points. This is useful when a path has been created but doesn't have a sufficient number of points to properly follow the desired shape. When the Add Point mode button is active, the mouse cursor changes to an arrow with a plus symbol below it whenever the cursor is close enough to a path segment to add a point. If the mouse button is not released when the point is added, the point can immediately be edited. In other words, if the mouse button remains pressed, the control handles will appear when you drag the mouse, and the Shift and Control keys can be used to manipulate the control point and the control handles. This is a handy feature because a control point can be added to a path and then immediately edited without having to return to the Paths menu.

The Delete Point mode button removes control points from a Bezier path. This can be used to delete extraneous control points or those that were added accidentally. When you use the Delete Point mode button, the mouse cursor changes to an arrow with a minus symbol below it whenever the cursor is close enough to a control point to delete it. If the Shift key is pressed while using the Delete Point mode button, the mouse click deletes the entire path.

Finally, the Edit Point mode button allows the control handles to be manipulated and the control points to be moved, as described in Section 3.1.1. That is, clicking and dragging on a control point moves the point's control handles in unison. Shift-clicking and dragging a control handle moves that handle independently of the other one. Control-clicking and dragging the mouse on a control point makes the control point move, following the mouse. Finally, Alt-clicking and dragging the mouse on a control point causes the entire path to follow the mouse. When you're using the Edit Point mode button, the mouse cursor changes to an arrow with the outline of a square below it whenever the mouse cursor is close enough to a control point to edit it.

3.4.3 THE PATHS MENU

Like the Layers dialog and the Channels dialog, the Paths dialog also has a menu that can be displayed by right-clicking anywhere in the Paths Palette area. Figure 3.24(a) shows the Paths dialog and Figure 3.24(b) the Paths menu. As shown in the figure, many of the functions available in the Paths menu can be accessed from the button bar. However, the functions Copy Path, Paste Path, Import Path, and Export Path are unique to the Paths menu.

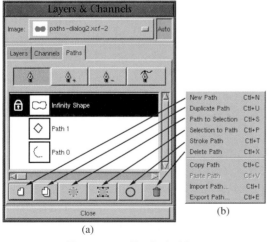

(a)

Figure 3.24: The Paths Menu

The Copy Path function copies the path in the active path strip to a buffer. This path can then be pasted into another path strip, either in the same image or in another, using the Paste Path function. The Export Path function brings up a dialog allowing the active path to be saved to disk. This saved path can later be recovered using the Import Path function.

Because the remaining functions are available in the button bar, they are described in the next section.

3.4.4   THE PATHS BUTTON BAR

The Paths dialog button bar provides access to six functions: New Path, Duplicate Path, Path to Selection, Selection to Path, Stroke Path, and Delete Path.

New Path and Duplicate Path are self-evident. The New Path button creates a new path, and the Duplicate Path button duplicates the current active path.

The Path to Selection button converts the active path to a selection. The path can also be converted to a selection by simply clicking inside the path in the image window. In either case, this causes the selection's Marching Ants to appear in the image window but does not necessarily cause the visibility of the path to toggle off. To toggle off the path's visibility, click on a tool icon, other than the one for `Bezier Path`, in the Toolbox.

The Selection to Path button is the same as the `To Path` function described in Section 3.3.12. Using this button converts a selection visible in the image window to a new path in the Paths dialog. This becomes the active path and can be seen in the image window.

The Stroke Path button is the same as the `Stroke` function described in Section 3.3.15. It is applied to the active path using the active brush and the active foreground color. In addition, the `Stroke` function in the Paths dialog will stroke the path using any painting tool selected from the Toolbox. To specify the painting tool, you select its icon in the Toolbox just prior to clicking the Stroke Path button in the Paths dialog. Using this technique the `Airbrush` tool can be used, for example, to stroke the path.

Finally, the Delete Path button removes the active path from the Paths Palette.

3.5   USING SELECTIONS EFFECTIVELY

This section begins the discussion of how to effectively use the selection tools presented in this chapter. The full story, however, won't be completed until we cover masks in Chapter 4.

3.5.1   GENERAL SELECTION TOOL GUIDELINES

This chapter has presented the six selection tools from the Toolbox as well as the `By Color` selection tool. This leaves you with quite a few choices. So, the question naturally arises, "Which is the best tool to use?" This section summarizes the tools discussed so far and describes their strengths and weaknesses.

The order of the summary is from the most useful selection tool to the least:

- `Bezier Path`: Of the seven choices, this is the most useful selection tool because it is the most flexible and the most versatile. Combined with the associated tools available in the Paths dialog, this is the selection tool that will usually get the job done in the least amount of time.

  The `Bezier Path` selection tool is not, however, a panacea. When the selection subject's boundary is not smooth, it is impractical to use the `Bezier Path` tool. Examples of difficult selections with this tool would be the image of a leafy tree or one of a woman's hair blowing in the breeze. For these types of selections, other approaches are necessary (see Chapter 4).

- `Lasso`: Although this tool is not useful for precision selection work, it is probably still the next most useful selection tool. The `Lasso` is the best selection tool when only a rough selection is needed. Good examples of using the `Lasso` to separate image elements is illustrated in Sections 4.5.3 and 7.4.

- `Rectangle Select`: This selection tool is about as useful as the `Lasso`. However, it is used for very different reasons. This tool is valuable for framing (see Section 2.6.2) and for the selective application of filters and gradients to layer edges (see, for example, Section 7.5.3).

- `By Color`: This selection tool is most useful for making selections in images that have several regions that consist of an almost uniform color. Examples of this would be trying to select a large-font, solid-color text on a photographic image background or a complicated bitmapped image. See Section 8.6 for a practical example.

- `Ellipse Select`: This tool, like `Rectangle Select`, is also used for framing. An example of using `Ellipse Select` in this way is shown in Section 3.1.2. It is also occasionally useful for selecting shapes that are known to be elliptical or circular, such as the clock illustrated in Section 3.5.4. This tool, however, is used less often than `Rectangle Select`.

- `Magic Wand`: This tool is based on a great concept but is difficult to use in practice. Fortunately, there is another technique based on almost the same idea but producing results with much greater control and flexibility. This technique is based on the `Threshold` tool, which is described in more detail in Section 4.5.3.

- `Intelligent Scissors`: In principle this tool should be good at selecting shapes that do not have smooth outlines, the shapes that are difficult for the `Bezier Path` tool. Unfortunately, the performance of this tool is poor and I, personally, never use it. I rank this tool as the least useful for making selections.

3.5.2 TOOL CONJUGATION

Often a selection is most efficiently made using a combination of tools. For example, beginning a selection with the Magic Wand or with By Color can produce a result that is almost right but may be missing a component or may have included an unwanted element. When this happens, the Lasso can often be used to correct the problem.

Figure 3.25(a) shows the selection of a flower made with the Magic Wand. As can be seen, the flower has been almost completely selected. However, it was impossible to include the central region of the flower by interactively adjusting the threshold without also including more of the background. The value of the threshold used in Figure 3.25(a) is seen in the Tool Options dialog for the Magic Wand, shown in Figure 3.25(b). The value of 59.9 seen in the dialog is just at the point where parts of the background started to be included in the selection.

Figure 3.25: Selection Tool Teamwork

Although the Magic Wand could not select all the desired parts of the flower, the remainder can be added to the selection using the Lasso. Figure 3.25(c) shows the process of making a selection with the Lasso. Pressing the Shift key before clicking and dragging in the image window causes the new selection to be added to the one created by the Magic Wand. The Shift key needs to be released before the selection is finished. Adding selections was described in Section 3.2. Notice that under these circumstances the selection made with the Lasso need not be precise, which corresponds to the guidelines given for the Lasso in Section 3.5.1.

The example of conjugating tools presented here is a little contrived because it is not often that the Magic Wand can be used practically in this way. But it is illustrative of how the tools can be used together. We will see much more of this in Chapters 4 and 7 where the Threshold tool takes the place of the Magic Wand.

3.5.3 USING ZOOM

One of the most useful tools that can be used in conjunction with the Bezier Path selection tool is the Zoom tool, found in the Toolbox and in the Image:View menu. This tool was covered in some detail in Section 1.8.1; however, its value for aiding selections is emphasized here.

When attempting to perform a precise selection of a subject, it is essential to get in close to the pixels. Figure 3.26(a) shows a Bezier path of an airplane that is to be converted to a selection. However, prior to the conversion it is desirable to examine the path to verify its accuracy.

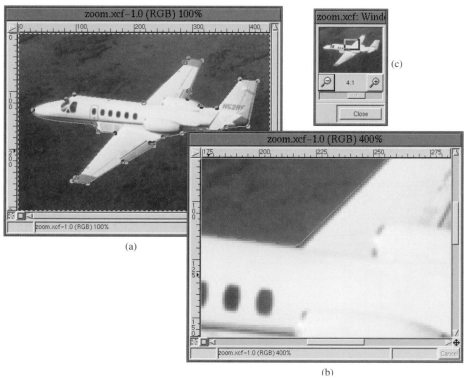

Figure 3.26: Using Zoom to Aid with Selections

Figure 3.26(b) is a 400% zoom of Figure 3.26(a). As can be seen, the control point of the Bezier path located at the junction of the right wing and the fuselage is not quite correctly positioned. It is only through the use of Zoom that such a careful examination of the selection can be made. It is quite easy to improve the positioning of the control point using the Edit Point mode button in the Paths dialog.

Although the Zoom tool was used in Figure 3.26(b) to verify a Bezier path, it is often a good strategy to draw the path from the start in a zoomed window. A useful tool for helping with this is the Navigation Window, found in the Image:View menu. Figure 3.26(c) illustrates this tool, which consists of a thumbnail of the image with a panning rectangle superimposed on it. This panning rectangle shows the part of the image that can be viewed in the zoomed image window. The panning rectangle can be dragged with the left mouse button, and this makes the image in the zoomed window move in tandem with it. In addition to the panning function of the Navigation Window it also contains + and − buttons, which can control the amount of zoom applied to the image window.

3.5.4 SELECTIONS AND GUIDES

The image window guides (see Section 2.6.1) can be used to accurately position a selection made with the Ellipse Select or Rectangle Select tools. An example of the former is illustrated in Figure 3.27. The figure shows a clock and also shows horizontal and vertical guides that have been positioned tangent to the perimeter of the clock's upper and left edges.

Figure 3.27: Positioning an Elliptical Selection Using the Guides

Choosing the Ellipse Select tool from the Toolbox, the selection is begun by clicking and dragging from the intersection of the two guides. If the Snap to Guides checkbox in the Image:View menu is toggled on, the initial point for the selection snaps to the guides' intersection. Because the guides are tangent to the clock's perimeter, dragging the mouse until the selection touches the two tangent points perfectly completes the selection.

3.6 COMMON PROBLEMS AND FREQUENTLY ASKED QUESTIONS

There are some problems with selection tools that everyone is tripped up by sooner or later. Here is a common list.

- **I choose a selection tool from the Toolbox and try to make a selection, but the Marching Ants don't appear, and the selection doesn't seem to have been made. What's wrong?**

  This is such a common problem! It is due to the Marching Ants having been toggled off in some prior operation. Toggle the Marching Ants back on by typing C-t in the image window or by clicking on the `Toggle Selection` checkbox in the `Image:View` menu.

- **I try to cut, paste, or filter a selection, but nothing happens. Why not?**

  Your image contains multiple layers, and the active layer is not visible. Operations in the GIMP are applied to the *active* layer (for more information, see Chapter 2). Thus, the selection in your image may be visible, but the active layer may not be. Open the Layers dialog and verify that the layer you are working on is active and is visible in the image window.

- **I've selected the `Bezier Path` tool from the Toolbox, but clicking in the image window with the mouse button doesn't produce any control points. What's going on?**

  Open the Paths dialog and verify that there is an active path in the Paths Palette. If there isn't, create a new one by clicking on the New Path button. Also, verify that the New Point mode button is toggled on.

4

MASKS

Masks are powerful GIMP tools, and it would be quite difficult to do many things without them. What are masks? They are selections! Actually, they are grayscale images that *represent* selections. In masks, the white regions represent selected pixels, the black regions unselected pixels, and the gray regions partially selected pixels.

You may be asking, "Why do we need another way of representing a selection? Weren't the selection tools presented in Chapter 3 good enough?" The selection tools are good, but masks provide a whole new set of options for creating and editing selections. This chapter demonstrates how the GIMP's painting tools, gradients, and filters can be used with masks to get selection results that would be impossible with the selection tools alone. Masks are complementary to the selection tools, and this chapter shows how the two can be used together to produce the most effective results.

In addition to the new capabilities for editing and creating selections that masks provide, they also have another very useful feature. A mask can be stored and used more than once. Selections created with the selection tools are more ephemeral. When created, they exist only until another selection is made or until they are canceled. Moreover, while a selection is present in the image window, it only allows operations to be applied to the pixels in the selected region. This means that active selections can impede the work flow because pixels outside the selected region cannot be processed. Thus, there is a need for selections that can be stored and reused. Masks provide this capability, and, as will be seen shortly, it is easy to convert selections to masks and vice versa.

There are two types of masks in the GIMP: channel masks and layer masks. A channel mask is an independent entity and can be applied to any image layer. Alternatively, a layer mask is associated with a single layer, on which it is totally dependent. Every layer in an image can have a layer mask, but each layer mask is specific to its own layer. In addition, the layer mask is directly linked to its layer's alpha channel. As was discussed in Section 2.2, the alpha channel controls the opacity of the layer. As will be developed more in this chapter, the alpha channel is just a special mask and, as a mask, it is just a special type of selection.

Selections, channel masks, layer masks, and alpha channels. They are the same, they are different, and it is all explained in this chapter. Read on!

4.1 CHANNEL MASKS

A channel mask is a special grayscale layer only 8 bits deep and is used to store and edit selections. This section describes the Channels dialog, how to save selections to channel masks, how to convert channel masks to selections, and the other GIMP functions used for organizing masks and operating on them.

4.1.1 THE CHANNELS DIALOG

As an image can have any number of layers, it can also have any number of channel masks. Thus, analogous to the Layers dialog, the Channels dialog is the the tool for organizing and working with channels. The Channels dialog is obtained by typing C-1 in the image window and clicking on the Channels tab in the resulting Layers & Channels window. Figure 4.1 illustrates the various elements of the Channels dialog.

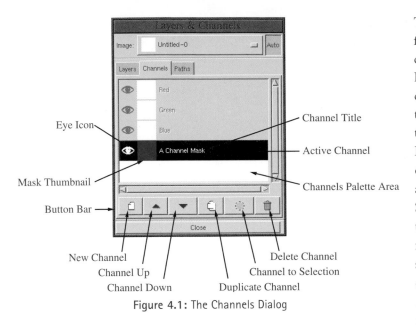

Figure 4.1: The Channels Dialog

The most important feature of the Channels dialog is the Channels Palette. This region of the dialog consists of horizontal strips where the top three entries are always the Red, Green, and Blue channels of the image, already described in Section 2.2.1. The rest of the strips are channel masks. Figure 4.1 shows a single channel mask. The channel mask strip displays a thumbnail image of the mask's contents, and the area to the left of the thumbnail contains an Eye icon. Analogous to layer strips in the Layers dialog, the visibility of the Eye icon for channel strips can be toggled on and off, making the channel mask either visible or invisible in the image window.

To the right of the thumbnail is the Channel Title Area. In Figure 4.1 the channel is named A Channel Mask. The title can be changed by double-clicking in the Channel Title Area. This brings up a dialog where the new title can be entered.

The channel strip in Figure 4.1 is highlighted in blue, indicating that it is the active channel. A channel mask is made active by clicking on its thumbnail or Title Area. Only a single channel mask can be active at a time, and when a channel mask is active, none of the image layers can be active. Because GIMP tools applied to the image window are applied to the active layer or the active channel, this can sometimes be a source of confusion. After working on a channel mask, to work on a layer it is necessary to explicitly switch to the Layers dialog and to make the layer active.

The remaining elements of the Channels dialog are the Channels menu and the button bar. These are described in more detail shortly.

4.1.2 SAVING SELECTIONS TO CHANNEL MASKS

One of the primary uses you will make of channel masks is to save selections. Why should you save a selection to a channel? There are many reasons. The first is that saving the selection protects your work, which is particularly important if you are making an involved and difficult selection. Second, it allows you to make your selections in parts. This helps divide and simplify the work. Third, it allows you to reuse a selection for several purposes. This is useful for all sorts of rendering operations, such as making drop shadows, high-lights, and special textures (for example, see Section 8.5). Fourth, it allows you to refine your selections in ways that would otherwise be impossible. Finally, many special effects can be had using filter plug-ins on masks. As you can see, saving a selection to a channel mask really has a very broad range of benefits.

After making a selection with any of the tools described in Chapter 3, we can save the selection to a channel mask using the Save to Channel function, found in the Image:Select menu. Figure 4.2(a) illustrates an image of a selected falcon, and Figure 4.2(b) shows the Channels dialog after having used the Save to Channel function. The thumbnail appears as a grayscale image, where white corresponds to fully selected, gray to partially selected, and black to unselected pixels. As seen in Figure 4.2(b), the default channel mask title is Selection Mask copy.

(a)

(b)

Figure 4.2: Saving a Selection to a Channel Mask

After using Save to Channel, the active focus changes from the Layers dialog to the newly created channel in the Channels dialog. Nevertheless, the selection in the image window remains active. This has several important consequences. First, since the new channel is active, all ensuing filtering or painting operations are applied only to this channel. Furthermore, since the original selection is still active, the only parts of the new channel that can be affected are those inside the selection area. For example, trying to paint outside the selection will have absolutely no effect. Thus, if the objective is to work on the newly created channel, the selection must be canceled by typing c-s-a in the image window, and the channel must be made visible by toggling on its Eye icon in the Channels dialog. If the objective is to save the selection as a channel and to move on to other image operations, the selection must be canceled, and the appropriate layer in the Layers dialog must be made active.

4.1.3 Making Channel Masks Visible

A channel mask's visibility can be toggled on or off by clicking on its Eye icon. Looking again at Figure 4.2(b), the Eye icon is not visible. Toggling it on, as shown in Figure 4.3(b), and toggling off the image layer's visibility produces the result shown in Figure 4.3(a). This figure shows that the channel mask is now visible in the image window.

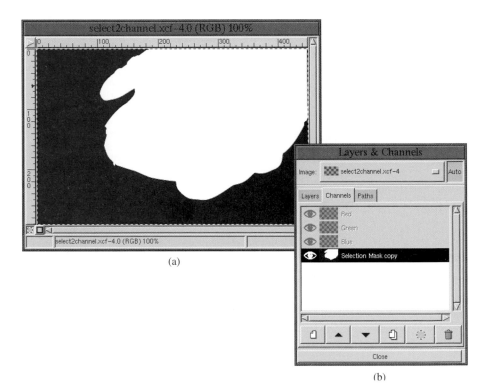

Figure 4.3: Viewing a Raw Channel Mask in the Image Window

If the Eye icon of the image layer is toggled back on, as shown in Figure 4.4(b), the resulting view in the image window is Figure 4.4(a). The image layer can now be seen through the channel mask. The parts of the image corresponding to the white region of the mask appear clearly, but the parts in the black region appear covered by a dark, semi-transparent film. This demonstrates why these channels are called masks; they allow the selected parts of the image to be clearly seen while "masking out" the unselected parts.

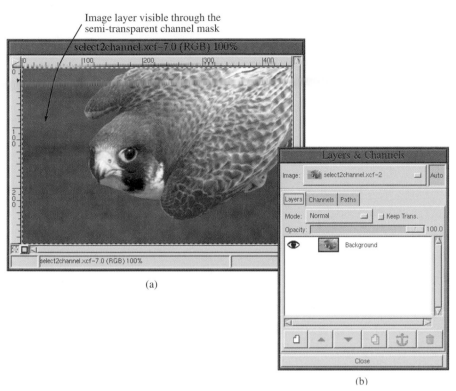

Image layer visible through the
semi-transparent channel mask

(a)

(b)

Figure 4.4: Viewing an Image Layer Through the Channel Mask

Being able to see the image through the filmy parts of the channel mask, as illustrated in Figure 4.4(a), makes it possible to edit the mask according to the features of the image behind it. In this way, the channel mask is like a piece of digital tracing paper placed over the image.

4.1.4 SETTING A CHANNEL MASK'S COLOR, TRANSPARENCY, AND TITLE

Double-clicking in the channel mask title area brings up the Channel Options dialog, shown in Figure 4.5(b). This dialog allows three mask attributes to be set: the Channel name, the Fill Opacity, and the mask color. Setting the name is self-explanatory, but the other two attributes merit some discussion.

The Fill Opacity slider sets the degree to which the image layer is visible through the filmy parts of the mask. The slider's units are in percent so if the opacity is set to 100, the only parts of the image that are visible are those that correspond to the white part of the mask, and the parts of the image corresponding to the black parts of the mask cannot be seen. Alternatively, if the opacity is set to 0, the image layer is completely visible, and the mask cannot be seen. An intermediate opacity setting allows the masked-out regions of the image to be seen through the black part of the mask. Adjusting the Fill Opacity slider allows an optimum working level to be set for the mask.

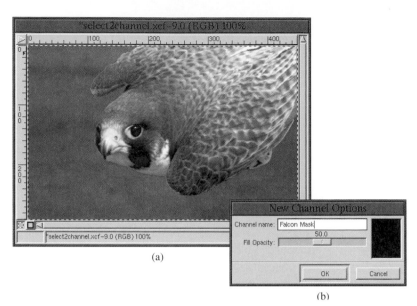

Figure 4.5: Changing a Channel Mask's Color, Opacity, and Title

If some of the image pixels seen behind the semi-opacity of the mask are dark, it will be difficult to see the details of these pixels. This may impede your ability to make useful edits to the mask, regardless of the Fill Opacity slider's setting. This is why the color of the mask can be changed. Changing the mask's color is done by clicking in the color patch of the Channel Options dialog. This brings up the Color Selection dialog, from which any color can be chosen. A good choice, of course, is one that contrasts well with the image layer pixels. Closing the Color Selection dialog changes the color in the Channel Options color rectangle. Closing the Channel Options dialog makes this color appear at the chosen opacity level in the image window. This is shown in Figure 4.5(a), where a 50%-transparent red has been chosen for the mask color.

4.1.5 THE CHANNELS MENU

The Channels dialog, like the Layers dialog, has a hidden menu that can be displayed by right-clicking in the title area of the Channels Palette. This menu is shown in Figure 4.6(b). As shown by the red arrows, many of the operations available in the Channels menu are directly accessible from the button bar. Most of the functions in the menu are organizational: New Channel, Raise Channel, Lower Channel, Duplicate Channel, and Delete Channel are all self-explanatory. Of particular importance is the Channel to Selection function, which is the inverse of the Save to Channel function. Channel to Selection creates a selection in the image window corresponding to the active mask in the Channels dialog.

The remaining functions in the Channels menu, Add to Selection, Subtract From Selection, and Intersect With Selection are described in the following section.

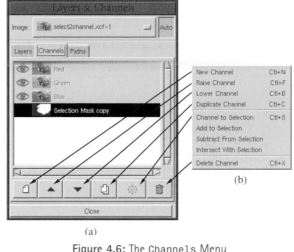

4.1.6 COMBINING CHANNELS

Section 3.2 describes how selections can be combined; selections can be added, subtracted, and intersected. These operations are useful because they allow the results from different selection tools to

Figure 4.6: The Channels Menu

be combined and because they also allow the work to be performed incrementally. This can be particularly important when selecting from a large image or when making a complicated selection.

Channel masks can also be combined. This is done by converting the masks to selections and then saving the combined result back to a mask. Figure 4.7 illustrates the procedure. Figure 4.7(a) shows an underwater scene for which two selections have been previously made and saved to channel masks. The channels strips for the two masks, labeled Fish and Rock, can be seen in the Channels dialog, shown in Figure 4.7(b).

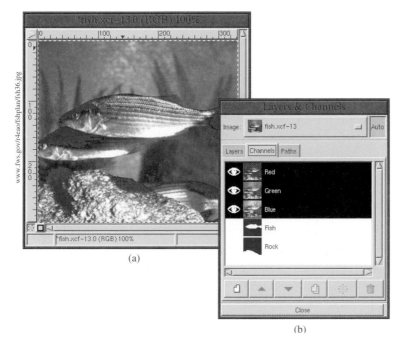

Figure 4.7: Two Channel Masks

After making the channel labeled Rock the active channel, it is converted to a selection by clicking on the Channel to Selection button (represented by the dashed circle icon) in the button bar. The active channel can be seen in Figure 4.8(b). Figure 4.8(a) shows the resulting selection in the image window. Note that it was not necessary nor useful to toggle on the visibility of the channel mask to do this.

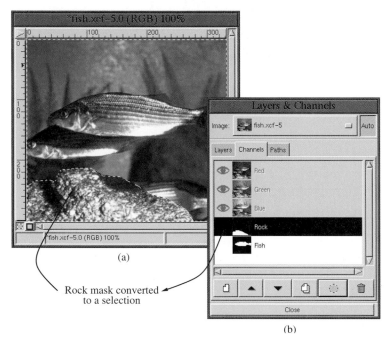

(a)

Rock mask converted
to a selection

(b)

Figure 4.8: Converting the First Mask to a Selection

A similar operation is performed with the channel mask labeled Fish. The mask is made active and then converted to a selection. Normally the conversion of a mask to a selection replaces any selection already active in the image window. However, the selection represented by the mask can also be added to the active selection. This is accomplished by choosing the Add to Selection function from the Channels menu, shown in Figure 4.6(b). The Add to Selection function can also be invoked by Shift-clicking the Channel to Selection button in the button bar. The result of adding the selection is shown in Figure 4.9(a), which shows the combined selection in the image window.

Two other combining modes are also available in the Channels menu. These are the Subtract From Selection and the Intersect With Selection functions. These can both be used from the Channel to Selection button in the button bar. Control-clicking the button produces a subtraction and Control-Shift-clicking produces an intersection.

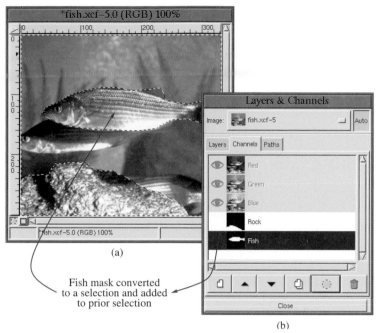

Figure 4.9: Converting the Second Mask to a Selection and Adding to the First

The final step to obtain a channel mask of the combined selection is performed by using Save to Channel from the Image:Select menu. The procedure is illustrated in Figure 4.10. The resulting channel mask, which has been labeled Rock+Fish, is shown in Figure 4.10(b).

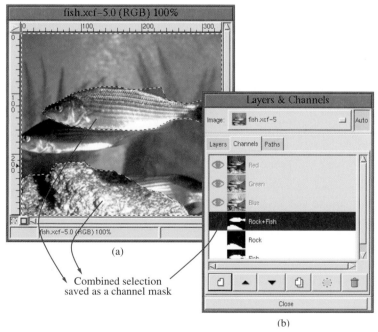

Figure 4.10: Creating the Combined Channel Mask

4.1.7 PARTIALLY SELECTED PIXELS

Partially selected pixels are especially important at selection edges because they allow the selection to blend more smoothly with other image layers. The subject of partially selected pixels has already been discussed to some extent in Section 3.1.2, which presented the concepts of antialiasing and feathering.

A powerful feature of masks is that they provide an easy way to create and to work with partially selected pixels. As has already been discussed, a white pixel in a channel mask represents a fully selected pixel in the image window, a black pixel fully unselected, and a gray pixel partially selected. Thus, channel masks allow for partially selected pixels, and, moreover, provide a framework on which any of the GIMP's filters and functions can be applied. This makes channel masks a particularly flexible and versatile medium for working with partial selections. Some examples of using GIMP filters on masks are illustrated in Section 4.3.5.

4.2 LAYER MASKS

Layer masks are special layers that are only 8 bits deep and that represent the alpha channel of an image layer. The main difference between channel and layer masks is that the layer mask represents the alpha channel of the layer it is linked to, whereas channel masks represent selections and exist independently of any particular layer. Nevertheless, as will be seen later in this chapter, there is an intimate relationship between alpha channels and selections and, by extension, between layer masks and channel masks.

The interpretation of white, black, and gray pixels in a layer mask is slightly different than that for a channel mask. A layer mask represents an alpha channel, which, in turn, controls the transparency of a layer. In this context, for the layer mask, white represents 100% opacity, black 100% transparency, and gray an intermediate level of opacity/transparency. This section describes the basic operations that can be performed on layer masks.

4.2.1 CREATING A LAYER MASK

To create a layer mask, make the desired layer active in the Layers dialog and choose Add Layer Mask from the Layers menu. This creates the layer mask, but only if the active layer already has an alpha channel. If it does not have an alpha channel, create one using Add Alpha Channel from the Layers menu.

Figure 4.11(a) illustrates the Layers dialog for an image consisting of an alpha-less background layer, and Figure 4.11(b) shows the associated Layers menu. As can be seen, all the functions in the two lowest groups of the Layers menu, including Add Layer Mask, are grayed out except for the function Add Alpha Channel. Selecting this function adds the required alpha channel, and bringing up the Layers menu a second time now produces the Layers menu shown in Figure 4.11(c). As can be seen, the function Add Layer Mask is now available.

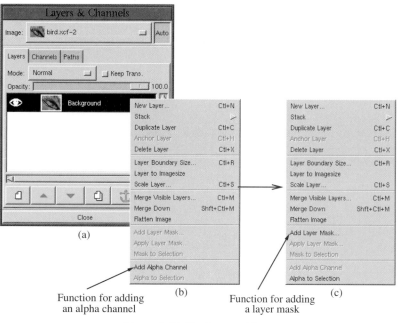

Figure 4.11: The Layers Menu

Selecting the Add Layer Mask function from the Layers menu brings up the Add Mask Options dialog. This dialog allows a choice of three initial states for the new mask. The default is White (Full Opacity), which is what you will choose most often. This choice produces a layer mask that leaves the image layer fully opaque. It can sometimes be useful to choose the second option, Black (Full Transparency), which creates a layer mask that makes the image layer fully transparent. The final option is Layer's Alpha Channel, which loads the active layer's alpha channel into the layer mask.

Figure 4.12 illustrates a layer mask created using the White (Full Opacity) option. Figure 4.12(a) shows the image window, and Figure 4.12(b) shows its associated Layers dialog. The layer strip for the image shows the thumbnail of the image and, next to it, the thumbnail of the newly created white layer mask. That a layer mask is associated with a single image layer is underscored by the fact that the mask's thumbnail appears in the same layer strip as the image layer's thumbnail.

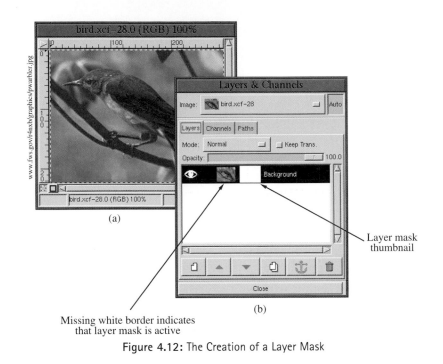

(a)

(b)

Layer mask
thumbnail

Missing white border indicates
that layer mask is active

Figure 4.12: The Creation of a Layer Mask

4.2.2 MANIPULATING THE LAYER MASK

As was first described in Section 2.1.1, the active layer in the Layers dialog is highlighted in blue. When the active layer consists of an image layer and a layer mask, only one of these two components can be active at a time. Operations performed in the image window affect the active component of the layer, either the image or the layer mask. The layer mask is made active by clicking on the layer mask thumbnail. The active focus is returned to the image by clicking on the image thumbnail.

You can determine whether the image or the layer mask is active by a white border drawn around the appropriate thumbnail in the layer strip. However, if the layer mask is white, it may be difficult to tell that there is an additional white border around it. Carefully examine Figure 4.12(b). Here it can be seen that the image thumbnail does not have a white border and that the layer mask thumbnail looks a little taller than the image thumbnail. This is a clue that the layer mask is active. Changing the active focus from the layer mask to the image by clicking on the image thumbnail is shown in Figure 4.13. It can be seen that the image thumbnail now has the white border.

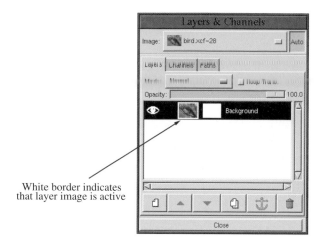

Figure 4.13: Toggling from an Active Layer Mask to an Active Layer Image

A layer mask is a direct way of editing an image layer's alpha channel. Thus, performing edits on the layer mask changes the opacity of the corresponding image layer. This is illustrated in Figure 4.14. Figure 4.14(b) shows that the image consists of a single layer with a layer mask. The layer mask has been constructed so that the white part of the mask corresponds to the bird shown in Figure 4.12(a) and the black part corresponds to the rest of the image.

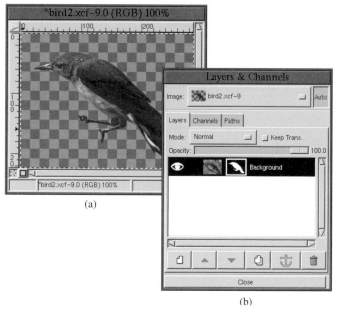

(a)

(b)

Figure 4.14: Editing a Layer Mask Edits the Image Layer's Alpha Channel

Figure 4.14(a) shows the effect of the layer mask; it makes the region around the bird's body completely transparent. It is important to note that the background part of the image has not been destroyed; it just can't be seen due to the modified values in the alpha channel. Section 4.3 describes in detail how a layer mask can be edited to produce a result like the one shown in Figure 4.14. However, before doing that, several additional features of layer masks must be described.

It is often useful to be able to examine the layer mask without the visual interference of the image layer. This can be accomplished by Alt-clicking on the thumbnail of the layer mask. Doing this toggles off the visibility of the image layer in the image window, leaving just the layer mask. In addition, the outline of the layer mask thumbnail in the Layers dialog becomes green. This is illustrated in Figure 4.15. The mask seen in the image window is shown in Figure 4.15(a), and the green border around the layer mask thumbnail is shown in Figure 4.15(b). The effect can be toggled off by Alt-clicking on the thumbnail a second time.

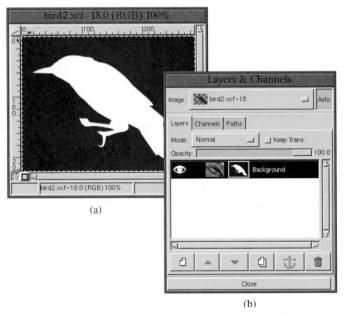

(a)

(b)

Figure 4.15: Viewing Only the Mask in the Image Window

Similarly, it can be useful to toggle off the visual effect the layer mask has on the image. This is done by Control-clicking on the layer mask thumbnail. When this is done, the effect of the layer mask on the image is toggled off, and the border of the layer mask thumbnail becomes red. Figure 4.16 illustrates this. The full image can now be seen in Figure 4.16(a) and a red border can be seen around the layer mask thumbnail in Figure 4.16(b).

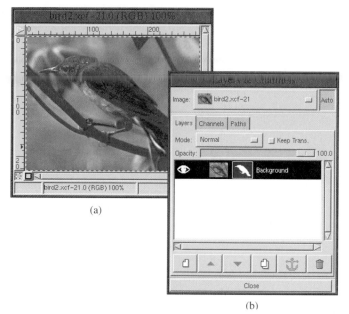

(a)

(b)

Figure 4.16: Suppressing the Effect of the Layer Mask in the Image Window

A layer mask can be converted to the image layer's alpha channel by choosing the `Apply Layer Mask` function from the `Layers` menu. This is not normally necessary, though, because the action of the mask is the same whether it remains a mask or is converted to the alpha channel. However, the Apply Layer Mask dialog also permits the layer mask to be discarded. This is the only way to remove a layer mask. Applying a layer mask by converting it to an alpha channel destroys the mask and removes it from the Layers dialog. It can be recovered, though, by choosing `Add Layer Mask` from the `Layers` menu and choosing Layer's Alpha Channel as the mask option.

Finally, a layer mask can be converted directly to a selection. This is done by choosing `Mask To Selection` from the `Layers` menu. This operation creates a selection by mapping the white pixels in the layer mask to selected pixels in the image window, black pixels in the layer mask to unselected pixels, and gray pixels in the layer mask to partially selected pixels. Note that applying the mask as a selection does not destroy the mask.

4.3 BASIC TOOLS FOR WORKING WITH CHANNEL AND LAYER MASKS

This section discusses techniques for editing channel and layer masks. Although layer masks are used to edit a layer's alpha channel, and channel masks are used to store and edit selections, these two mask types behave similarly. Thus, the techniques for editing and filtering them can be treated in a somewhat unified manner.

4.3.1 Painting Tools

One of the most direct ways to modify masks is with the GIMP's painting tools. The Paintbrush, Pencil, Airbrush, Eraser, Ink Pen, Dodge and Burn, Smudge, and Bucket Fill tools can all be used. The versatility of these tools allows masks to be created that could not be duplicated using the selection tools alone. This is one of the reasons why masks are complementary to the selection tools.

Figure 4.17 illustrates the use of the Paintbrush tool to edit a channel mask. As can be seen from Figure 4.17(a), the Paintbrush tool has been selected from the Toolbox, and white is the Active Foreground Color. Furthermore, as shown in Figure 4.17(b), a medium hard brush has been selected from the Brush Selection dialog. Figure 4.17(c) illustrates the Channels dialog, which shows that an active channel mask labeled Butterfly has been created. The mask's color is set to yellow, its opacity is 50%, and its Eye icon is toggled on, which means the the channel mask can be seen in the image window. The effect of the mask in the image window is shown in Figure 4.17(d).

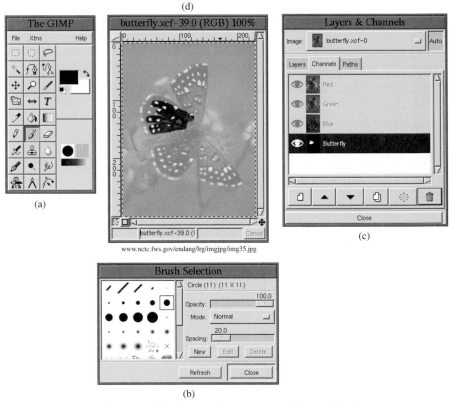

www.nctc.fws.gov/endang/lrg/imgjpg/img35.jpg

Figure 4.17: Using Painting Tools on a Channel Mask

The partial transparency of the mask makes it easy to paint in the image window while following the butterfly's outline. As already noted, the mask acts like digital tracing paper. Some white strokes can be seen in the channel mask thumbnail shown in Figure 4.17(c). These were created by painting with the `Paintbrush` tool in the image window. Because the channel mask is active, the `Paintbrush` modifies the mask, not the image layer. However, the effect in the image window is to reveal parts of the image layer, as can be seen in Figure 4.17(d). Regions that have been painted white can be repainted black, which restores the mask. Note that although the mask appears yellow in the image window, it actually remains a grayscale image. For this reason, white, black, and grays are the only colors that should be used when painting in channel masks.

4.3.2 SELECTION TOOLS

Selection tools can also be used to modify masks. Cutting a selection while a mask is active fills the selected region of the mask with the current `Active Background Color`. Like the painting tools, selections can be used to add or subtract parts of the mask.

Figure 4.18 shows how a selection in the image window can be used to add white pixels to the mask and, consequently, add to the set of selected pixels represented by the mask. Figure 4.18(a) shows that a selection has been made in the image window, and Figure 4.18(b) indicates that it was made using the `Bezier Path` tool. Figure 4.18(b) also shows that the `Active Background Color` is white. Cutting the selection while the channel mask is active produces the result shown in Figure 4.18(c). The selected part of the mask has been removed from the image window. Furthermore, the corresponding part of the mask has been changed to white, as can be seen from the mask thumbnail shown in Figure 4.18(d).

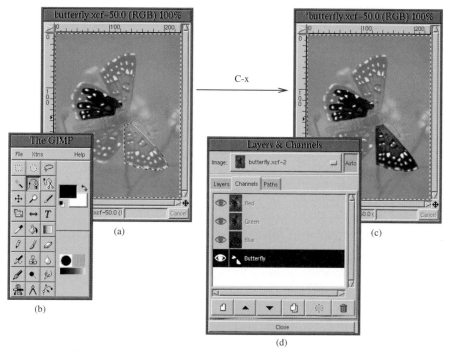

Figure 4.18: Using Selection Tools on a Channel Mask: Addition

Alternatively, Figure 4.19 shows how a selection can be used to add black pixels to the mask, thus subtracting from the set of selected pixels represented by the mask. Figure 4.19(a) shows the selection in the image window and, as indicated by Figure 4.19(b), the selection was made using the Rectangle Select tool. Figure 4.19(b) also shows that the Active Background Color is set to black. The result of cutting the selection using C-x is shown in Figure 4.19(c). All the pixels in the interior of the rectangle selection have been filled with black, which results in the removal of these pixels from the set of selected pixels represented by the mask.

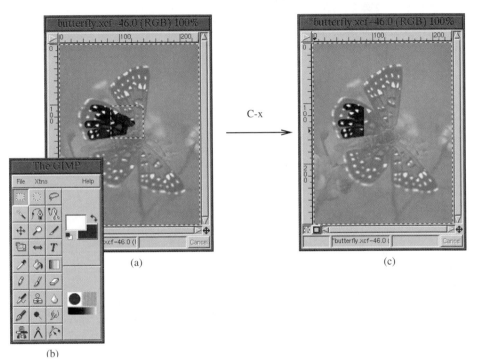

Figure 4.19: Using Selection Tools on a Channel Mask: Subtraction

4.3.3 GRADIENTS

When used in layer and channel masks, gradients are very useful blending tools. Figure 4.20 is used to illustrate how two images can be blended together using a gradient in a layer mask. To begin, a new transparent layer is created in the lunar module image (Figure 4.20(a)), and the space shuttle image (Figure 4.20(b)) is copied and pasted into it. The paste actually creates a float-ing selection that is subsequently positioned and anchored to the transparent layer. The result of the paste is illustrated in Figure 4.21(a), and the image's Layers dialog is shown in Figure 4.21(b). It can be seen from the Layers dialog that the space shuttle is in the upper layer and that, in preparation for the next step, a layer mask has been created for it.

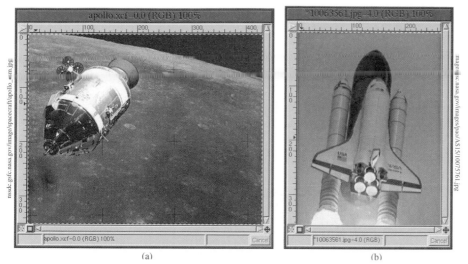

(a)   (b)

Figure 4.20: Two Images

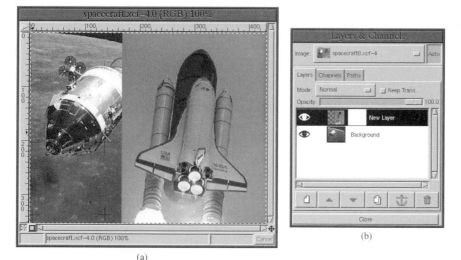

(a)   (b)

Figure 4.21: Pasting and Positioning the Shuttle Over the Lunar Module

The blending of the two layers is performed by constructing a gradient in the layer mask. The following steps are used to accomplish this:

1. The layer mask is made active by clicking on its thumbnail in the Layers dialog.

2. The Gradient tool is chosen from the Toolbox, and the Active Foreground Color and the Active Background Color are set to black and white, respectively.

3. The Tool Options dialog is opened by double-clicking on the Gradient icon in the Toolbox, and the Blend option is set to FG to BG (RGB).

4. The gradient is applied by clicking and dragging in the image window starting at the leftmost edge of the space shuttle layer, and releasing slightly to the left of the left shuttle rocket.

The resulting gradient can be seen in the layer mask's thumbnail, shown in Figure 4.22(b).

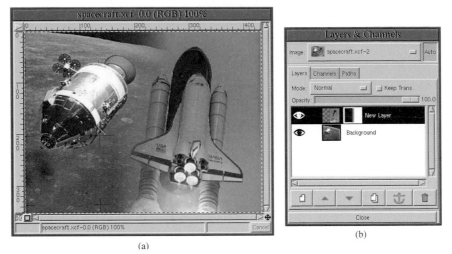

(a)   (b)

Figure 4.22: Two Images Blended Using a Gradient in a Layer Mask

Several points are worth noting here. First, the gradient is created in the layer mask by clicking and dragging in the *image* window. The gradient is applied to the *layer mask* because it was made active in the first step of the preceding procedure. Second, as seen in Figure 4.22(a), the gradient in the layer mask blends the upper layer with the lower one by creating a gradual transition from black to white in the mask. The black pixels of the mask make the upper layer completely transparent. The trend from dark gray to light gray pixels in the mask gradually blends the upper layer into the lower until the mask is totally white, at which point the upper layer is totally opaque. The width of the blend is controlled by the width of the gradient.

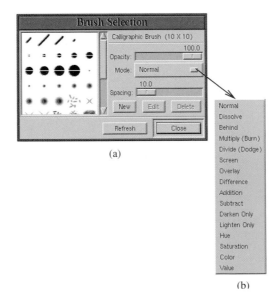

(a)

The blend made in Figure 4.22 produces a straight, horizontally varying gradient, but what if a more complicated blending interface is desired? This can be solved using the Mode menu found in the Brush Selection dialog. Figure 4.23(a) shows the Brush Selection dialog, and Figure 4.23(b) shows the Mode menu's choices.

(b)

Figure 4.23: The Brush Selection Dialog and the Mode Menu

The Mode menu controls how the paint of the gradient combines with what is already active in the image window (whether that be an image layer, a channel mask, or a layer mask). The Normal mode is the default, and this mode just replaces anything that was in the layer with the paint from the gradient. The other modes combine the paint from the gradient in various ways, which are described in depth in Chapter 5. For the moment, however, let's turn our attention to the Multiply and Screen modes. These modes will permit us to create gradients with tailor-made interfaces. To illustrate this, Figure 4.24(a) shows a horizontally varying gradient created by clicking and dragging with the mouse in the image window, beginning at the tail of the red arrow and releasing at its tip. (Note that the red arrow is just for illustrative purposes and is not part of the image or the gradient.)

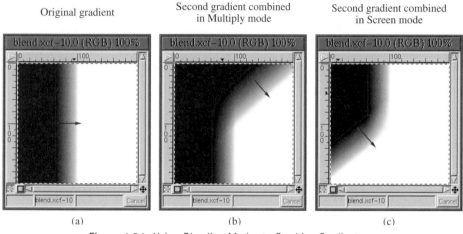

Figure 4.24: Using Blending Modes to Combine Gradients

Choosing the Multiply mode from the Brush Selection dialog's Mode menu and applying a second gradient to the first is shown in Figure 4.24(b). The direction of the applied gradient is indicated by the red arrow. If the normal combining mode had been used, the second gradient would have replaced the first. However, setting the blending mode to Multiply has produced a completely different effect. The two gradients have been multiplied together. What does it mean to multiply two gradients? Assigning a value of 0 to black, a value of 1 to white, and proportional values for grays provides us with a definition. This numerical correspondence is used to create a gradient that is the product of the first two. More precise definitions for the blending modes are given in Chapter 5.

Figure 4.24(c) shows the result of using the Screen mode, applied as shown by the red arrow in the figure. This mode works in a manner similar to Multiply mode. It performs a multiplication, except that it is white and is assigned the value of 0 and black the value of 1. As can be seen in Figure 4.24, the Multiply and Screen blending modes can be used to create custom gradient interfaces.

The Multiply mode can be used to make a black pivot around the point of application, and the Screen mode to make a white pivot.

Figure 4.22 shows an example of using a gradient in a layer mask to blend two layers. In the upper part of this figure, the blend seems too abrupt because the black space of the lunar module image contrasts strongly with the gray-blue sky of the space shuttle launch. This can be softened by making the gradient interface curve around the space shuttle image, letting more of the lunar module's black show through from below. Using the Multiply and Screen blending modes to do this produces the effect shown in Figure 4.25(a). The corresponding curved gradient interface can be seen in the layer mask thumbnail shown in Figure 4.25(b).

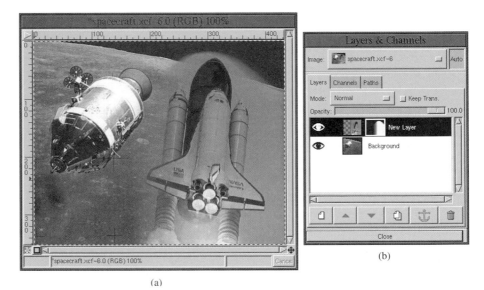

(a)

(b)

Figure 4.25: Custom Blending in the Upper Portion of the Image by Combining Additional Gradients Using the Multiply and Screen Modes

Effects similar to what were achieved with Multiply and Screen can be had using two other blending modes: Darken Only and Lighten Only. The results are a little different from those obtained with Multiply and Screen because these two modes provide more angular, predictable results at the corners of intersection. The result is more like a mitred picture frame than a fluid, smooth transition. Figures 4.26(a), (b), and (c) illustrates the application of the Darken Only and Lighten Only modes. Compare them with the application of the Multiply and Screen modes, shown in Figure 4.24.

Original gradient	Second gradient combined in Darken Only mode	Second gradient combined in Lighten Only mode

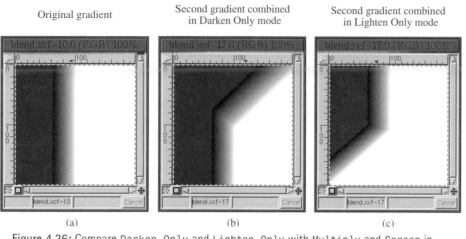

(a) (b) (c)

Figure 4.26: Compare Darken Only and Lighten Only with Multiply and Screen in Figure 4.24

Blending modes are discussed in more detail in Section 5.6. A sophisticated use of gradients and blending modes in layer masks is illustrated in Section 7.3.

4.3.4 TRANSPARENCY AS A TOOL FOR EDITING MASKS

To effectively edit masks, the image layer must be partially visible behind the mask so that it can be used as a guide for editing. The semi-transparency of channel masks was discussed in Section 4.3.1, but how is it done for layer masks? It is done by using the Opacity slider in the Layers dialog. The following example demonstrates its use.

Figure 4.27 illustrates an image consisting of two layers. The Layers dialog shown in Figure 4.27(b) shows that the lower layer is a photo of a woods and the upper layer an image of a fish, on an otherwise transparent layer. The upper layer also has a layer mask, which is to be used to edit the fish image.

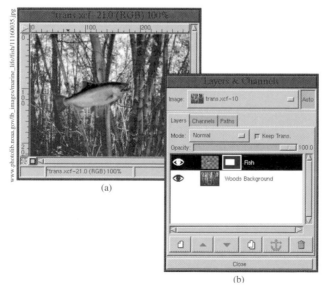

Figure 4.27: Image with Two Layers and a Layer Mask

The goal is to make parts of the fish transparent to create the illusion that the fish is partially behind some of the trees in the woods. This can be done with the layer mask by painting with black on the desired areas of the mask (see Section 4.3.1) or by cutting away parts of the mask with a selection (see Section 4.3.2). However, to effectively edit the layer mask using either approach, you must be able to see the outline of the trees through the fish. This is achieved by making the Fish layer active, and then lowering the value of the Opacity slider.

Figure 4.28(a) illustrates the effect of lowering the Fish layer's opacity. Because the trees can be perceived through the fish, it is easy now to edit the layer mask to achieve the desired effect. The result of using the Bezier Path tool to make a selection is shown in Figure 4.28(b). (Note that the opacity of the Fish layer has been reset to 100%.)

(a)

(b)

Figure 4.28: Decreasing the Opacity of the Top Layer and the Selection Obtained Using the Bezier Path Tool

Making sure that the Active Background Color in the Toolbox is set to black and that the layer mask is active in the Layers dialog, the selection is cut by typing C-x in the image window. The result on the image is shown in Figure 4.29(a), and the thumbnail of the resulting mask can be seen in Figure 4.29(b).

(a)

(b)

Figure 4.29: Result of Editing the Layer Mask

4.3.5 BLURRING OF MASKS AND OTHER EFFECTS

Section 3.1.2 discussed an edge-softening technique called antialiasing and an edge-blending technique called feathering. Effects similar to antialiasing and feathering can be had by applying blur filters to masks.

White pixels in a mask correspond to selected pixels in an image layer, and black pixels in the mask correspond to unselected image pixels. If there are no gray pixels between the black and white zones, this gives the selection edges represented by the mask the harsh edge already seen in the discussion on antialiasing. Blurring a mask softens the sharp edges in the mask by creating a graded zone of gray between the regions of black and white pixels. The width of the gray zone is controlled by the blur radius. The gray zones correspond to partially selected pixels in the image layer, and this is what creates the antialiasing/feathering effect for masks.

Figure 4.30 is used to illustrate the use of blur filters on masks. Figure 4.30(a) shows an image of a wood duck, and Figure 4.30(b) shows a channel mask representing a selection of it. Figure 4.30(c) shows the associated Channels dialog.

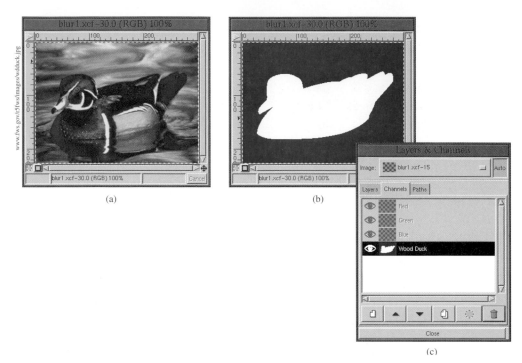

(a)

(b)

(c)

Figure 4.30: An Image and a Mask

A closer examination of the wood duck mask is shown in Figure 4.31(a). As can be seen, the mask has an unpleasant, hard, and aliased edge. This can be softened by blurring the mask. Figure 4.31(c) shows the result of applying the Gaussian Blur (IIR) filter to the mask. The filter dialog is displayed in Figure 4.31(b), which shows the choice of blur radius. In general, a small radius produces an antialiasing effect, and a large blur radius creates a feathering effect. A blur radius of 1 was used for this example.

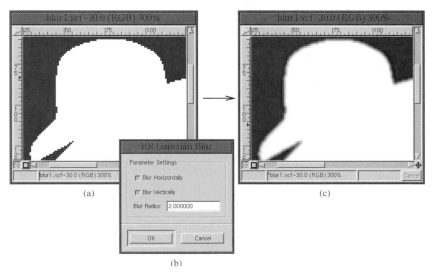

(a)

(b)

(c)

Figure 4.31: Aliased Mask Edge Softened Using Blur Filter

Other interesting and artistic edge effects can be obtained by processing masks with one or more of the GIMP's large collection of filters, found in the Image:Filters menu. Figures 4.32, 4.33, and 4.34 illustrate some examples.

Figure 4.32(a) illustrates the Waves filter dialog, found in the Image:Filters/Distorts menu. The resulting effect on the wood duck mask is shown in Figure 4.32(b), and the result of applying this mask as a selection to cut away the image's background is shown in Figure 4.32(c). Figure 4.33(a) shows the Glass Tile filter dialog, found in the Image:Filters/Glass Effects menu. Figures 4.33(b) and (c) show the effect of this filter on the mask and the image. Figure 4.34(a) shows the Spread filter dialog, found in the Image:Filters/Noise menu. Figures 4.34(b) and (c) show the effect of this filter on the mask and the image.

Many other interesting filter possibilities can be found. Have fun! Experiment!

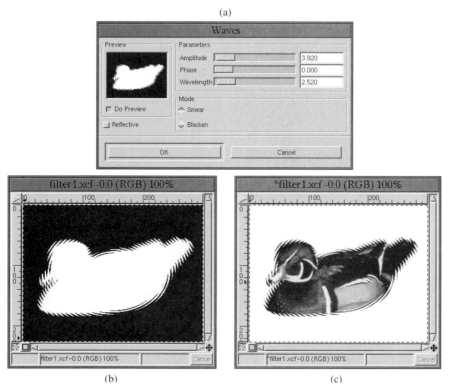

Figure 4.32: Applying the Waves Filter to the Wood Duck Mask

(a)

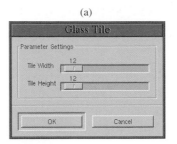

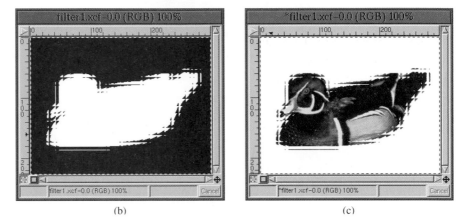

(b)   (c)

Figure 4.33: Applying the `Glass Tile` Filter to the Wood Duck Mask

(a)

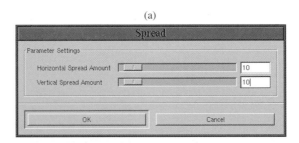

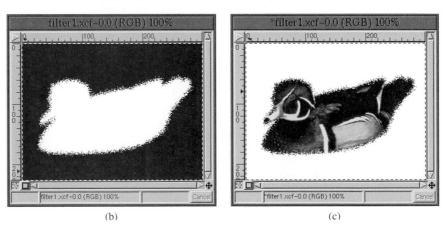

(b)   (c)

Figure 4.34: Applying the `Spread` Filter to the Wood Duck Mask

4.4 CONVERSIONS OF SELECTIONS, CHANNEL MASKS, LAYER MASKS, AND ALPHA CHANNELS

As has been discussed many times already, selections, channel masks, layer masks, and alpha channels are all different implementations of the same thing. They partition a layer into selected pixels, partially selected pixels, and unselected pixels. Although they all do the same thing, they do it in slightly different ways…ways that are remarkably complementary.

Being able to convert a selection to a layer mask or an alpha channel to a channel mask is often useful, however, it may not always be obvious how to go about it. As an aid to the reader, the table shown in Figure 4.35 describes the steps required to convert from any one of the four types to any other. You may want to bookmark this page.

To / From	Selection	Channel Mask	Layer Mask	Alpha Channel
Selection		Image: Select/Save To Channel	(1) Layers Menu: Add Layer Mask (2) Image: Edit/Cut (C-x)	Image: Edit/Cut (C-x)
Channel Mask	Channels Menu: Channel To Selection		(1) Channels Menu: Channel To Selection (2) Layers Menu: Add Layer Mask (3) Image: Edit/Cut (C-x)	(1) Channels Menu: Channel To Selection (2) Image: Edit/Cut (C-x)
Layer Mask	Layers Menu: Mask To Selection	(1) Layers Menu: Mask To Selection (2) Image: Select/Save To Channel		Layers Menu: Apply Layer Mask
Alpha Channel	Layers Menu: Alpha To Selection	(1) Layers Menu: Alpha To Selection (2) Image: Select/Save To Channel	Layers Menu Add Layer Mask (Layer's Alpha Channel)	

Figure 4.35: Selections, Channel Masks, Alpha Channels, and Layer Masks: Table of Conversions

4.5 MASKS AND SELECTIONS

Chapter 3 described in detail the use of the GIMP's selection tools; however, that discussion is incomplete. A full understanding of how to effectively work with selections requires a discussion on how to integrate masks. This section shows how masks are complementary to the selection tools and illustrates why the combination of selections and masks is so powerful.

4.5.1 Using Masks to Refine Selections

Masks are terrific tools for refining selections. A careful examination of a mask can often reveal several problems. Figure 4.36 illustrates a selection made with the Bezier Path tool. As will be seen in a moment, this selection exhibits the three basic types of selection problems. To better examine these problems, the selection is converted to a channel mask, and the selection itself is canceled.

The resulting channel mask is shown in Figure 4.37(a), and Figure 4.37(b) shows the associated Channels dialog. Because it is difficult to make out the light blue water background through a 50% transparent, black channel mask, the color of the mask has been changed to yellow, as shown in Figure 4.37(c).

Figure 4.36: Image Illustrating a Selection

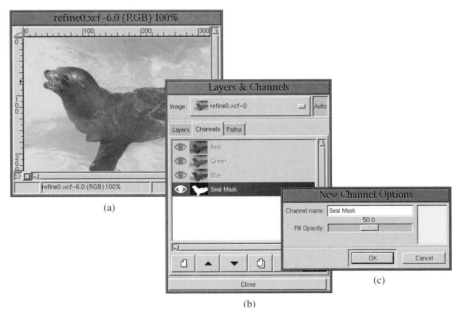

Figure 4.37: A Mask Converted from the Selection

To see the problems associated with the selection, the Zoom tool is used to magnify the image window. This produces the result shown in Figure 4.38(a). This figure shows that in several regions the light blue color of the background is showing through from around the edges of the yellow mask. This means that these pixels have been erroneously included as part of the selection.

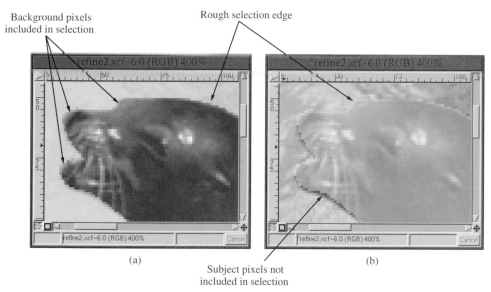

Background pixels
included in selection

Rough selection edge

(a)

(b)

Subject pixels not
included in selection

Figure 4.38: Illustrating the Three Basic Selection Problems

Figure 4.38(b) shows the same image as in Figure 4.38(a), but with the colors of the mask inverted. The color inversion is done by making the channel mask active and then using the `Invert` function found in the `Image:Image/Colors` menu. Inverting the colors inverts the regions of the mask that correspond to selected and unselected pixels in the image. Now it can be seen that in some places, the dark pixels from the subject are showing through around the mask edges. This means that they are mistakenly not included in the set of selected pixels.

Finally, in both Figures 4.38(a) and (b), a rough-edge, aliasing effect can be seen.

Each of these three problems can be solved by refining the mask. This can be accomplished using several different methods, but for this type of fine work near a mask edge, the best choice is the `Airbrush` tool from the Toolbox. The `Airbrush` can apply a very light coat of paint, so it is a great touch-up tool. Working near the edge requires some blending of the background with the subject to avoid aliasing. When used with a light pressure the `Airbrush` is perfect for this.

Figure 4.39(a) shows the `Tool Options` dialog for the `Airbrush`. It is the Pressure option that interests us here. The Pressure slider is in units of percent, and the default value of 10% is shown in Figure 4.39(a). The effect of using 10% pressure in conjunction with the soft brush chosen in Figure 4.39(b) produces the top line painted in Figure 4.39(c). Each of the other lines is painted with the Pressure value labeled to the right of the line. This figure shows that for low pressures, the `Airbrush` tool produces a very light layer of paint, great for touching up imperfect and aliased edges like the ones seen in Figure 4.38.

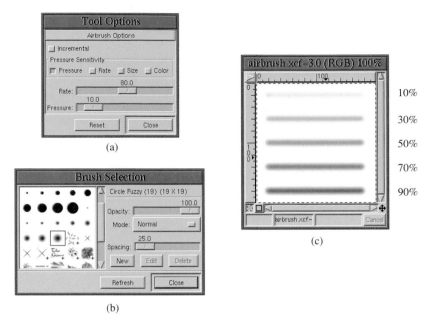

Figure 4.39: Introducing the Airbrush Tool

Using the Airbrush tool on the problem pixels shown in Figure 4.38 produces the results shown in Figure 4.40. The technique used in applying the Airbrush tool is as follows:

1. Make the channel mask active.

2. Use the Zoom tool to magnify the image to a sufficient resolution so that the paint can be applied to the problem edge areas with precision.

3. Set the Active Foreground Color to black by typing d in the image window.

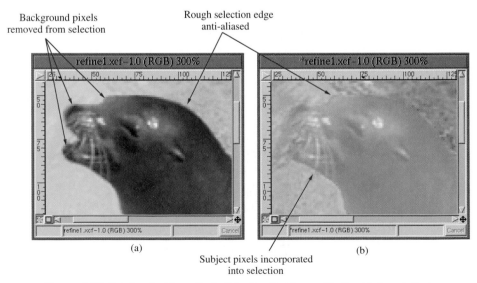

Figure 4.40: Solving the Three Basic Selection Problems with the Airbrush Tool

4. Lightly apply black paint to the problem areas with the `Airbrush` tool. The black paint is useful for removing pixels which should not be part of the selection.

5. Invert the mask colors using `Invert` from the `Image:Image/Colors menu`, and work the new problem areas. Because of the inversion of color, now the black paint is useful for including pixels that should be part of the selection.

6. Evaluate the precision of the applied paint, and correct for mistakes by making liberal use of the `Undo` (`C-z`) and `Redo` (`C-r`) functions.

4.5.2 THE QUICK MASK

The previous section showed you how a channel mask could be used to refine a selection. This is so useful that the GIMP has a special pair of function buttons on the image window allowing a selection to be quickly converted to a channel mask and vice versa. These are called the `Quick Mask` buttons.

Figure 4.41(a) illustrates an image with a selection. It also shows a button circled at the lower–left side of the image window containing a red square icon. This is the `Quick Mask` button. Clicking on it converts the selection to a mask, as shown in Figure 4.41(b). The button shown circled in Figure 4.41(b) contains an icon showing a square drawn in a dashed line and resembling the Marching Ants. Clicking on this button reverts the quick mask to a selection. Thus, the `Quick Mask` buttons can be used to quickly convert a selection to a mask that can then be edited, as described in Section 4.5.1, before being converted back to a selection.

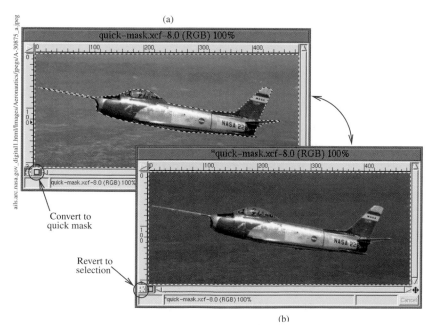

Figure 4.41: Using the Quick Mask

Figure 4.42 shows two features of the Quick Mask buttons. Double-clicking either of the buttons brings up the Edit Qmask Attributes dialog. This dialog, shown in Figure 4.42(a), permits the default opacity and color of the mask to be modified. The second feature of the quick mask is shown in Figure 4.42(b). When the quick mask is created, it also appears in the Channels dialog with the label Qmask in the Channel Title area. This channel exists only as long as the quick mask and disappears as soon as the mask is reverted to a selection.

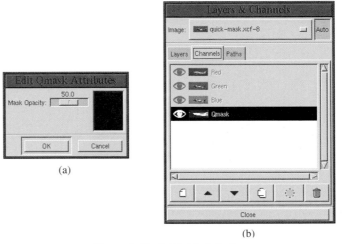

(a)

(b)

Figure 4.42: Quick Mask Options

4.5.3 FINDING THE NATURAL MASK

Performing a selection requires separating the subject, the part of the image that interests us, from the background. Often the subject has colorspace features that differentiate it from the background, and the goal of this section is to explain how to exploit this fact. Since the techniques described in this section depend on using an image's natural color features to make the selection, I call this *finding the natural mask*. The methods are based on using two primary tools: Threshold, found in the Image:Image/Colors menu, and Decompose, found in Image:Image/Mode. The natural mask approach often allows the subject to be extracted in a single, bold operation.

WORKING WITH THE THRESHOLD TOOL

The Threshold tool allows you to specify a range of values in an image. All the pixels that are in the range of the selected values are mapped to white, and the rest are mapped to black. Threshold is a powerful tool for automatically creating masks. This is illustrated in the following example.

Figure 4.43 illustrates the first step of using Threshold to create a natural mask. In the example, we want to make a selection of the partially blooming flower. We begin by copying the image in Figure 4.43(a) into a channel mask. This is done by creating a new channel mask in the Channels dialog, and then copying and pasting the image layer to the mask using c-c and c-v (see Section 2.4). Figure 4.43(b) shows the resulting Channels dialog, and Figure 4.43(c) shows that yellow is chosen as the mask color. This color was chosen to contrast against the dark background of Figure 4.43(a). Since a channel mask is only 8 bits deep, pasting the color image into the channel mask immediately converts it to a grayscale. This can be seen in Figure 4.43(d), which was obtained by toggling on the channel mask's Eye icon and toggling off the image layer's Eye icon.

Figure 4.43: Pasting the Image into Its Own Channel Mask

The Threshold dialog works by clicking and dragging out a part of the range of values in the histogram. The range of values in the histogram is in [0,255], and, as can be seen in Figure 4.44(b), the range that has been selected is from 72 to 253. Sweeping out values in the Threshold dialog's histogram immediately maps to white the pixels in the active layer (here the channel mask) having these values. The pixels having values outside the swept range are mapped to black. Thus, the channel mask that was a continuously varying grayscale image is converted to a binary black-and-white one. Figure 4.44(a) shows the channel mask before the application of Threshold, and Figure 4.44(c) shows the channel mask after the application of Threshold.

Figure 4.44: Applying Threshold to the Channel Mask

Mask defects

Mask defects

Figure 4.45: The Resulting Mask
Defects as Seen in the Image Window

Toggling the image layer's Eye icon back on
allows the channel mask to be seen over the
image, as illustrated in Figure 4.45. The parts
of the image layer corresponding to the white
parts of the channel mask can be seen clearly
in the image window. The parts of the image
corresponding to black parts of the channel
mask are masked by a partially transparent
yellow film.

As shown in Figure 4.45, the result of using
Threshold produces an almost perfect mask for
the flower. However, several defect regions
remain. There are certain parts of the image
that should be masked but aren't, and there are
parts that are masked but that shouldn't be.
These regions are easily removed using the
Lasso and the Paintbrush tools.

Figure 4.46(a) shows how the Lasso has been used to select parts of the image that should be masked but aren't. Because there are several offending regions, their selections have been combined using the methods described in Section 3.2. The parts of the channel mask that are in the selected regions are repaired (that is, converted to black) in three steps. The channel mask is made active by clicking on its thumbnail in the Channels dialog, the Active Background Color is set to black, as shown in Figure 4.46(b), and the selections are cut by typing C-x in the image window. The result is shown in Figure 4.46(c).

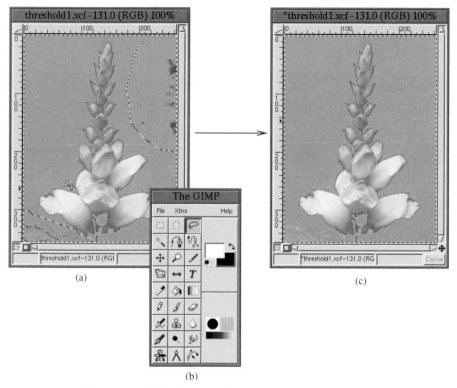

Figure 4.46: Using the Lasso Tool to Remove Defect Regions

Figure 4.47 shows how the stalk of the flower, which was not included in the mask, is restored using the Paintbrush tool. Figure 4.47(a) shows the stalk of the flower zoomed by 300%, and Figure 4.47(b) and (c) show that white is chosen as the Active Foreground Color and that a small hard brush has been chosen from the Brush Selection dialog. The Paintbrush cursor can be seen applying white paint to the mask over the region of the flower stalk in Figure 4.47(a). The semi-transparency of the mask facilitates the painting process. Figure 4.47(d) shows the result of having fully restored the flower stalk.

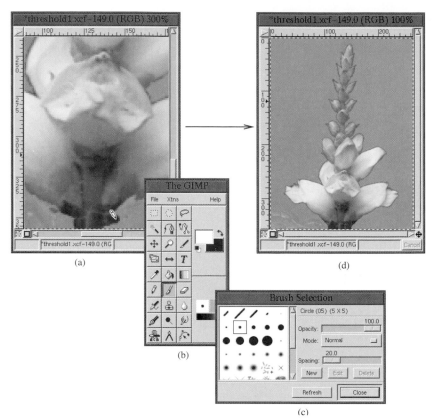

Figure 4.47: Using the Paintbrush Tool to Fill In Missing Regions

For the final step in this example, Figure 4.48(a) shows how the Channel to Selection function is applied by clicking on its icon in the Channel dialog's button bar. By turning off the visibility of the channel mask, the resulting selection is seen in Figure 4.48(b).

Channel to Selection

Figure 4.48: Converting the Mask to a Selection

This example shows how using Threshold can produce a selection much more quickly than would have been possible with the Bezier Path tool. Making a Bezier path would have required placing and refining a large number of control points. In contrast, the procedure employed with the Threshold tool required some experimentation with values in the tool's dialog, followed by some rough selections with the Lasso and some painting with the Paintbrush.

A key element to making the Threshold tool work efficiently is finding a reasonable range of values in the tool dialog's histogram. The example used in this section shows that it is not necessary to find a perfect mask. Rather, the goal is to find a mask that separates the subject from the background enough so that tools such as Lasso and Paintbrush can be used to easily clean up the defects.

The range of values used to create the mask in this example is shown in Figure 4.44(b). It is important to understand that this result was obtained by using a trial-and-error, experimental approach. Several contiguous regions of the histogram were swept out by the mouse, and each time the parts of the image that mapped to white and black were observed. A tip for finding useful regions is to examine the ranges of values supporting the main bumps in the histogram. These are usually associated with major image features, and it is often the case that one of these bumps is the solution to our search. When a reasonable range has been discovered, the data entry boxes can be used to refine the end points of the range.

Although the Threshold tool is not a panacea and isn't guaranteed to work, it is often successful. It is worth trying to apply the Threshold tool before launching into a long selection process with the Bezier Path tool. Some good examples of using Threshold to make selection masks are illustrated in Sections 7.3 and 7.4.

THRESHOLD TOOL VERSUS THE MAGIC WAND

The Magic Wand, presented in Section 3.1.1, is very similar in principle to Threshold but not nearly as effective. As already described, the Magic Wand works by choosing a seed pixel in the image and interactively setting a threshold that controls how many pixels around the seed are included in the selection. Thus, if the value of the pixel at the seed is S, and the value of the threshold is T, then the range of pixel values that are included in the selection is $[S-T, S+T]$.

Now suppose that the range of pixel values that separates the subject from the background is $[R_1, R_2]$. To make the Magic Wand work on this image, the threshold must have the value $T=(R_2-R_1)/2$ and the seed must have the value $S=(R_1+R_2)/2$. The problem then is finding a pixel in the subject having the correct seed value that, when experimenting with threshold values, will produce an acceptable result. This is impractical for several reasons, the main difficulty being that there is no way to use the visual feedback from several tries of the Magic Wand to discover a more refined solution. On the other hand, Threshold requires only that the end points of the range be specified, so it's much better adapted to experimentation. It is easy to try several contiguous value-regions, and the visual feedback from this is very useful for improving the search. In addition, the histogram in the Threshold dialog provides important clues as to which regions may be most useful.

Finally, the algorithm used by the Magic Wand is slow, because for each change in the threshold value, it must recursively grow the selected region around the seed. In comparison, the algorithm for Threshold is very fast, because it must only compare each pixel in the image with a threshold.

THRESHOLD AND DECOMPOSE

In the previous sections, Threshold was applied directly to the image. However, this tool can often be more effective when applied to an image color component. The function Decompose, found in the Image:Image/Mode menu, can be used to separate an image into its RGB and HSV components. When the decomposition is RGB, Decompose creates three grayscale images containing the red, green, and blue channels of the image. For HSV, three grayscales are also created, but now they represent the hue, saturation, and value components of the image. (See Chapter 5 for an in-depth discussion of the relationship between an image and its RGB and HSV color components.)

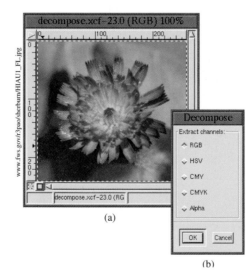

(a)

(b)

Figure 4.49: A Flower Image and the Decompose Dialog

Figure 4.49(a) illustrates an image of a flower, and Figure 4.49(b) shows the Decompose dialog. Either an RGB or HSV decomposition of the image can be performed by clicking on the appropriate radio button. The CMY decomposition is not useful because it produces results that are identical to RGB when used with the Threshold tool. CMYK may produce interesting results, but only RGB and HSV are discussed here.

Figure 4.50(a), (b), and (c) show the red, green, and blue components of the flower shown in Figure 4.49(a). Figures 4.50(d), (e), and (f) show the hue, saturation, and value components. Note that for each of the components, the relationship between the flower and its background is different. For example, the flower in both the red component and the saturation component seems to be better separated from the background than for the other components. Because the flower is a brightly saturated orange-red, this should not be a surprise. However, the point of using the Decompose tool is that it gives the Threshold tool an advantage that can be exploited when trying to extract a natural mask. Examples of using this technique can be found in Sections 7.3 and 7.4.

(a) Red   (b) Green   (c) Blue

(d) Hue   (e) Saturation   (f) Value

Figure 4.50: The RGB and HSV Decompositions of the Flower

4.6 COMMON PROBLEMS AND FREQUENTLY ASKED QUESTIONS

Masks can be tricky and, as with layers, it is sometimes possible to run into seemingly incomprehensible difficulties. The reason is almost always because the active layer is not what you think it is. The following lists some common problems you might run into with masks.

- **I just saved a selection to a channel mask, and I can't modify certain parts of the mask. Why not?**

  The problem is that the selection is still active. This means that modifications to the mask are allowed only in the selected region. Cancel the selection using Image:Select/None or by typing C-S-a in the image window.

- **I just saved a selection to a channel mask and I can no longer paint or filter my image. What's wrong?**

  Saving a selection to a channel automatically makes the new channel mask the active layer; however, if you check the Channels dialog, you'll see that the active channel is not visible. Thus, the paint and filtering operations you are trying to use have been applied to the channel mask, which can't be seen. Either toggle on the channel mask visibility by clicking on its Eye icon in the Channels dialog, or make the desired image layer active in the Layers dialog.

- **I try cutting a selection in a mask or channel and nothing happens. What's going on?**

  Cutting a selection in a mask has the effect of making the selected mask pixels the background color (as shown by the `Active Background Color` patch in the Toolbox). If the selection is made in a black part of the mask, make the background color white. If it is made in a white part of the mask, change the background to black. Typing `d` in the image window sets the default colors, which are black for the `Active Foreground Color` and white for the `Active Background Color`. Typing `x` switches the foreground and background colors.

- **I try painting in a layer mask, but the associated image doesn't become transparent/opaque where I painted. I only get paint marks on the image. Why?**

  The layer mask is not active. Make sure you select it by clicking on its thumbnail in the Layers dialog.

- **I am trying to use the paint tools, but the results are strange. Sometimes I don't get the color indicated by the `Active Foreground Color` patch, and other times I don't get anything at all. Is my GIMP broken?**

  No, the GIMP is not broken. Check the `Mode` menu in the `Brush Selection` dialog. If the blend mode is not set to `Normal`, this explains your problem.

5

COLORSPACES AND BLENDING MODES

I t is amazing that almost every color we see can be decomposed into a mixture of just three primary colors. Most children learn this at school and know that the primary colors are blue, yellow, and red. Using finger paints, kids can experiment making the so-called secondary colors green, orange, and purple. If hearing worked this way, every musical note could be decomposed into a sum of just three tones. Three tones might make a nice guitar chord, but it's not enough to rock-and-roll.

The interesting fact that three colors suffice is due to the way human vision functions. There are three different types of cones in the eye (red, green, and blue); this is what accounts for only three colors being needed. The fact that all the colors can be reproduced by mixing only three is extremely useful. It's like an alphabet. With a small collection of letters, any word can be made and any meaning can be conveyed. The lesson is the same for color. With only three color phosphors a computer monitor can, in principle, express any color; with only three color inks, in principle, a printer can print any color.

There are some practical limitations to the concept of reproducing all colors with only three primaries. However, without going into more detail, it suffices to know that the set of colors that can be made by adding different amounts of three primaries is called a colorspace. The shape of the space defined in this way is a cube.

In principle, the three primaries used to produce a colorspace are not unique. In theory, any triple of independent colors can be used to decompose a colorspace. However, in practice, colorspaces created by two different sets of primaries are not identical. Typically, there is a part of the color range of one space that cannot be reproduced by the other.

The best choice of primaries usually depends on the type of physical device used to create the color. Monitors use red, green, and blue phosphors to create a colorspace called RGB. Printers use cyan, magenta, and yellow inks and work in a colorspace called CMY. It is the physical way colors are combined that explains the two spaces. Monitors *emit* light, whereas inks only *reflect* light. When we shine a white light on ink, what we see is the color component of the white light that is reflected and not absorbed by the ink.

Knowing about colorspaces is important in the GIMP for several reasons. To effectively correct color in an image requires some notions about how colors interact. Furthermore, looking at different color components of an image can often be quite useful for making selections and masks.

This chapter is composed of two main parts. The first part begins with a tutorial on three colorspaces: RGB, HSV, and CMYK. The RGB space is discussed in detail, and this is followed by a description of the relationship between the RGB and HSV spaces. HSV is a more perceptually useful space than RGB and finds many uses in the GIMP. Although the GIMP is not CMYK-capable, this important pre-press colorspace is also discussed. Its benefits and drawbacks are described and its importance to pre-press is explained.

The second part of the chapter presents transparency and the GIMP's 16 blending modes from a colorspace perspective. Blending modes are powerful tools for combining colors between layers. You can also use them to control how the painting tools apply color. The colorspace presentation in the first part of this chapter will be very useful in understanding how these modes work. The final section of this chapter presents some practical uses of the blending modes.

5.1 THE RGB COLORSPACE

The RGB colorspace is important to us because it is what we see when we look at a color monitor. The monitor mixes together different amounts of red, green, and blue primaries. Because of this, the colors that can be seen on a computer monitor can be represented as triples of numbers or as vectors in a three-dimensional cube. The amount of each primary contained in a color can be represented by a number in a fixed range. Because the GIMP uses 8 bits per primary color channel, the range per primary is 0 to 255 (2^8=256). Here, 0 means no primary is used and 255 means that there is as much primary as the monitor can produce. Although there are issues with white balance, calibration, and human visual perception, it is presumed that the three primaries combined at full strength produce white and the three combined at zero strength produce black. Of course, the black produced is no deeper than that of the monitor when turned off.

When it is useful to talk about colors in numeric terms, as it is in Chapter 6, which discusses color correction, we will use a special notation to designate colors. For example, the purple composed of a red at 172, a green at 83, and a blue at 232 will be denoted $172^R83^G232^B$. This color is illustrated in Figure 5.1, which shows how the color is composed using the `Color Selection` tool. This tool is opened by clicking on the `Active Foreground Color` or `Active Background Color` patches in the toolbox. The tool dialog can be used to display RGB colors. These are dialed in using the sliders or can be entered numerically. The selected color appears in a patch at the upper right of the dialog. What we have here is digital finger paint!

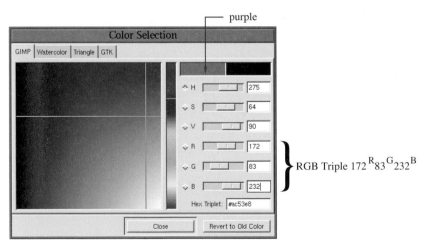

Figure 5.1: Representing a Color with an RGB Triple: Purple=$172^R83^G232^B$

As you will see later in this chapter, it is useful to think of the triples formed by the primaries as a color cube where each of the primaries forms one of the principle axes. The RGB color cube is illustrated in Figure 5.2. Each axis of the cube represents values of red, green, or blue in the range [0,255]. The red axis, labeled R, shows the associated color scale beneath it. The green and blue axes are illustrated similarly. As mentioned earlier, 0 means that the monitor does not emit the primary color and 255 means that it emits the maximum. Values between 0 and 255 yield gradations in the color's intensity.

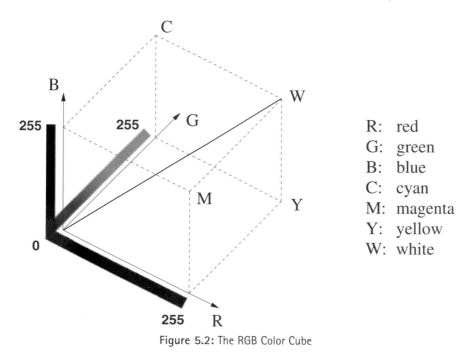

R: red
G: green
B: blue
C: cyan
M: magenta
Y: yellow
W: white

Figure 5.2: The RGB Color Cube

As the word colorspace implies, colors act like vectors. They can be combined by addition and subtraction to obtain other colors in the cube. Thus, the origin of the cube, or 0^R 0^G 0^B, represents the total absence of color, which is black. The far corner from the origin is the sum of the highest intensities of red, green, and blue, or $255^R255^G255^B$. This produces the color white, which is why this corner of the cube is labeled W in Figure 5.2. The other corners of the cube represent the various primary and secondary colors. We've already encountered red, green, and blue. The remaining three are cyan, magenta, and yellow. From the labels in Figure 5.2, it can be seen that adding 255 red to 255 green makes $255^R255^G0^B$ or yellow, adding 255 red to 255 blue makes 255^R0^G 255^B or magenta, and adding 255 green to 255 blue makes $0^R255^G255^B$ or cyan.

Note that the main diagonal of the RGB cube is illustrated in Figure 5.2 as a line drawn between the black origin at 0 and white at W. This line represents the colors in the RGB cube that consist of equal amounts of red, green, and blue. All the points on this line are gray. The closer to the origin, the darker the gray; the closer to W, the lighter. It is for this reason that the main diagonal of the RGB cube is referred to as the *neutral axis*. Grays are neutral because they prefer no hue; they contain equal quantities of red, green, and blue.

5.2 THE HSV COLORSPACE

The perception of color and our way of talking about it in everyday life is not well served by the RGB colorspace. If we're thinking of repainting the walls of the living room, for example, we usually think about what shade of color it should be, how bright we want it, and whether it should be pastel or vivid.

Typically, the first thing we usually notice about a color is its hue. Hue describes the shade of color and where that color it is found in the color spectrum. Red, yellow, and purple are words that describe hue. Figure 5.3 illustrates the range of hues, H, as a circle represented by values from 0 to 360. The reasons for this will become clear shortly.

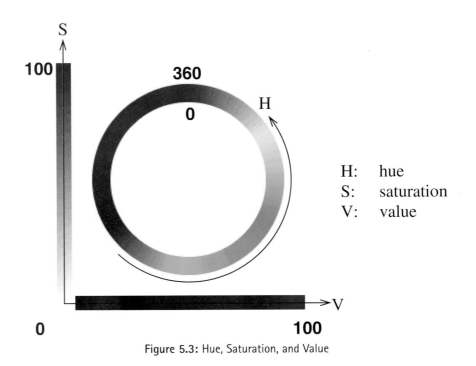

H: hue
S: saturation
V: value

Figure 5.3: Hue, Saturation, and Value

The next most significant aspect of color is typically the saturation, S. The saturation describes how pure the hue is with respect to a white reference. For example, a color that is all red and no white is fully saturated. If we add some white to the red, the result becomes more pastel, and the color shifts from red to pink. The hue is still red but it has become less saturated. This is illustrated in the vertical bar of Figure 5.3. Saturation is a percentage that ranges from 0 to 100. A pure red that has no white is 100% saturated.

Finally, a color also has a brightness. This is a relative description of how much light is coming from the color. If the color reflects a lot of light, we would say that it is bright. Imagine seeing a red sportscar during the day. Its color looks bright. Compare this with the perception of the car as night is falling. We can see that the car is red but it looks duller because ambient illumination is reflecting less light into the eye. Less light means the color looks darker. In the GIMP, the most important measure of brightness is measured by a quantity called value. However, there are also other measures of brightness that will be introduced shortly. For the moment, though, the horizontal bar in Figure 5.3 illustrates a range of red values. Value, like saturation, is a percentage that goes from 0 to 100. This range can be thought of as the amount of light illuminating a color. For example, when the hue is red and the value is high the color looks bright. When the value is low it looks dark.

Thus, hue, saturation, and value are like an alternative colorspace. Any color can be decomposed into these three components and, similar to RGB, it is possible to represent this space as a cube. Figure 5.4 illustrates the result of using `Image:Image/Mode/Decompose` on the color image in Figure 5.4(a). Choosing the HSV option in the `Decompose` dialog produces the hue, saturation, and value decomposition shown in Figures 5.4(b), (c), and (d). It is interesting to note that hue really doesn't change much. It is almost constant over broad regions of the image. For, example, although there is significant detail in the saturation and value components of the sky, the hue is quite uniform there. Of the three, it is the value component that is the most detailed.

Figure 5.4: Decomposing a Color Image into its HSV Components

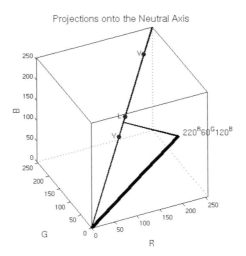

Figure 5.6: Different Projections Onto the Neutral Axis

Next, we define saturation. The definition of saturation is related to that of brightness. Saturation is the relative colorfulness of an area with respect to its brightness. What is colorfulness? An answer can be given in the context of the RGB cube and the neutral axis. As already noted, the neutral axis is the diagonal in the cube going from $0^R0^G0^B$ to $255^R255^G255^B$, and which consists of black, white, and the grayscale between them. Thus, in the usual sense, this axis has no color (that is, hue). The colorfulness of any point in the RGB cube, then, is proportional to its perpendicular distance to the neutral axis. Points closer to the axis are less colorful (that is, closer to gray) and those that are further away are more colorful. The saturation, then, of a point in the RGB cube is the ratio of its colorfulness to its brightness.

This means that surfaces of constant saturation in the RGB cube are cones centered around the neutral axis. Figure 5.7 shows two instances of the RGB cube. The cube in Figure 5.7(a) shows the cone corresponding to 20% saturation and that in Figure 5.7(b) to 70% saturation. Note that the colors on the rightmost cone seem more vivid because they are more saturated. The colors of the leftmost cone are much paler because their colors are more relatively neutral. When a color is more neutral we call it pastel.

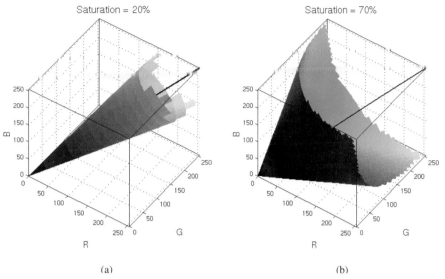

Saturation = 20%   Saturation = 70%

(a)   (b)

Figure 5.7: Cones of Constant Saturation in the RGB Cube

Finally, the definition of hue is related to what we colloquially think of as color. The hue of a point in the RGB cube is defined to be its angular position around the neutral axis. Looking at the corners of the RGB cube shown in Figure 5.2, you can see that red, yellow, green, cyan, blue, and magenta are distributed equally in angles around the neutral axis. Thus, the wedge defined by the neutral axis and any point on the surface of the cube is a plane of constant hue.

Figure 5.8 illustrates three instances of the RGB cube with different wedges of constant hue. Because hue is a function of angle, its range is from 0 to 360 degrees. The red corner of the cube is defined to be the hue at 0, which, forcibly, is also the hue at 360. This hue is shown in Figure 5.8(b). The cube in Figure 5.8(a) shows a hue of 330, which is purple, and that in Figure 5.8(c) a hue of 30, which is orange. Note that although the hue of each wedge is constant, the brightness and saturation vary over the range of possible values.

Figure 5.9 summarizes the relationship between RGB and HSV. Although, the neutral axis represents brightness and not value, I will often abuse this notion and refer to it as the value axis. The model shown in Figure 5.9 will be useful for understanding the explanations of the color blending modes described later in this chapter.

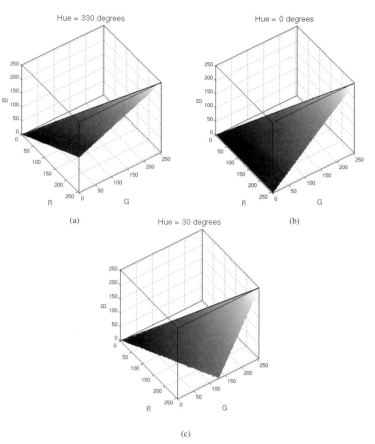

Figure 5.8: Wedges of Constant Hue in the RGB Cube

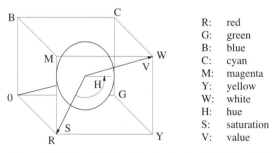

R:	red
G:	green
B:	blue
C:	cyan
M:	magenta
Y:	yellow
W:	white
H:	hue
S:	saturation
V:	value

Figure 5.9: The HSV Coordinates in the RGB Color Cube

With the HSV coordinate system in mind, several observations can be made about regions of color in the RGB cube. The first is that the cyan, magenta, and yellow vertices of the cube represent brighter colors than red, green, and blue because these latter project lower down onto the neutral axis. Similarly, all colors in the pyramid defined by the C, Y, M, and W vertices correspond to lighter colors, and the pyramid defined by the origin and the R, G, and B vertices correspond to darker colors. Colors near the neutral axis in the cube will have a more pastel or washed out look because they are less saturated, and colors further away from this axis will appear more vivid.

5.4 THE SUBTRACTIVE COLOR SYSTEMS CMY AND CMYK

A color monitor emits light and consequently relies on the RGB colorspace, which is an additive color system. Ink on paper, however, is a totally different story. Ink absorbs light and the color we see from it is the light that was reflected and not absorbed. If we shine a white light on an area and the color seen is cyan, it is because the red component of the white light was absorbed leaving only cyan to be reflected. Similarly, magenta absorbs green, and yellow absorbs blue. Thus, the cyan, magenta, and yellow colors make a subtractive color space, which is the anti-space of RGB. This colorspace is called CMY for cyan, magenta, and yellow. For a pixel that has R, G, and B components in the RGB colorspace, the corresponding C, M, and Y components are just (255-R), (255-G), and (255-B).

Due to the physical nature of colored inks, the CMY colorspace is perfect for working with printed images. Or almost. In principle, the addition of equal amounts of cyan, magenta, and yellow is like subtracting equal amounts of red, green, and blue. We know that equal amounts of R, G, and B make a neutral color, so equal amounts of C, M, and Y do too. Thus, adding large and equal amounts of cyan, magenta, and yellow makes black, and adding very small amounts makes a color that is close to white. At least this is true when CMY is used to print on white paper.

In practice, due to imperfections in inks, adding equal amounts of cyan, magenta, and yellow does not make a deep dark black. Rather, it produces a muddy brown. To remedy this problem, printers subtract out some of the cyan, magenta, and yellow from an image and replace it with black. This new colorspace is called CMYK, and it significantly improves the depth and tonal range of printed images. Here, the K in CMYK stands for black.

How much cyan, magenta, and yellow can be subtracted out and replaced by black? Because neutral colors require equal amounts of cyan, magenta, and yellow, the most that can be subtracted out for a pixel is the minimum of its C, M, and Y components. Thus, $K=min(C,M,Y)$ is the maximum black that can be extracted, and the resulting new values of C, M, and Y are just the old values less this value of K. Although choosing K to be the minimum of C, M, and Y is reasonable, it is not necessary; it can also be chosen to be less than this value.

In addition to CMYK's natural relationship to printing because its subtractive qualities mirrors that of inks, it also has another important, more pragmatic advantage. Replacing equal amounts of three colored inks with a single black one can significantly reduce the amount of ink printed on the paper. This means that the ink will dry faster and the printing presses can produce more copy in the same amount of time.

There are also significant advantages to CMYK when doing color correction on an image that will end up in a printed format.[6] The most significant is that the range of colors, known as the color gamut, that can be produced with inks is significantly smaller than what can be created on a color monitor. Thus, it isn't sensible to invest a lot of time working on an RGB image only to convert it to CMYK for printing at the end. This will more than likely produce many out of gamut colors. When the final result is a *printed* image it is more sensible to convert to CMYK before performing any color transformations.

Unfortunately, the GIMP provides very little support for working in CMYK. There is the `Decompose` function, found in the `Image:Image/Mode` menu, which offers a CMYK option in its dialog. This is not terribly useful, though. To make the GIMP truly pre-press capable, the following is needed:

- The ability to set K in the range 0 to $min(C,M,Y)$.
- The ability to convert RGB to CMYK while applying color gamut limitations.
- The ability to work in CMYK space just like in RGB space. This means a Channels dialog with C, M, Y, and K components and color editing functions and tools like `Curves`, `Levels`, `Color Picker`, and so on, which work in CMYK.

There is also the perception that spot colors are needed to make an effective pre-press image manipulation tool. Although there is much pageantry about the colorimetry, device calibration, and Pantone ink systems available for Adobe's Photoshop, these are somewhat of a red herring. Making these systems work is difficult and unreliable. Physical printing devices like presses tend to produce different results from day to day and even from run to run. In the printing process, there are many problems that can change the color balance so carefully calibrated on the monitor. The amounts of ink the printer uses, the capability of the press to apply the specified percentages of ink uniformly across the printing surface, and many other environmental and press health factors make for significant variability in the final result. No amount of calibration and proprietary ink systems can fix that.

Thus, the main hurdle to cross before the GIMP can become a viable pre-press tool is the functionality given in the preceding bulleted list.

5.5 CONVERSION TO GRAYSCALE

From the previous discussions, it is clear that every color image has a grayscale component that can be separated out from the hue and saturation components. There are actually three different functions in the GIMP for converting an image to grayscale. These are the Grayscale function, the Desaturate function, and the value component of the HSV option of the Decompose function. To illustrate these functions, each one is applied to the color image shown in Figure 5.10(a).

(a) Color Original   (b) Convert to Grayscale

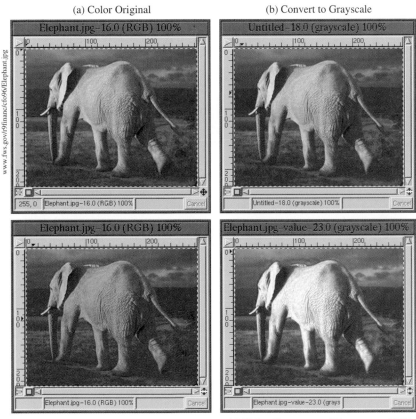

(c) Desaturate   (d) Value Component of Decompose HSV

Figure 5.10: The Three Methods for Converting to Grayscale

To begin, the most obvious choice for converting a color image to grayscale is to use the Grayscale function found in the Image:Image/Mode menu. This function transforms a 24-bit, three-channel, color image to an 8-bit, single-channel grayscale image by forming a weighted sum of the red, green, and blue components. The formula used in the GIMP is $Y = 0.3R + 0.59G + 0.11B$; this result is known as luminance.[4, 5] The weights used to compute luminance are related to the monitor's phosphors. The explanation for these weights is due to the fact that for equal amounts of color the eye is most sensitive to green, then red, and then blue. This means that for equal amounts of green and blue light the green will, nevertheless, seem much brighter. Thus, the image obtained by the normal averaging of an image's three color components produces a grayscale brightness that is not perceptually equivalent to the brightness of the original color image. The weighted sum that defines Y, however, does.

The result of converting the color image of Figure 5.10(a) using the `Grayscale` function is shown in Figure 5.10(b). When you compare it to the two other grayscale images, the `Grayscale` function does seem the most representative of the color image's brightness.

From previous discussion, the removal of the saturation from an image should also produces a grayscale. One way to desaturate an image is to replace the RGB value for each pixel with that of the closest point on the neutral axis. This point on the neutral axis is illustrated in Figure 5.6. In the GIMP, the `Desaturate` function, found in the `Image:Image/Colors` menu, does something like this. Actually, it uses an approximation to this idea; it chooses the point on the neutral axis determined by computing `L={max(R, G, B) + min(R, G, B)}/2`, which corresponds to the definition of lightness. After applying `Desaturate`, the image remains in RGB space and continues to have three color channels, but now the channels have identical values, which is why the image appears as a grayscale.

The result of applying `Desaturate` to the color image in Figure 5.10(a) is shown in Figure 5.10(c). Of the three methods for converting an image to grayscale, this one produces the flattest (that is, with the least contrast) and the darkest conversion.

Finally, it is possible to get a slightly different grayscale conversion by using the HSV option of the `Decompose` function. This decomposes the original image into three new images, each an 8-bit grayscale image representing the hue, saturation, and value components of the image. The value component is a conversion to grayscale that is based on moving to the neutral axis by selecting the maximum RGB component. Thus, `V= max(R, G, B)`.

Figure 5.10(d) shows the value component of the HSV decomposition for Figure 5.10(a). This grayscale is clearly the brightest of the three, which makes sense because the value is defined as the maximum of the R, G, and B components (see Figure 5.6).

So, which conversion to grayscale is best? I'm tempted to say that `Grayscale` is best because it produces the result whose brightness is the most perceptually similar to the brightness of the original color image. However, the answer must depend on what *you* want to do with the image. Furthermore, the two other methods for converting to grayscale are useful, and, in particular, the value component of the `Decompose` HSV function is used for many operations in the GIMP (for examples, see Sections 6.2.6 and 6.4.4).

5.6 THE BLENDING MODES

Usually layers are opaque, which means that upper layers cover and visually block lower ones. Blending modes change this behavior and allow some color features of a layer to be combined with the colors of layers below it. Blending modes can also be used to affect how color from a painting tool combines with the layer the paint is applied to.

Figure 5.11(a) illustrates the blending mode menu for layers, which is found in the Layers dialog. Figure 5.11(b) shows the Blending Mode menu for painting tools, which is found in the Brush Selection dialog.* The menu in the Brush Selection dialog applies the selected blending mode to all the paint tools: the Pencil, Paintbrush, Airbrush, Ink Pen, and Xinput Airbrush tools. In addition, this menu controls the way the Bucket Fill, Gradient, and Clone tools apply their paint.

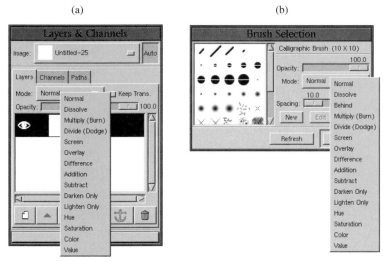

Figure 5.11: The Blending Mode Menus

The different blending modes are described in this section, and their practical uses and applications are described in the next. The GIMP has 16 different blending modes. They are listed in the following five logical groups:

- Normal, Dissolve, and Behind (available in paint mode only)

- Difference, Addition, and Subtract

- Multiply (Burn), Divide (Dodge), Screen, and Overlay

- Darken Only and Lighten Only

- Hue, Saturation, Color, and Value

---

* Actually, the GIMP preferences can be set so that each painting tool has individual access to the Mode menu. This is set by toggling off the Use Global Paint Options checkbox in the Tool Options branch of the Preferences dialog. Doing this makes the Mode menu available in the Tool Options dialog for each painting tool.

In the following descriptions of the blending modes, the pixels of the upper layer (or of the applied paint) are referred to as the foreground pixels and those of the lower layer or layers as the background pixels. The notations F and B are used to represent their respective values. Blending the foreground pixel value F with the background value B yields the resultant pixel value R.

5.6.1 THE NORMAL, DISSOLVE, AND BEHIND BLENDING MODES

Normal, Dissolve, and Behind are pseudo-blending modes because they don't really combine the foreground and background pixel values of the image.

Normal mode is the default GIMP behavior where the foreground pixels are visible and the background pixels are not. Of course, this can be changed by adjusting the opacity slider in the Layers dialog (more on opacity and transparency is discussed in Section 5.7).

Dissolve mode works by allowing a percentage of background pixels to be seen through the foreground. It does this by making some parts of the foreground partially transparent and the rest fully transparent. These two sets are intermingled in a random way. For the Dissolve mode to have an effect, the foreground layer must have an alpha channel with values less than 255. The alpha channel for a layer can be modified with a layer mask. The details of working with layer masks are discussed in Section 4.2.

Figure 5.12 illustrates the use of Dissolve. Figure 5.12(a) shows the Layers dialog, which illustrates how this example is constructed. The image consists of two layers: a red background and a white foreground. The foreground has a uniform alpha channel set to a value of 191 (about 75% opaque). The Mode menu in Figure 5.12(a) shows that the Dissolve mode has been chosen for the foreground.

Figure 5.12(b) shows the result of the Dissolve blending mode. Due to the value of the foreground's alpha channel the result is that 75% of the white pixels are 75% opaque and 25% are fully opaque. The details of the effect can be more clearly seen in the small region framed by the black box shown in Figure 5.12(b). This region is zoomed 900% and redisplayed in Figure 5.12(c), which makes the relationship of the red and white pixels more apparent.

Unlike all the other blend modes in the GIMP, the Behind mode only works with painting tools. It is not available as a blending mode for layers. To understand how it works, imagine a pane of glass that has something painted on the front surface but there are some parts of the pane that are bare, or have only a partially transparent paint on it. Painting on the back surface of the pane lets the color from this new paint show through to the front wherever the front is not fully opaque. Figure 5.13 illustrates this effect.

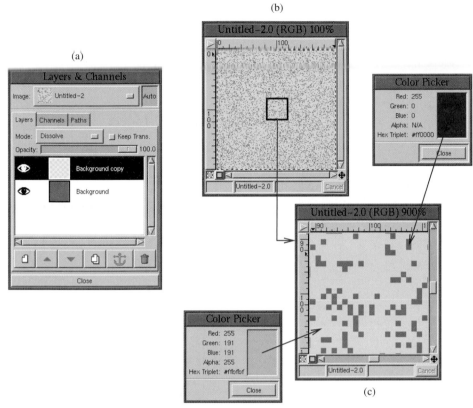

Figure 5.12: The Dissolve Blending Mode

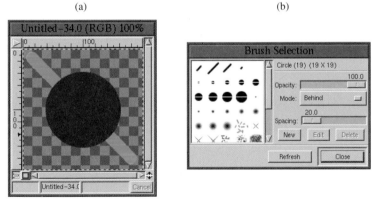

Figure 5.13: The Behind Blending Mode

In Figure 5.13(a), a single-layer image with a centered red circle is displayed. The rest of the layer is transparent. The Brush Selection dialog, shown in Figure 5.13(b), has been used to choose a large, hard brush and to set the blending mode to Behind. The figure shows the result of painting a bright green stripe, using the Paintbrush tool, through the red circle. In Behind mode, however, the green is only seen through the transparent parts of the layer. This mode only works for layers with alpha channels.

5.6.2 THE ADDITION, SUBTRACT, AND DIFFERENCE BLENDING MODES

Addition, Subtract, and Difference are blending modes that add and subtract foreground and background pixel values in RGB colorspace. Figure 5.14 illustrates the effect of addition and subtraction for two pixels in the RGB cube.

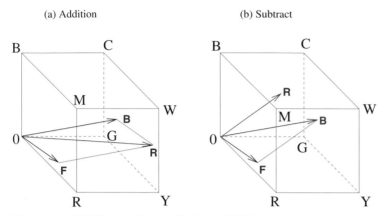

Figure 5.14: Addition and Subtraction in the RGB Cube

The Addition blending mode works as follows: Given a foreground and background pixel, represented by the RGB vectors $F=[r_1,g_1,b_1]$ and $B=[r_2,g_2,b_2]$, the pixel obtained from the Addition blending mode is $R=F+B=[r_1+r_2,g_1+g_2,b_1+b_2]$. Thus, in Figure 5.14(a), the two blue arrows represent a foreground and background pixel, and the red arrow is the vector sum of the two. Addition always produces a resultant color that is as light or lighter than either the foreground or background colors. This is because the vector sum must have a projection onto the neutral axis that is closer to white than the projection for either the background or foreground colors.

In the event that the vector sum produces a result outside of the color cube (that is, by producing any RGB component greater than 255), its value is clipped to the surface of the cube. The equation describing the Addition blending mode is

$$R=\min\{F+B,W\}$$

where W is the vector [255,255,255] and the min function performs component-wise minimization of the two vectors.

Cyan, magenta, and yellow are the sums of green and blue, red and blue, and red and green, respectively. Thus, cyan, magenta, and yellow appear lighter than red, green, or blue because they project higher up onto the neutral axis. Furthermore, any of these secondary colors (cyan, magenta, yellow) summed with the complementary primary color (red, green, blue) produces white, the lightest color of all.

Figure 5.15 illustrates an application of the Addition blending mode. Figure 5.15(a) displays the image of a flower, and Figure 5.15(b), showing the associated Layers dialog, indicates that this image consists of two-layers. The upper layer is the flower image, and the lower layer is filled with a medium gray whose pixel values are uniformly $127^R127^G127^B$.

(a)   (c)

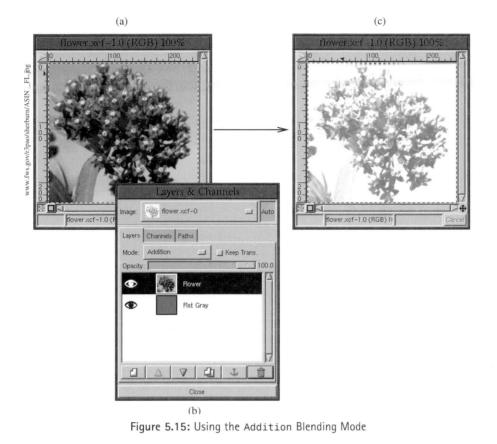

(b)

Figure 5.15: Using the `Addition` Blending Mode

Figure 5.15(a) shows the flower image for the `Normal` blending mode. Figure 5.15(c) shows the same image when the blending mode of the upper layer is changed to `Addition`. This has the effect of adding $127^R 127^G 127^B$ to every pixel in the flower layer, which lightens the entire image considerably. In fact, some parts of the image are completely blown out to white.

The effect of the `Subtract` blending mode is illustrated in Figure 5.14(b). This blending mode works as follows: Given a foreground and background pixel, we'll again represent each as an RGB vector $F = [r_1, g_1, b_1]$ and $B = [r_2, g2_2, b_2]$. The pixel obtained from the `Subtract` blending mode is $R = B - F = [r_2 - r_1, g_2 - g_1, b_2 - b_1]$. Thus, for the two blue arrows labeled F and B in Figure 5.14(b), the result of subtracting the foreground from the background is given by the red arrow labeled R.

Unlike the `Addition` blending mode, `Subtract` is not symmetrical (that is, subtracting F from B is not the same as subtracting B from F). The result of subtracting the foreground from the background can produce negative values. If a component of the resulting RGB vector is less than zero, it is clipped to the surface of the cube. Thus, the equation representing the `Subtract` blending mode is

$$R = \max\{B - F, 0\}$$

where 0 represents the color $0^R0^G0^B$ and max is the function that performs component-wise maximization of the two vectors. Because the foreground color is always a positive number, the result is always darker than the background (unless either the foreground or background are black, and then there is no change).

The Difference blending mode is like Subtract, but the result is symmetrical between the foreground and the background. Difference is symmetrical because it applies an absolute value to the difference of the foreground and background values. Thus, if one of the RGB components is negative after subtraction, its sign is reversed to make it positive. The resulting mathematical expression for the Difference blending mode is

$$R = |F - B|$$

where the vertical bars in the equation represent the absolute value function.

Figure 5.16 illustrates the application of the Subtract and Difference blending modes. The modes are applied to the image from Figure 5.15(a), which consists of the flower in the upper layer and a medium gray in the lower layer. You can see that the result of using Subtract, shown in Figure 5.16(a), has regions that are totally black. This is where the difference between the foreground and background creates negative values that are clipped to zero. Difference, shown in Figure 5.16(b), however, has no clipped values because it employs the absolute value of the difference. Note that for both the Subtract and Difference modes, the results are darker than the original flower image.

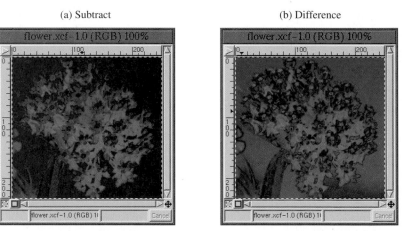

Figure 5.16: Using the Subtract and Difference Blending Modes

5.6.3 THE MULTIPLY (BURN), DIVIDE (DODGE), SCREEN, AND OVERLAY BLENDING MODES

Multiply, Divide, Screen, and Overlay are all multiplicative blending modes. The resulting pixel values are the product, or a function of the product, of the foreground and background pixels.

The actions of the `Multiply` and `Screen` modes on pixels represented in the RGB cube are illustrated in Figure 5.17. For a foreground pixel whose position in the RGB cube is $[r_1, g_1, b_1]$ and a background pixel whose position is $[r_2, g_2, b_2]$, the resultant pixel for `Multiply` mode is the component-by-component product of the two, or $[r_1r_2/255, g_1g_2/255, b_1b_2/255]$, where the division by 255 is necessary to normalize the result back into the RGB cube. This can be succinctly expressed by the equation

$$R = \frac{1}{255}(F \times B)$$

where the $\times$ symbol means component-wise multiplication.

(a) Multiply   (b) Screen

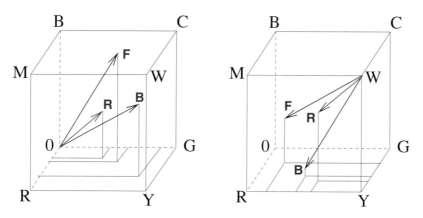

Figure 5.17: The `Multiply` and `Screen` Modes in the RGB Cube

Due to the scale factor of 255, the component values of one RGB vector are normalized to the range [0,1]. Thus, R is component-wise smaller than either F or B. From previous discussions, you know that smaller means darker because the projection onto the neutral axis is closer to the origin. This is illustrated in Figure 5.17(a) which shows two blue arrows representing the foreground and background pixel positions and a red arrow representing the component-wise product.

Figure 5.18(a) illustrates an example of applying `Multiply` mode to the flower image from Figure 5.15(a). As before, the lower layer of this image is a uniform gray equal to $127^R 127^G 127^B$. The result, shown in Figure 5.18(a), is the image has been made uniformly darker. In fact, because the lower layer is a medium gray, the pixels values in the flower layer have been scaled by $127/255 \approx 1/2$ everywhere.

(a) Multiply   (b) Divide

(c) Screen   (d) Overlay

Figure 5.18: An Example of Multiply, Divide, Screen, and Overlay Modes

For a foreground pixel whose position in the RGB cube is $[r_1,g_1,b_1]$ and a background pixel whose position is $[r_2,g_2,b_2]$, you might imagine that the resultant pixel for the Divide blending mode would be analogous to that for the Multiply mode. This would suggest something like $[255r_2/r_1, 255g_2/g_1, 255b_2/b_1]$. However, this expression presents two problems. The first problem is that when the foreground pixel has a zero component, the result is not defined; the second problem is that when the foreground pixel value is small, the result can be so large that it is no longer inside the RGB cube. The first problem is solved by adding one to each component of the foreground pixel. This prevents a division by zero. The second problem is solved by clipping values that are too large to the surface of the cube.

A succinct expression for the Divide mode is

$$R = \min\{W, B \div \frac{(F+1)}{256}\}$$

where W is $255^R 255^G 255^B$, $\div$ represents component-wise division of two vectors, and min represents component-wise minimization. Figure 5.18(b) illustrates the application of Divide to the flower image from Figure 5.15(a).

Here, you can see that some parts of the resulting image are blown out to white. This occurs in regions where the original flower image has small (that is dark) pixel values. Note that Divide always lightens an image because it divides each pixel component by a number less than 1.

The Screen blending mode has a lightening effect that is exactly analogous to the darkening effect created by Multiply. This concept is illustrated in Figure 5.17(b). As shown in the figure, Screen mode redefines the origin to be 255^R $255^G 255^B$, the white point in the cube. Thus, the vectors to the foreground and background pixels are as shown by the two blue arrows in Figure 5.17(b). Screen then multiplies the two vectors, producing a resultant shown as a red arrow in Figure 5.17(b). As with the Multiply mode, the resulting vector of the Screen mode is shorter than either the foreground or background vectors—but with respect to the white point in the cube. Thus, the resulting vector is closer to the white point, and, consequently, lighter than either the foreground or background colors. The mathematical expression for Screen mode is

$$R = W - \frac{1}{255} (W-F) \times (W-B)$$

Again, the factor of 255 is introduced to keep the resultant pixel values inside the RGB cube.

Figure 5.18(c) illustrates an example of applying the Screen mode to the flower image from Figure 5.15(a). As predicted, the result is brighter than in the original image of the flower. Also notice that unlike Divide, Screen mode does not blow out to white. Thus, although both Divide and Screen have similar lightening characteristics, they have very different personalities.

Finally, the Overlay mode is a combination of both Multiply and Screen. The equation for overlay mode is

$$R = \frac{1}{255} [B \times R_s + (1-B) \times R_m]$$

where R_s represents the resultant pixel value for Screen mode and R_m represents that for Multiply. This equation says that the resultant pixel value for Overlay mode is a combination of the Screen and Multiply modes. The mix of the two modes is proportional to the background pixel value.

Thus, if the background is dark (that is, has an RGB value close to zero in all three components), the result of Multiply mode will dominate and the result of Screen mode will be suppressed. The opposite is true if the background pixel is light (that is, has an RGB value close to white in all three components). Overall, Overlay mode tends to make an image darker where it is already dark and lighter where it is already light. Figure 5.18(d) illustrates an example of applying Overlay mode to the flower image from Figure 5.15(a).

5.6.4 THE DARKEN ONLY AND LIGHTEN ONLY BLENDING MODES

Darken Only creates a resultant pixel that retains the smallest components of the foreground and background pixels. Thus, if the foreground pixel has the components $[r_1, g_1, b_1]$ and the background has $[r_2, g_2, b_2]$, the resultant pixel is $[\min(r_1, r_2), \min(g_1, g_2), \min(b_1, b_2)]$. This is expressed more compactly as

$$R = \min\{F, B\}$$

where min means component-wise minimization. Not surprisingly, Darken Only mode makes an image darker.

Figure 5.19(a) illustrates the use of Darken Only mode on the flower image from Figure 5.15(a). Because the grayscale layer below the flower is uniformly $127^R 127^G 127^B$, everything in the flower that has an RGB component darker than 127 retains its character in the image. The parts of the flower image that are lighter are replaced by the flat gray.

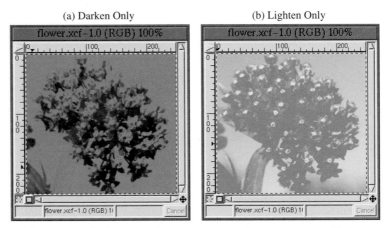

Figure 5.19: An Example of Darken Only and Lighten Only Modes

Lighten Only mode has the opposite action of Darken Only. It selects the maximum of each component from the foreground and background pixels. The mathematical expression for Lighten Only is

$$R = \max\{F, B\}$$

where max means component-wise maximization. Lighten Only mode makes an image lighter.

Figure 5.19(b) illustrates the use of Lighten Only mode on the flower image from Figure 5.15(a). Now, everything in the flower that has an RGB component lighter than 127 retains its character in the image. The parts of the flower image that are darker are replaced by the flat gray.

5.6.5 THE HUE, SATURATION, VALUE, AND COLOR BLENDING MODES

The Hue, Saturation, Value, and Color blending modes all work similarly. For each mode, one HSV component is taken from the foreground pixel and the other two components from the background pixel. For example, if the Hue blending mode is chosen, the result is the hue of the foreground pixels combined with the saturation and value of the background pixels. The same process is used for the Saturation and Value blending modes. The Color blending mode, however, is slightly different. For this mode, the hue and saturation of the foreground pixels are used in conjunction with the lightness of the background pixels. Lightness, defined in Section 5.3, is less bright than value, and is simultaneously more true to the human perception of brightness.

Thus, the action of the Hue blending mode can be expressed as

$$R=[h(F),s(B),v(B)]$$

where $h(F)$ means the hue of the foreground, $s(B)$ represents the saturation of the background, and $v(B)$ is the value of the background. An example of applying the Hue blending mode is illustrated in Figure 5.20. The flower image from Figure 5.15(a) is shown in Figure 5.20(a). This image is the foreground to the Hue mode, and the background is the blue layer shown in Figure 5.20(b). This blue layer varies horizontally in value and vertically in saturation. The result of applying the Hue mode is shown in Figure 5.20(c). Here, it can be clearly seen that the saturation and value variations of the blue layer are combining with the hue of the flower layer.

Figure 5.20: An Example of Hue Mode

Similar to Hue, the Saturation blending mode produces resultant pixels that are a combination of the saturation of the foreground and the hue and value of the background. The expression for this is

$$R = [h(B), s(F), v(B)]$$

where $s(F)$ is the saturation of the foreground, $h(B)$ is the hue of the background, and $v(B)$ represents the value of the background. An example of applying the Saturation blending mode is illustrated in Figure 5.21. We see again our flower image in Figure 5.21(a) playing the role of the foreground layer. However, now the background layer, shown in Figure 5.21(b), has been constructed to vary only in hue and value. In this layer, the hue changes along the horizontal direction and the value along the vertical. The result of applying the Saturation mode is shown in Figure 5.21(c).

Figure 5.21: An Example of Saturation Mode

The Value blending mode produces resultant pixels that are a combination of the value of the foreground and the hue and saturation of the background. The expression for this is

$$R = [h(B), s(B), v(F)]$$

Here, $v(F)$ represents the foreground value, $h(B)$ the background hue, and $s(B)$ the background saturation. An example of this blending mode is shown in Figure 5.22. The background layer, shown in Figure 5.22(b), varies in hue in the horizontal direction and saturation in the vertical direction. The result of this mode is shown in Figure 5.22(c).

Figure 5.22: An Example of Value Mode

The final example in this section illustrates the Color blending mode. This mode combines the foreground hue and saturation with the background lightness. Lightness was defined earlier in Section 5.3; lightness is always a bit less bright than value. The expression for this blending mode is

$$R=[h(F),s(F),l(B)]$$

where $h(F)$ and $s(F)$ are the hue and saturation of the foreground, and $l(B)$ is the lightness of the background. An example of this blending mode is shown in Figure 5.23. Here, the background, shown in Figure 5.23(b), varies only in value. The result is shown in Figure 5.23(c).

Foreground

Background

Figure 5.23: An Example of Color Mode

5.7 OPACITY AND TRANSPARENCY

Transparency is usually not considered to be a blending mode, however, it works just like one! Transparency is just a combination of the Multiply and Addition blending modes; it takes a percentage of the foreground and adds it to the complementary percentage of the background. Thus, if you want the foreground to be 75% opaque (opacity is just the opposite of transparency), you multiply the foreground by 0.75, the background by (1–0.75), and add the two. This relationship can be expressed as

$$R = \alpha F + (1 - \alpha)B$$

where α represents the opacity. The percentages used in scaling the foreground and background pixels are called complementary because $\alpha + (1 - \alpha) = 1$.

By the way, can you guess why the percentage of opacity is represented by the Greek letter alpha in the preceding equation? It is because the opacity of a layer is controlled by its alpha channel. The alpha channel takes values in the range [0,255] where a value of 255 represents 100% opacity, and 0 represents 100% transparency.

Different amounts of transparency/opacity can be obtained by adjusting the value of α. For a foreground and background pixel pair, the effect of opacity can be illustrated in the RGB cube. Figure 5.24 shows how combining a percentage of the foreground with a complementary percentage of the background creates a resultant pixel that is somewhere on a line between the two points. The two blue arrows in Figure 5.24 show the locations in the RGB cube of a foreground and background pixel. The line between the two points represents the set of pixels obtained for varying degrees of opacity. The three red arrows show the pixels corresponding to 25, 50, and 75% opacity of the foreground with respect to the background pixel.

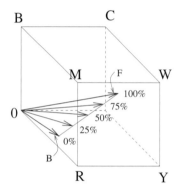

Figure 5.24: Explanation of Opacity in the RGB Cube

Figure 5.25 illustrates an example of setting the opacity of a layer. Figure 5.25(a) shows a two-layer image consisting of herons in the upper layer and flowers in the lower. When the Opacity slider for the upper layer is set to 75%, as shown in the Layers dialog in Figure 5.25(b), the result is as shown in Figure 5.25(c).

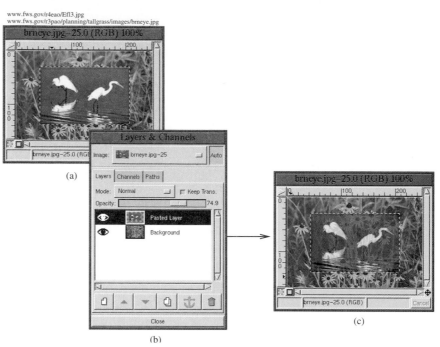

Figure 5.25: An Example Application of Transparency

Transparency/opacity can also be controlled for the GIMP's painting functions. The Opacity slider for these are found in the `Brush Selection` dialog.

5.8 PRACTICAL USES OF BLENDING MODES

Blending modes are fascinating toys that are lots of fun and can stimulate creative play with color. Results of experimenting with the blending modes often produce surprising and very aesthetic results.

Blending modes, however, are a lot more than toys for playing with color; some very useful operations would be impossible without them. Examples of practical uses for blending modes can be found in Sections 7.2, 7.3, and 7.4. This section describes two great applications of blending modes that do not appear elsewhere in this book.

5.8.1 COLORIZATION

It is often desirable to completely change the color of a subject—the color of a car, a lip gloss, eyes, a dress. The problem with changing the color of any real world image is that there are always lots of variations in the shading of a color. This is due to natural color gradations, lighting conditions, and textures. Figure 5.26(a) illustrates such an image. Notice the subtle variations in the kitten's fur. The gray color of her coat has highlights and shadows as well as natural variations due to the texture of her fur. Changing the color of her coat requires choosing the new color and applying it in such a way that these natural looking variations are preserved.

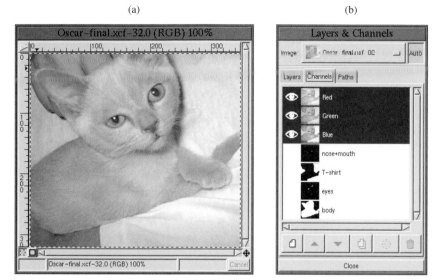

(a)   (b)

Figure 5.26: Image Whose Color Is to Be Changed

The `Color` blending mode is purr-fect for this type of operation. This mode combines the hue and saturation of the foreground with the lightness of the background. Thus, the natural dark and light areas of the kitten's coat are preserved and only the color changes. The following illustrates how the technique is applied.

The objective is to change the kitten into a tabby colored cat with blue-ish eyes and to make the T-shirt of the person holding her a khaki green. To do this, a separate selection is made of the kitten's body, her eyes, her nose and mouth, and of the T-shirt. Each of these image components are selected using any of the techniques from Chapters 3 or 4 (I used the `Bezier Path` tool). Each selection is stored as a channel mask, as shown in the Channels dialog displayed in Figure 5.26(b). The four channel masks are labeled Body, Eyes, T-shirt, and Nose+Mouth.

The next step is to create a transparent layer above the kitten image where the new colors can be applied. The new layer is created by clicking on the `New Layer` button in the Layers dialog. When the `New Layer Options` dialog appears, the Transparent option is used, and the resulting layer is labeled Colorization Layer. Changing the blending mode of this new layer to `Color`, the color surgery can begin.

The Body channel mask is used to recover the selection of the kitten's body by applying the function `Channel to Selection` from the Channels menu (see Section 4.1.5). The Marching Ants for this selection can be seen in Figure 5.27(a). Now, making sure that the Colorization layer is active by clicking on its thumbnail in the Layers dialog, the `Color Selection` tool, as shown in Figure 5.27(b), is used to pick the desired color, and the `Bucket Fill` tool is used to apply the color to the selected region. Figure 5.27(a) shows the result of this process. Note that the lightness variations of the kitten's coat from the lower layer are applied to the color and saturation choices in the upper one. Also note that in the Layers dialog, shown in Figure 5.27(c), the Colorization Layer shows the thumbnail of the `Bucket Fill` operation.

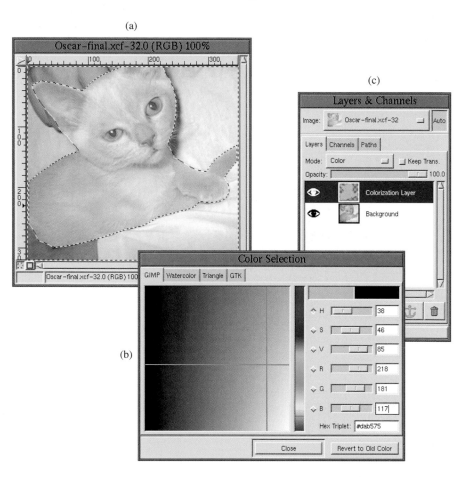

Figure 5.27: Making the Kitten's Coat Tabby-Colored

The color of the kitten's eyes are changed using a similar operation. After applying the selection from the Eyes channel mask and making the Colorization layer active, you can apply the desired color to the eyes. Figure 5.28(b) shows the color selection, Figure 5.28(a) shows the result of the eye-coloring procedure, and Figure 5.28(c) shows the corresponding Layers dialog.

Figure 5.28: Making the Kitten's Eyes Blue

Before proceeding to the final operation, that of changing the T-shirt color, an important touch is needed to make the kitten's nose, mouth, and inner ear look natural. These parts are not the same color as her fur and require a little pink to make them look correct. The nose and mouth are colored by converting the Nose+Mouth mask to a selection and by using the Bucket Fill tool to apply an appropriately chosen pink color. As for the kitten's inner ear, the color is applied a little differently. The inside of her ear consists of both fur and skin, and, consequently, the Airbrush tool is more suitable than the Bucket Fill tool for locally applying the pink paint.

Making the T-shirt a khaki green is a little different from the previous colorization efforts. Because the T-shirt's color in the original image is so light, it is impossible to make it any darker using the Color blending mode, which uses the lightness of the lower layer. This problem can be solved by changing blending modes. Creating a new transparent layer and setting the mode to Multiply allows darker color to be applied to the T-shirt. The result of this is shown in Figure 5.29(a). Figure 5.29(b) shows the color chosen for the T-shirt, and Figure 5.29(c) shows the thumbnail of the new layer and the choice of the `Multiply` blending mode. Note that I set the Opacity slider to 50% for this layer, which adjusted the color to a value I liked.

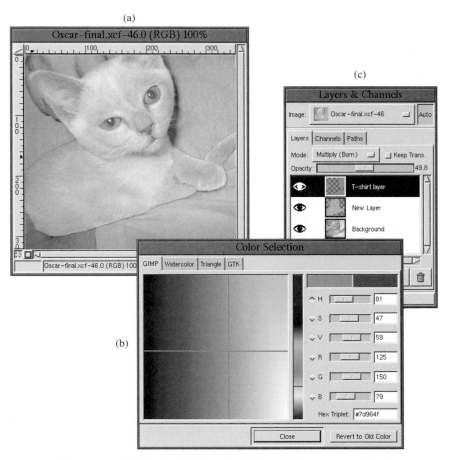

Figure 5.29: Making the T-shirt a Khaki Green Using `Multiply` Mode

5.8.2 REALISTIC SHADOWS AND HIGHLIGHTS

A strong specular reflector illuminated by a point source creates a strong highlight and well defined shadows. However, more diffuse lighting produces less well-defined effects. Under these circumstances, the `Multiply` and `Screen` blending modes can be used to create realistic shadows and highlights in an image. These modes can be used to darken and lighten parts of an image without the risk of blowing out the tonal range, as is the case for specular reflectors and point source illumination. The following example illustrates this application of these blending modes.

Figures 5.30(a) and (b) illustrate two selected colors that are used to make the red circle on the yellow background shown in Figure 5.30(c). The goal is to give the circle a 3D look, to produce the effect of depth and light by creating a natural, diffuse looking highlight and shadow. The idea is to use each color itself to create the shadow and highlight. Applying a color to itself in Multiply mode tends to slightly darken the spot where the paint is applied. In Screen mode, it tends to slightly lighten it. This darkening and lightening, then, appears visually as a diffuse shadow and highlight. Repeated applications increase the shadow/highlight intensity until the desired effect is achieved.

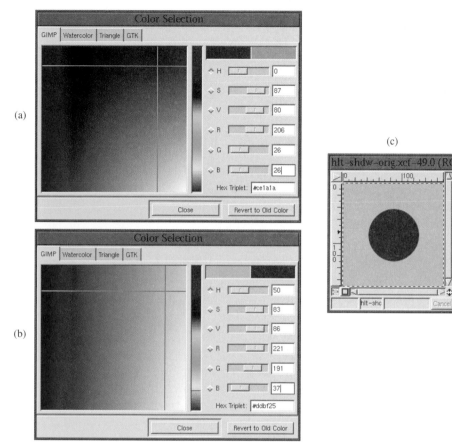

Figure 5.30: Original Circle with Measured Colors Shown in Color Selection Dialogs

Using the Color Picker tool, the measured colors of the image are $221^R 191^G 37^B$ for the yellow background and $206^G 26^G 26^B$ for the red circle. Because the colors are not fully saturated, they can be used. However, if either color were fully saturated (that is, a pure red, green, blue, cyan, magenta, yellow, or white), it would be necessary to select a color that is slightly off pure for this technique to work. This is easily done, however, using the Color Selection tool.

To make the highlight shown in Figure 5.31(a), a large fuzzy brush is chosen from the Brush Selection tool, as shown in Figure 5.31(b). Note that in the Brush Selection dialog, the blending mode has been set to Screen and the opacity to 60%. These numbers were chosen with some experimentation to achieve results I liked. A light application of the Paintbrush tool to the side of the red circle where I imagine the light to be coming from produces the high-light shown in Figure 5.31(a). Note that the Airbrush tool is also an excellent device for this type of work.

(a)   (b)

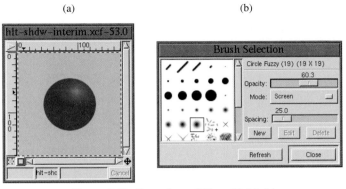

Figure 5.31: Screening a Diffuse Highlight

The shadow shown in Figure 5.32(a) is made with the same brush; however, now the Multiply blending mode is used, as shown in Figure 5.32(b). Here, the opacity slider in the Brush Selection dialog is set to 100%. Again, the numbers depend on the aesthetic sensibilities of the individual. Light application of the Paintbrush tool to the opposite side of the highlight and below the circle produces a believable, diffuse shadow.

(a)   (b)

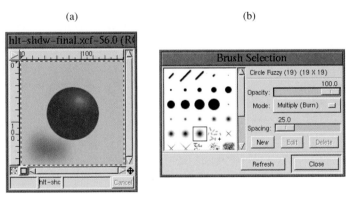

Figure 5.32: Multiplying in a Diffuse Shadow

5.9 COMMON PROBLEMS AND FREQUENTLY ASKED QUESTIONS

The following are a few common problems that arise when working with colorspaces and blending modes:

- **I want to apply a blending mode with the Paintbrush (Pencil, Bucket Fill, and so on) tool. Although I've set the blending mode in the Layers dialog, it doesn't seem to work.**

  The problem is that the blending modes for the painting tools are controlled from the Brush Selection dialog, not from the Layers dialog. Type C-S-b in the image window or click on the Active Brush in the Toolbox window to bring up this dialog.

- **I'm using the Paintbrush (Pencil, Bucket Fill, and so on) tool, and I'm getting strange color results. What's going on?**

  Check that the Brush Selection dialog's blending mode is set to Normal.

- **I want to color a black-and-white image, but no matter what color I apply it comes out as a shade of gray in my image. Why?**

  You are working on a grayscale format image. Convert the image to RGB by selecting the function RGB from the Image:Image/Mode menu.

6

TOUCHUP AND ENHANCEMENT

Photos that are scanned or come from a PhotoCD or digital camera can suffer from both aesthetic and processing defects. These defects can be due to problems of contrast, color casts, color saturation, tonal range, blur, scratches, and so on. Furthermore, most photos, no matter how carefully composed, typically need some enhancement to achieve their full potential. Ansel Adams, one of America's most renowned photographers, spent as much time in the darkroom enhancing his negatives and prints as he did in composing and taking his shots. Adams' books on working with the negative and the print are classics in photography.[7, 8]

Photo touchup and enhancement are part science and part art, and the GIMP is an excellent tool for these on both counts. This chapter describes the main ideas for aesthetically improving photos and explains how to use the GIMP to achieve terrific results. Following are the topics addressed in this chapter:

- Improving tonal range
- Removing color casts
- Repairing blemishes
- Sharpening

Each of these subjects is described in detail in the following sections, and a case study is presented at the end of the chapter.

6.1 IMPROVING TONAL RANGE

Improving the tonal range of an image is the first step that should be taken in almost every effort to touch up and enhance a photo. To do this, it is necessary to understand the basic elements of tonal range and the tools the GIMP provides to measure and affect it.

6.1.1 HIGHLIGHTS AND SHADOWS

What is tonal range? To answer this question, let's look at the grayscale photo shown in Figure 6.1(a). The figure shows a tiger image consisting of a complete range of grayscale values from 0, or completely black, to 255, fully white. Furthermore, from the histogram shown in Figure 6.1(b), you can see that the distribution of pixel values in the image smoothly covers the entire available range. The histogram shown in Figure 6.1(b) is part of the Levels tool, which is discussed in detail in the next section.

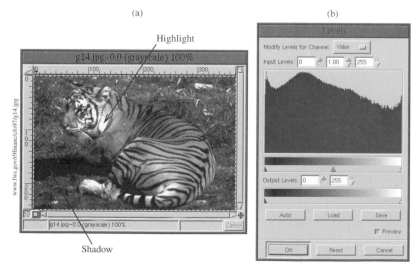

Figure 6.1: Highlights and Shadows in a Grayscale Image

The lightest part of an image is called the *highlight,* and the darkest is called the *shadow.* It is important to note that not all images will have the maximum highlight of 255 and/or the minimum shadow of 0. Thus, the tonal range of an image is just the numeric difference between the image's maximum highlight and its minimum shadow. You will see shortly that measuring highlight and shadow values is useful for performing image enhancement, but before developing this idea, let's examine why tonal range is so important.

Having a full tonal range is generally a good thing. A full tonal range means that the image has, in a general sense, the fullest possible contrast. To illustrate this idea, the tonal range of the image in Figure 6.1(a) can be synthetically diminished by setting the output sliders of the Levels tool to values well inside the range of 0 to 255. This adjustment is shown in Figure 6.2(b), and the result on the image is shown in Figure 6.2(c). Here, you can see the effect of compressing the tonal range. Figure 6.2(b) shows the settings of the Levels tool used to limit the tonal range. Notice that the resulting contrast of the image in Figure 6.2(c) is much poorer than the contrast in Figure 6.2(a). The image with the smaller tonal range looks muddy and washed out in comparison to the original.

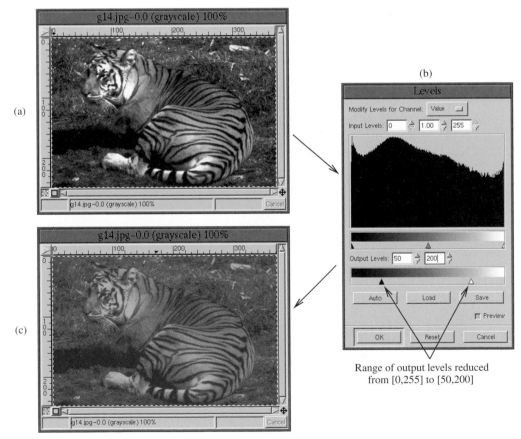

Figure 6.2: Limited Tonal Range

This example is based on a grayscale image whose tonal range has been synthetically impoverished. Nevertheless, the conclusions that can be drawn from it are general. That is, maximizing tonal range is usually a great way to enhance an image. However, sometimes it is better not to maximize the tonal range. An image of white lace gloves on a white linen tablecloth background is such an example. Under these circumstances, there is a subtle interplay of whites and off-whites in the image, and a deep black shadow is most likely undesirable. In most cases, however, getting the most tonal range out of an image improves contrast, which in turn significantly enhances the image.

6.1.2 USING THE LEVELS TOOL

The Levels tool is found in the Image:Image/Colors menu, and it was used in the previous section to examine the tonal range of a grayscale image. The features of this tool and how it can be applied to color images is discussed in detail here.

Figure 6.3 illustrates the Levels dialog. Note that the Channels menu is open in the figure, showing five different channels that can be displayed and modified. Because we are interested in color correction, only the Red, Green, and Blue channels apply in this section.

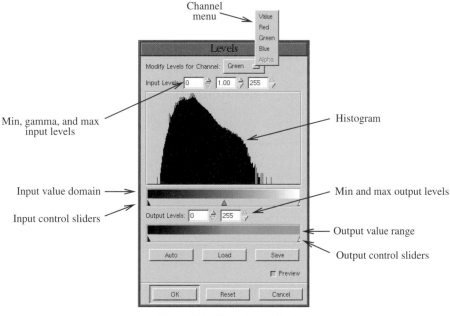

Figure 6.3: The Levels Tool

The histogram is a very important feature of the Levels tool because it immediately shows whether a channel occupies its entire tonal range or not. Just below the histogram is a grayscale called the *input value domain*. In this grayscale, black represents pixel values of 0 and white values of 255. Thus, for the Green channel shown in Figure 6.3, the black of the input value domain represents dark values of green and the white represents bright values of green. Having no histogram over a part of the input value range means that there are no pixels in the image having these values. Thus, in Figure 6.3, you can see that there is a lack of tonal range because there are significant parts of the upper and lower input value range that have no histogram values over them.

The remaining features of the Levels dialog are for adjusting the distribution of the histogram. The leftmost and rightmost arrows of the *input control slider* are used for stretching the tonal range of the image; the middle arrow can be used to warp the range. The leftmost arrow is called the shadow control arrow, the rightmost is the highlight control arrow, and the middle is the midtone control arrow. The arrows of the *output control slider* are used for shrinking the tonal range. Adjustments to the control arrows can be made interactively by clicking and dragging them. The arrows can also be controlled numerically by entering values for the min, gamma, and max input levels or for the min and max output levels.

The following example shows how the adjustment features of the Levels tool function. Figure 6.4 shows an image that has a severely compressed tonal range. This can be seen by looking at the distribution of pixel values in the Red, Green, and Blue channels shown in Figures 6.5(a), (b), and (c), respectively. The figure shows that the Red channel has the poorest tonal range. The Green and Blue channels, which are similar to each other, have tonal ranges that are hardly much better.

Figure 6.4: Image of Deep Sea Turtle Having Compressed Tonal Range

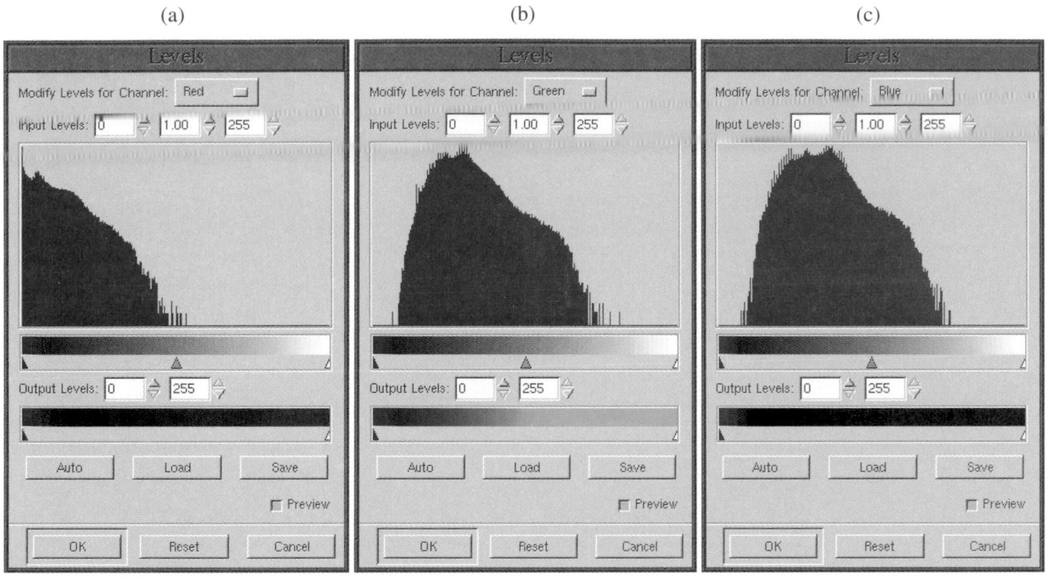

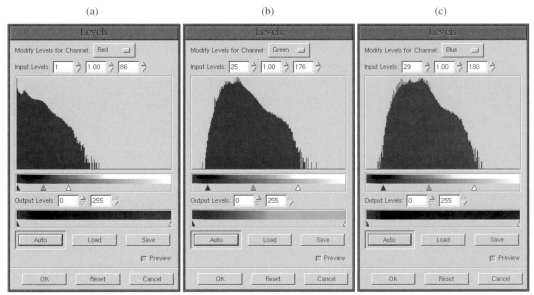

(a)   (b)   (c)

Figure 6.5: Levels for R, G, and B Channels

Figure 6.6 shows how the input shadows and highlights have been set for each of the channels, and the resulting image is shown in Figure 6.7 which shows that this simple readjustment of levels, producing a maximum tonal range, has greatly improved the image. The turtle now seems to pop right off the page, and the depth of field seems almost three dimensional. In comparison, the turtle in Figure 6.4 seems flat, the colors are muddy, and the image lacks life.

(a)   (b)   (c)

Figure 6.6: Levels for R, G, and B Channels with Adjusted Input Control Arrows

Figure 6.7: Deep Sea Turtle with Maximized Tonal Range

The maximization of an image's tonal range using the Levels tool can introduce color casts (see Section 6.2 for a definition of color casts). In fact, the turtle in Figure 6.7 appears to have a slight magenta cast. But don't worry! Color casts introduced using the Levels tool can be corrected using the Curves tool, which is treated in the next section.

A final note before leaving this section is appropriate. The Levels dialog shown in Figure 6.3 shows a button labeled Auto Levels. This button pretty much automates what has been described in this section. That is, it maximizes the tonal range in the Red, Green, and Blue channels. In fact, it moves the shadow and highlight input control sliders for each channel to about the 5% and 95% points of the histogram. After applying Auto Levels, any of the Red, Green, or Blue channels can be reviewed and modified.

6.2 REMOVING COLOR CASTS

A color cast occurs when the Red, Green, and Blue channels of an image are not properly balanced. The cast can be across the entire range of pixel values or can limit itself to the highlight, shadow, or midtones of the image. Color casts are common in photographs. They occur because, under certain circumstances, the sensitivity of film to color is different than the sensitivity of the human eye. The film just doesn't record the same scene as your eye.

Removing color casts requires being able to identify where the color in an image has gone wrong. I often have a hard time telling, simply by looking at an image, if it is suffering from a color cast. This is due to many reasons. First, color is a perceptual issue that is strongly affected by surrounding light conditions. Second, the representation of color varies from one computer monitor to another because settings such as brightness, contrast, gamma, and color temperature can be quite different. Furthermore, the ability of a monitor's phosphors to create levels of red, green, and blue light will differ from monitor to monitor and change over time as the monitor ages.

All this makes the perceptual evaluation of color casts difficult for the average person. Fortunately, the GIMP provides some analytical and interactive tools for determining whether color casts exist and for correcting them. There are several techniques for identifying, measuring, and correcting color casts. Each approach uses the powerful Curves tool, which is reviewed in the first part of this section.

6.2.1 THE CURVES TOOL

The Curves tool is found in the Image:Image/Colors menu. Figure 6.8 illustrates the basic components of this tool. As with the Levels tool, the Curves tool can be applied to any of five different channels; however, for removing color casts, we are mainly concerned with the Red, Green, and Blue channels.

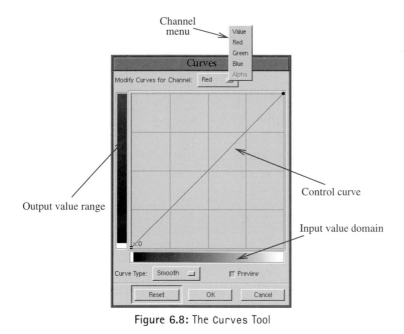

Figure 6.8: The Curves Tool

The main elements of the tool consist of an *input value domain*, an *output value range*, and a *control curve* drawn on a graph. The graph has a grid divided into quarters, and the range of values is from 0 to 255. Thus, the value of each grid line moving horizontally from left to right, is 0, 64, 128, 192, and 255. The values moving vertically from bottom to top are the same.

The control curve represents a map of the input value domain to the output value range. That sounds pretty abstract! What good is mapping input to output values? The executive, top-level answer is that curve mapping of input to output values is the most powerful color correcting tool in the GIMP, and learning how to use it is definitely worth your while. More about mapping input to output values and what it's good for in a moment...

Figure 6.9 illustrates the main operation we will be performing with the Curves tool—that is, adding a *control point* to the control curve as in Figure 6.9(a), and then moving it to a new position as in Figure 6.9(b). Control points can be added to the curve simply by clicking on the curve at the desired location. The point can be moved by clicking and dragging it. If the mouse cursor is not on the curve when the mouse button is clicked, a control point is added to the curve at the position directly above (or below) the cursor. This new point is then automatically positioned to the cursor location.

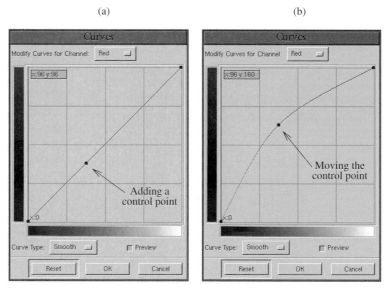

Figure 6.9: Adding and Moving a Control Point

Every control curve has two default control points located at the curve's upper right and lower left. These can be moved just like user-created control points. All control points except the defaults can be removed by clicking on the Reset button in the dialog. If many control points have been positioned and a single one needs to be removed you can remove it by dragging it with the mouse to the left or right edge of the dialog. This pulls the control point right off the curve.

The Curves tool also has an Information Field that interactively indicates the X and Y positions of the mouse cursor whenever it is in the graph area of the dialog. This field is located in the upper-left corner of the graph area, and, as you will see, this information is essential for performing precise color correction. But first, it is important to get an intuitive feel for how the Curves tool works.

Figure 6.10 illustrates a special test case that will help you understand how the Curves tool affects an image. The figure shows two gradients each using up half the tonal range of a grayscale. The upper gradient has values from 0 to 127, and the lower gradient has values from 128 to 255.

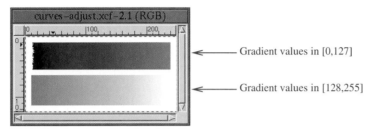

Figure 6.10: Image with Shadow to Midtone and Midtone to Highlight Gradients

The following illustrates how the Curves tool is used to change the tonal range of these two gradients. Figure 6.11(a) shows the Value channel of the Curves tool. A control point has been placed at the midpoint of the curve and pulled downward to a position one quarter of its original height. Initially, when it is a straight line, the curve of the Curves tool maps each input value to the identical output value. However, the curve shown in Figure 6.11 changes that map. Now the input values from 0 to 128 are mapped to one quarter of the scale they were before. That is, these values are now compressed into the range of 0 to 32. At the same time, the input values in the domain 128 to 255 are stretched to the range of 32 to 255. This is emphasized by the red dashed lines superimposed on the Curves dialog.

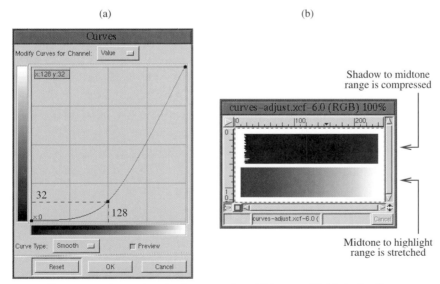

Figure 6.11: Improving the Contrast of the Midtone to Highlight Gradient

This means that all the pixels that had values in 0 to 128 in Figure 6.10 are compressed to a new range of 0 to 32. Thus, much of the detail and contrast between neighboring pixel values in this range is lost. This effect can clearly be seen in the upper gradient in Figure 6.11(b), which is the result of applying the curve in Figure 6.11(a) to the image in Figure 6.10. Simultaneously, the pixel values in the domain 128 to 255 are stretched to a new range of 32 to 255. Consequently, the contrast of the detail of these pixels is increased, as you can see in the lower gradient in Figure 6.11(b).

A similar analysis can be made for Figure 6.12, which illustrates the opposite effect. Here, as shown in Figure 6.12(a), the input value domain from 0 to 128 is stretched and the input domain from 128 to 255 is compressed. The effect on the gradients is shown in Figure 6.12(b). Although these two examples are illustrated using the Value channel, the same conclusions hold for the Red, Green, and Blue channels.

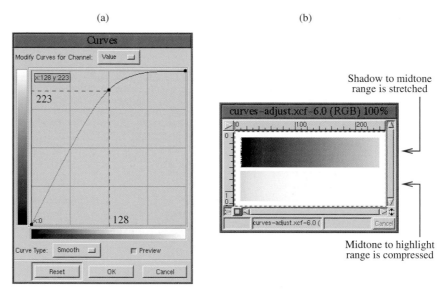

Figure 6.12: Improving the Contrast of the Shadow to Midtone Gradient

The conclusion that can be drawn from these two examples is that the Curves tool can be used for two things. First, ranges of pixel values can be remapped. This is particularly valuable when a color channel is out of balance with the others. When color imbalances occur, we try to measure which range is out of balance, determine what the range should be, and use the Curves tool to remap one range to the other. This approach is developed in detail in Section 6.2.2.

The second use is to improve contrast where it is most needed. Often an image has a subject that is much more important than the rest of the image. When this is the case, it is desirable to give the subject the most detail and contrast possible. From the examples, you can see that the Curves tool can be used to improve contrast. Note, however, that in improving the contrast in one range of values, there must simultaneously be a loss of detail and contrast in the complementary range of values. This was clearly demonstrated in Figures 6.11(b) and 6.12(b). Fortunately, improving the contrast of the subject while simultaneously impoverishing the contrast of the background is typically what we want to do. This draws the viewer's eye to the part of the image we most want to convey. The idea of improving subject contrast is developed more in Section 6.2.6.

6.2.2 COLOR CORRECTING BY BALANCING THE NEUTRALS

A powerful method for identifying color casts is to measure the color of pixels that, in principle, should be neutral gray. Neutrals must have equal components of red, green, and blue. If they don't, that indicates the presence of a color cast, and you know that a color correction must be made.

Figure 6.13 illustrates a case where the identification of neutral pixels allows us to color correct the image. In the image, the arcade of palm trees casts shadows over a white sand path and, in principle these shadows should be neutral in color.

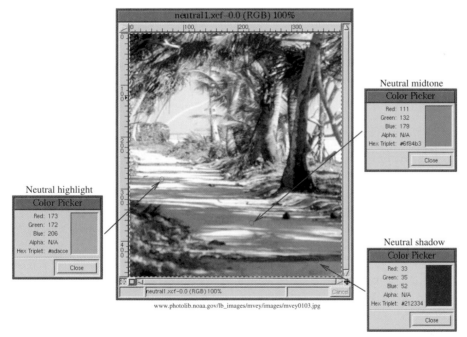

Figure 6.13: Image with a Color Cast? The Measured Pixels Say Yes!

There are a wide range of values for the shadow along the path, and it is possible to measure dark, mid-range, and light shadow values. In Figure 6.13, these are referred to as shadow, midtone, and highlight neutrals, and their values, measured with the Color Picker, are shown at three different points.

(The `Color Picker` is located in the Toolbox and is represented by the eye-dropper icon.) Measuring color in an image with the `Color Picker` displays the color in a rectangular patch in the `Color Picker` dialog and gives its R, G, and B values. Measuring a color with the `Color Picker` also has the effect of setting the `Active Foreground Color` patch, in the Toolbox window, to the measured color.

For the three measured pixels shown in Figure 6.13, you can see that there is a distinct blue tinge for each one. Not only do the color patches shown in the `Color Picker` dialog look blue, the measured R, G, and B values show that there is a significant deviation of the blue values from the red and green ones—too much for the color of these pixels to be neutral. Using the color notation introduced in Section 5.1, the color patches shown in the `Color Picker` dialogs have the values $33^R35^G52^B$ for the shadow, $111^R132^G179^B$ for the midtone, and $173^R172^G206^B$ for the highlight. The measured R, G, and B values for each point clearly indicate that there is too much blue.

It is true that shadows sometimes appear blue. However, this is usually true in winter away from the equator and is due to the natural filtering of the sun's rays by the earth's atmosphere. The blue color cast measured in Figure 6.13 is more likely due to the tendency of film, especially slide film, to produce blue casts when photographing under natural sky light. In any case, at an equatorial location on the earth, we would expect the fuller spectrum of the sun's light to create neutral shadows when these are seen on a neutral background.

In addition to the blue cast, there may also be a slight red deficiency in the midtone range. In the following discussion, the blue color cast and the red midtone deficiency are corrected using the `Curves` tool.

Figures 6.14 and 6.15 illustrate how the `Curves` tool is used to correct these color problems. Figure 6.14 shows a modification to the red curve and Figure 6.15 to the blue. For each, the procedure is identical. The red and blue components of the measured pixel values are used to place control points on their respective curves. This is shown in part (a) of each figure. The accurate placement of the points is facilitated by the Information Field found in the upper-left corner of the graph area. The control points are then moved vertically up or down to new positions, which remaps the ranges of pixel values between them and makes the measured pixels neutral in value. The displaced control points are shown in part (b) of the figures.

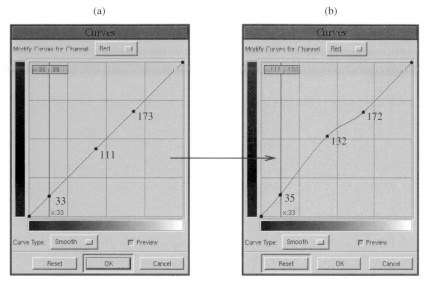

Figure 6.14: Using the Measured Pixel Values to Modify the Red Curve

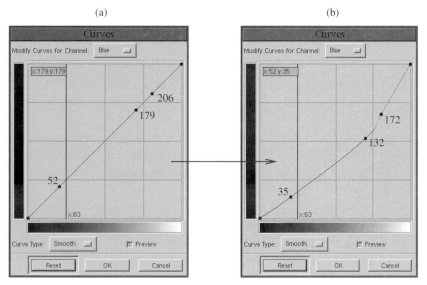

Figure 6.15: Using the Measured Pixel Values to Modify the Blue Curve

Again, the goal in displacing the control points is to make each of the measured pixel values neutral. This means making their red, green, and blue components equal. In this example, this is accomplished by moving the red and blue control points so that their values are made equal to the measured green values. The accurate repositioning of the points is made possible by the position Information Field displayed in the upper-left corner of the graph area. Note that the numbers positioned near the control points in Figures 6.14 and 6.15 are not a feature of the Curves tool; they are placed there to clarify the procedure.

Thus, on the red control curve, the shadow, midtone, and highlight values are moved from 33, 111, and 173 to the measured green values of 35, 132, and 172. On the blue control curve, the shadow, midtone, and highlight values are moved from 52, 179, and 206, again, to the green values of 35, 132, and 172. After the operation, the color values for the three measured pixels are $35^R 35^G 35^B$ for the shadow, $132^R 132^G 132^B$ for the midtone, and $172^R 172^G 172^B$ for the highlight—all three neutral grays.

The result of color correcting the neutral pixel values is shown in Figure 6.16(b). For comparison, the original image is shown in Figure 6.16(a). It is quite clear now that the original image did have a blue cast and that this has been eliminated in the corrected image. Measuring the pixel values along the tree-lined path shows that, overall, the balance is much better and most of the tree shadow values are now neutral. Furthermore, the rest of the image has taken on a much warmer look. The trees are now bathed in a yellow light, corresponding better to what we might expect from a tropical sunlit scene.

(a)   (b)

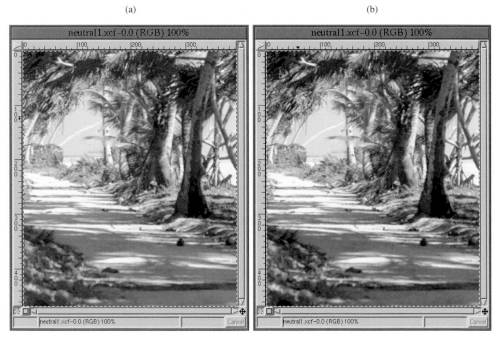

Figure 6.16: Comparison of the Original and Color Corrected Images

There are some practical questions about the color correcting procedure just described. The first is, why were the blue and red channels matched to the green? For the three measured pixels there are a total of nine ways to make the three neutral. However, in practice, it is typical that two of the channels are almost the same and that one is quite different. When this is the case, as it is for the the measured shadow and highlight values in the preceding example, the choice is clear. When it is not the case, some experimentation may be necessary.

The second question about the procedure is, why measure three points? The method doesn't require three points and, amazingly, often a single point can suffice to color correct the entire image. However, matching a shadow, midtone, and highlight image point provides additional insurance that the color in each range is properly balanced.

The Curves tool has several features that facilitate the positioning of points on the control curves. Clicking the mouse button in the image window produces a vertical bar in the graph area of the Curves tool. The bar position corresponds to the pixel value the mouse cursor is over in the image window. Clicking and dragging the mouse button interactively updates the position of the vertical bar. In this way, it is possible to see where different pixel values in the image are located on the control curve and helps to discover the locations of shadow, midtone, and highlight pixels. In addition to input position information, Shift-clicking in the image window automatically creates a control point on the curve in the active channel of the Curves dialog. Control-clicking on a point in the image window produces control points on each of the Red, Green, Blue, and Value control curves.

In addition to the Curves tool features, a very useful tool for exploring and discovering color problems in an image is the Info Window dialog. This dialog is found in the Image:View menu and can also be invoked by typing C-S-i in the image window. The Extended tab of this dialog interactively reports the R, G, and B pixel-color components when the mouse is in the image window. The advantage of the Info Window over the Color Picker for measuring pixel values in the image window is it remains open while using the Curves tool.

There are two lessons to be learned from this section. First, color correction can be very easy. Measuring only a few pixel values across the shadow to highlight range can color correct an entire image in a few minutes time. Second, the color correction obtained in this way not only fixes the individual measured pixels, but usually corrects the entire image. Third, the Curves tool is the only one that can be used to correct the image based on measured pixel values. For these reasons, the Curves tool is the most precise and the most powerful tool for color correction in the GIMP.

6.2.3 FINDING THE SHADOW, MIDTONE, AND HIGHLIGHT

To do color correction using the techniques of the previous section, it is important to be able to identify shadow, midtone, and highlight colors. To be frank, I sometimes have difficulties finding them for some images. When this happens, the Threshold tool is useful because it can show where any range of values is hidden in an image. The Threshold tool is found in the Image:Image/Colors menu. Figure 6.17 shows how this tool can be used to help locate critical shadow and highlight values.

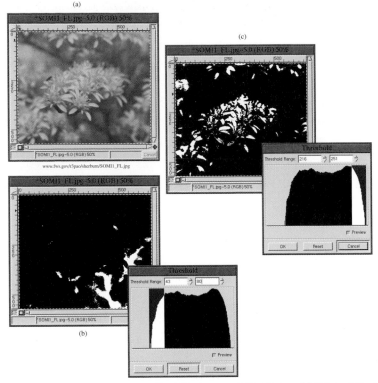

Figure 6.17: Using Threshold to Find Shadows and Highlights: (a) Original Photo
(b) Darkest Shadows (c) Lightest Highlights

Figure 6.17(a) illustrates an image and Figures 6.17(b) and (c) show how to use the `Threshold` tool to identify its darkest shadows and lightest highlights. The `Threshold` tool, which was introduced in Section 4.5.3, consists of a dialog that displays the histogram of the image's pixel values. Clicking and dragging the mouse through a range of histogram values has the effect of mapping all the pixel values in the image to either black or white. The image pixel values corresponding to the selected histogram range become white, and the rest become black.

In this way, it is easy to localize the pixel values we are searching for. Starting with an image like the one in Figure 6.17(a), a duplicate of the image is made by typing c-d in the image window. Then, the `Threshold` tool is applied to the duplicate, and a range of shadow values is swept out with the mouse, as shown in Figure 6.17(b). The resulting white pixel values in the duplicated image window show the locations of the darkest shadows. Using the duplicated image as a guide, the `Color Picker` can now be used in the original image window to measure pixel values at the appropriate locations. A similar procedure is used to accurately find and measure the lightest highlights of the image using the duplicated image shown in Figure 6.17(c).

Note that this procedure, using the `Threshold` tool to find value ranges in the image, can also be used on the image's individual RGB components.

The decomposition is made using the `Decompose` function, found in the `Image:Image/Mode` menu (see Section 4.5.3).

6.2.4 OTHER COLORS WE KNOW

If there are identifiable colors other than neutrals in an image, these, too, can be used to perform color correction. Examples are the colors of flags, logos, or certain animals. A Canadian flag whose famous maple leaf emblem were not red would be a good point of reference for color correction.

Another important class of colors that can be found in many images are flesh-tones. A medium Caucasian fleshtone has a green around 192, a red that is about 20% more (234), and a blue about 10% less (176). Darker-skinned people have skin colors with more blue and less red, and Asians have less blue. Because of the variability of skin tones, relying on them as guides is more uncertain than using neutrals. Nevertheless, for some images this may be the only point of reference available for color correction.

6.2.5 THE PERTURBATION TECHNIQUE

Sometimes it is impossible to positively identify a color in an image but it seems clear that a color cast is present. This means there are no color references that can be used to do color correction. Under these conditions, an alternate approach is needed. The method proposed here is what I call the perturbation technique. It relies on the visual feedback that the preview checkbox in the `Curves` dialog provides. In a nutshell, the method makes incremental perturbations to the shadow, midtone, and highlight regions for each of the red, green, and blue curves. The perturbations that improve the image are kept and those that do not are discarded.

Figure 6.18 illustrates the idea. In Figure 6.18(a), the Red channel of the `Curves` tool is displayed, and three control points have been added to the curve at the quarter, half, and three-quarter positions. The regions of the curve around these points roughly control the shadow, midtone, and highlight regions of the Red channel. The perturbation technique works by moving the control points up or down and seeing whether the change improves the image. Figure 6.18(b) shows a perturbation of the midtone control point.

Note that, in moving the midtone control point, the only parts of the curve that move are those between the shadow and highlight control points. The rest of the curve is constrained by the two other control points. This is very useful because it allows the `Curves` tool to act on a select part of the image's tonal range.

The perturbation technique is not scientific and relies on the perceptual abilities of the user to see changes that improve or deteriorate an image. Nevertheless, cycling among the nine control points, making only gradual changes to each, can often produce marvelous results. The following example illustrates this approach.

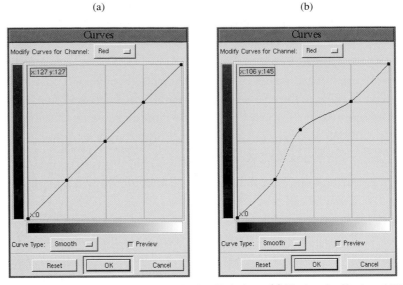

Figure 6.18: Implementation of the Perturbation Technique: (a) Placing the Shadow, Midtone, and Highlight Region Control Points (b) Perturbation of the Midtone Control Point

Figure 6.19 shows an image of a tiger that has a problem (the image, not the tiger). It has a subtle, overall green color cast. The color cast is so subtle, at first, I didn't even recognize it.

Figure 6.19: Image with a Color Cast...Can You See It?

The perturbation technique is an approach to color correction that requires experimentation. Thus, the steps are difficult to present in book format. The best that I can do is to show you the results. For this, Figure 6.20 shows the final curves for the Red, Green, and Blue channels (shown in parts (a), (b), and (c), respectively). The resulting effect on the image is shown in Figure 6.21. Comparing Figure 6.21 with Figure 6.19 makes the green color cast in the original image readily apparent. Furthermore, you can see that the application of the perturbation technique has simultaneously improved the contrast of the image's subject. The tiger looks significantly enhanced.

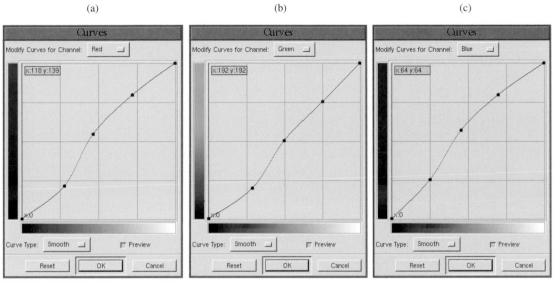

Figure 6.20: The Three Adjusted Curves Using the Perturbation Technique

Figure 6.21: The Color Corrected Image

There is an important caveat to the perturbation technique. Because this method relies on the visual feedback you get from your monitor, the technique is highly dependent on the monitor's individual characteristics. What looks great on your monitor might not look as great on another. The method described earlier in this chapter that measures pixel values and then makes adjustments accordingly does not depend on the monitor. The earlier method is the preferred approach whenever possible.

6.2.6 GETTING MORE DETAIL INTO THE SUBJECT

Sometimes one part of an image is more important than the rest. We often refer to this part of the image as the image subject. It is typical to want the subject to have as much contrast as possible. This makes the subject stand out and look much more interesting. As was discussed in Section 6.2.1, the Curves tool can be used to improve the contrast of certain parts of the tonal range in an image. This can be applied to the subject of the image by determining its lightest highlight and deepest shadow, and then steepening the part of the control curves covering this range.

However, if a lot of work has already gone into maximizing tonal range and correcting color, you might be reticent to play with the curves to get additional contrast into the subject. Clearly, manipulating a part of the curves in an attempt to improve contrast can damage the color balance obtained with much hard work.

Fortunately, there is a way to have your cake and eat it too. Up to this point, the red, green, and blue control curves have monopolized our attention. As you have already seen, modifying any of these changes the overall balance of color in the image. However, the Curves tool can also be used to modify the image's Value channel. As discussed in Section 5.3, the Value channel has no effect on color; it only affects brightness. This, then, is the perfect channel for improving contrast while preserving the image's color balance.

To illustrate the use of the Value channel to improve contrast, Figure 6.22(a) shows an original image that lacks tonal range and has a terrible yellow color cast. Figure 6.22(b) shows the corrected image, which was obtained simply by applying the Auto Levels button of the Levels tool (see Section 6.1.2). Although the image is much improved, it lacks detail in the eagle's white head feathers. It would be nice to improve this part of the eagle to give it more visual depth. This can be done by modifying the Value channel of the Curves tool.

To improve the contrast of the head feathers, it is necessary to determine the value range that this part of the image is contained in. The Threshold tool is perfect for this (see Section 6.2.3). Figure 6.23 illustrates the use of Threshold for determining an appropriate range of values. Figure 6.23(a) shows the Threshold dialog applied to the color corrected image in Figure 6.22(b), and Figure 6.23(b) shows the result of having swept out the range [174, 255] in the Threshold dialog. This range, which was determined by experimentation, pretty much covers the part of the eagle image where we want to improve the contrast.

(a)   (b)

Figure 6.22: Original and Color Corrected Images

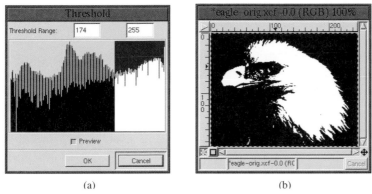

(a)   (b)

Figure 6.23: Using Threshold to Find the Correct Value Range

The value range determined with the Threshold tool is noted, and the tool is then canceled. The next step is to invoke the Curves tool and to improve the contrast of the Value channel curve using the range determined using Threshold. Figure 6.24 illustrates the procedure. Figure 6.24(a) shows the Curves dialog for the Value channel. A control point has been added to the curve at the input value of 174, and this point has been moved to the output value of 140. This has the effect of steepening the Value curve in the range [174, 255], which is the range of values where we want to improve contrast. From previous discussion, we know that steepening the Value curve in a range has the effect of improving this range's contrast.

The result of applying the curve shown in Figure 6.24(a) is shown in Figure 6.24(b). Comparing this result to the image in Figure 6.22(b) shows that the contrast of the eagle's head feathers has been significantly improved. As a final, practical note, the amount that the Value curve is steepened is determined experimentally by moving the control points on the curve and evaluating the effect on the image.

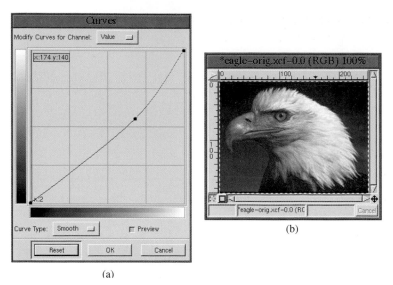

Figure 6.24: Using Curves to Improve Contrast in the Subject Value Range

6.2.7 OTHER COLOR CORRECTING TOOLS

The GIMP has several other color correcting tools. These all live in the Image:Colors menu and their names are Color Balance, Brightness-Contrast, and Hue-Saturation. In this book, these tools are not covered in detail, and for good reason. Although they can be used for touchup and enhancement, these tools are like working with a dull knife, especially when compared to the Curves tool, which has the precision of a surgeon's scalpel. Let's see why.

THE COLOR BALANCE TOOL

Figure 6.25(a) shows the dialog for the Color Balance tool. This allows an image to be adjusted in the shadow, midtone, or highlight regions for the red-cyan, green-magenta, or blue-yellow balance. Curves does exactly the same thing except with much greater precision. Raising a curve at a point adds more of the color it represents at the expense of the complementary color around that point. Lowering the curve has the opposite effect, that of shifting the balance towards the complementary color.

The Curves tool can do anything the Color Balance tool can, only better. The reason Curves is more powerful is that the Color Picker can be used to identify exactly which input values need color balancing. The Color Picker is shown in Figure 6.25(b), and it is displaying a value for a measured pixel in an image. This value can be precisely placed and manipulated in the Curves tool. Figure 6.25(c) shows how a control point, corresponding to the green component the measured pixel, has been placed on the Green channel curve. This placement of a control point, corresponding to a measured pixel value, permits the subsequent, precise correction of color balance at this point. By comparison, the `Color Balance` tool only allows for the gross selection of input regions (shadow, midtone, and highlight) and is incapable of performing the precision color corrections described in detail in Section 6.2.2.

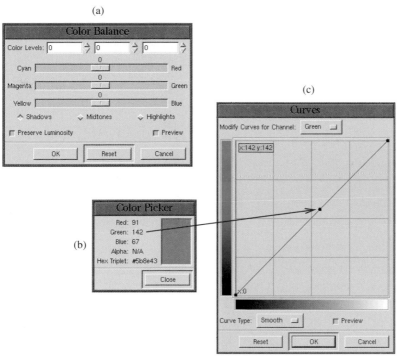

Figure 6.25: Comparing `Color Balance` to the `Curves` Tool

The conclusion is that the `Curves` tool is much more precise and versatile than the `Color Balance` tool.

THE BRIGHTNESS–CONTRAST TOOL

Figure 6.26(a) displays the dialog for the `Brightness-Contrast` tool. The way this tool functions can be fully simulated using the `Curves` tool. Figure 6.26(b) illustrates the Value channel of the `Curves` tool, showing that the curve has been displaced upward. Moving the value curve up maps the input value domain to an output range that is uniformly brighter. This modification to the value curve exactly simulates the action of the `Brightness-Contrast` tool when the Brightness slider in the dialog is moved to the right. Moving the Brightness slider to the left corresponds to displacing the value curve downward.

(a)

Controlling Brightness   Controlling Contrast

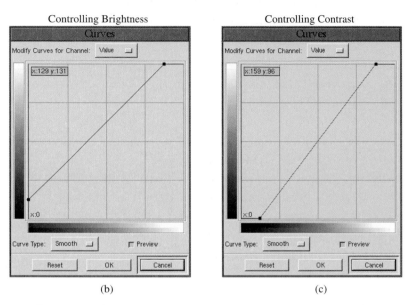

(b)   (c)

Figure 6.26: Comparing `Brightness-Contrast` with the `Curves` Tool

Thus, brightening or darkening an image using the Brightness slider has the effect of diminishing tonal range because the result maps the input value domain to a smaller output range. From the discussion in Section 6.1, this is clearly a disadvantage. The `Curves` tool, on the other hand, can be used to increase or decrease brightness without loosing tonal range. To brighten an image, place a control point on the Value curve and displace the point upwards. This brightens the image without losing tonal range. To darken the image, drag the point downwards.

Figure 6.26(c) also shows the Value channel of the `Curves` tool. Here, the curve has been rotated counter-clockwise around the center of the input-output dialog. This has the effect of increasing contrast in the midtones of the image. However, it simultaneously eliminates detail in the shadow and highlight ranges. This action is exactly what the `Brightness-Contrast` tool does when the Contrast slider of the dialog is moved to the right. Moving the slider to the left corresponds to rotating the curve in a clockwise direction.

The conclusion is that the `Curves` tool performs much better than the `Brightness-Contrast` tool.

The Hue–Saturation Tool

The Hue-Saturation dialog is shown in Figure 6.27. This tool is more complex than either the Color Balance or Brightness-Contrast tools, and its action cannot be simply reproduced using Curves. Nevertheless, there is rarely any reason to use this tool for touchup or enhancement. The Hue-Saturation tool allows hue, lightness, and saturation to be adjusted for an image. The adjustment can be made for the entire image or for any combination of the image's red, green, blue, cyan, magenta, or yellow components.

The reason Hue-Saturation is not useful for color correction is that it is difficult to know how to make adjustments with it to enhance an image. With the Curves tool, the measurements made with the Color Picker can be used to make precise changes that will result in predictable improvements to an image. By contrast, there is no way to measure what is wrong in an image in a way that can then be used to make precise

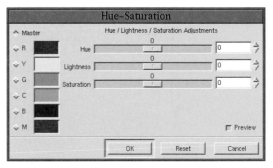

Figure 6.27: The Hue-Saturation Tool

corrections with the Hue-Saturation tool. Furthermore, as has already been pointed out, color problems are rarely uniform over the shadow, midtone, and highlight regions. The Hue-Saturation tool has no capability for varying color components in different ranges of the image.

Thus, for color correction, the Hue-Saturation tool is of little use. Nevertheless, unlike Color Balance and Brightness-Contrast, the Hue-Saturation tool *can* be used to do useful and interesting things that would be difficult to do with any other color tool. Figure 6.28 illustrates an application of the Hue-Saturation tool that doesn't fit into the category of touchup or enhancement but is of considerable stylistic and artistic interest.

Figure 6.28(a) displays a beach scene consisting of vivid colors, and Figure 6.28(b) shows the Hue-Saturation dialog where the Saturation slider for the Cyan radio button has been adjusted to -100%. The result, shown in Figure 6.28(c), is to completely desaturate the sky and water while leaving the color of the beach untouched. Similarly interesting modifications can be made with the Hue and Lightness sliders. Try experimenting!

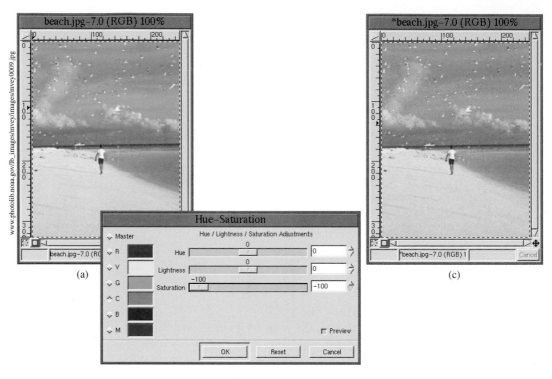

(a)

(b)

(c)

Figure 6.28: Hue-Saturation

6.3 REPAIRING BLEMISHES WITH THE CLONE TOOL

Sometimes an image has elements you'd prefer weren't there. A telephone pole and wires might ruin an otherwise lovely composition of a New England cottage on Cape Cod. Fortunately, these sorts of annoyances can be easily removed using the Clone tool. The Clone tool is found in the GIMP Toolbox, and its icon resembles a rubber stamp. The following illustrates how this powerful tool is used.

Figure 6.29(a) illustrates an idyllic scene we've seen already. It shows a long, deserted stretch of beach, blue waters, and a sky dotted with white fluffy clouds on the horizon. Well, the beach is not quite deserted. There is a lone person promenading along the water's edge. This might not be a problem for some uses of this picture. On the other hand, it might be desirable to have an image like this without a single soul on the beach. If that's the case, you can still use this image by simply removing the person from the scene using the Clone tool. To do this, begin by choosing a brush from the Brush Selection dialog, as shown in Figure 6.29(b). For this example, the second to smallest hard brush has been selected. As usual, the choice is dictated by need.

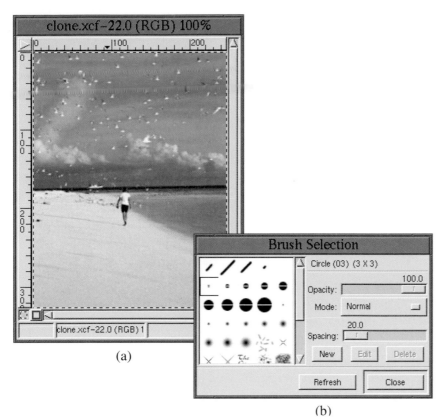

(a)

Brush Selection

Circle (03) (3 X 3)

Opacity: 100.0

Mode: Normal

Spacing: 20.0

New   Edit   Delete

Refresh   Close

(b)

Figure 6.29: Image with Unwanted Content

The idea for working with the Clone tool is to cover over the offending part of the image using colors from the background. Where do the background colors come from? From the background itself. The Clone tool covers up one part of an image using another part of the same image. When this is done carefully, it can be used to completely and convincingly remove offending elements.

Figure 6.30(a) shows a zoom of the image from Figure 6.29(a). Notice the small + cursor on it. The cursor shows the center of the image source reference patch that will be used to cover other undesirable parts of the image. The size and character of the patch around this point is controlled by the brush size and type. Selecting the Clone tool from the Toolbox, the image source reference point is specified by Control-clicking on it.

Now, when (simple) clicking and dragging on another part of the image, the neighborhood around the reference point is copied to the new mouse location. If the choice of reference point is made carefully, it can be made to look as if the foreground is being removed to reveal the natural background. The effect is shown in Figure 6.30(b), which shows part of the person's leg being removed. (Don't worry, the process is completely painless, and no one was harmed to present this example.)

(a) (b)

Figure 6.30: Zoom of Image Showing (a) Clone Reference Point and (b) Application of `Clone` Tool to Unwanted Image Area

The pencil icon is over the region being covered, and the size of the region being affected is equal in size to the area of the brush chosen from the `Brush Selection` dialog. Note that a smaller + sign cursor is visible in Figure 6.30(b). While painting with the `Clone` tool, the location of the reference patch is indicated by this cursor. The + sign moves in tandem with the mouse cursor, always remaining exactly the same distance away, as long as the mouse button is held down. This feature aids in producing a more natural looking result because different parts of the image are being used in the cover-up.

Figure 6.31 shows the final result of using the `Clone` tool for this example. Figure 6.31(a) shows the original image, and Figure 6.31(b) shows that the person has been completely removed, including his shadow! The boat seen on the horizon in the original image has also been removed. Good examples of practical uses for the `Clone` tool are presented in Sections 7.4 and 7.5.

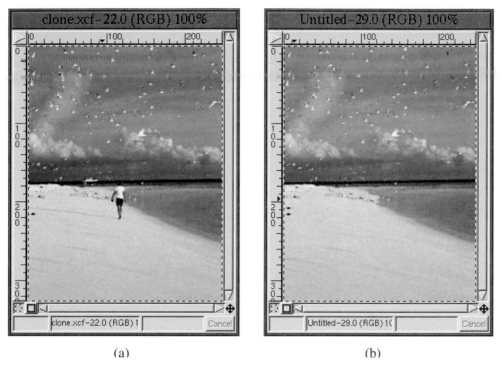

(a)   (b)

Figure 6.31: Original Image and Final Image with Unwanted Image Content Removed

6.4 SHARPENING

Due to a whole range of issues, the acquisition and digitization of an image
can often produce a slightly blurred or out-of-focus result. Furthermore, the
ensuing processing to improve tonal range and contrast can also deteriorate
the crispness of the image. To remedy this, it is desirable to sharpen things up.
Sharpening is usually applied at the end of the processing sequence after all
other modifications have been made.

In the GIMP, there are two tools for sharpening an image; they are both
located in the Image:Filters/Enhance menu. These tools are called Sharpen and
Unsharp Mask. Although the underlying principles of the two are the same,
I prefer Unsharp Mask because it has several parameters that have intuitive
meanings and that provide more control over the sharpening process. The
remainder of this section describes in detail how to use Unsharp Mask.

6.4.1 THE UNSHARP MASK CONCEPT

Before knowing the sharp, little grasshopper, you must first become one with the unsharp. Wheeew…that sounds like a bad episode of Kung Fu. I'm expecting David Carradine to peak out from behind my monitor any moment now! The truth is, though, that Unsharp Mask, as arcane and counter-intuitive as its name may sound, is an excellent tool for sharpening. The principle of the Unsharp Mask and the ins and outs of this special filter are covered in this section.

Figure 6.32 illustrates the principle of the Unsharp Mask. The upper black line graphed in the top part of the figure represents pixel values as a function of pixel index. For example, this line could represent the color values along the row of an image. The graph shows a transition from a lower to a higher pixel value at the middle of the graph. Visually, if you were looking at this row of pixels in an image, it would appear as an edge between regions of constant value.

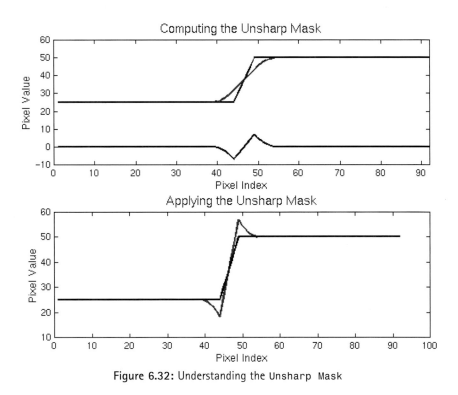

Figure 6.32: Understanding the Unsharp Mask

The red line in the upper graph of Figure 6.32 illustrates how the pixel values change if the row of pixels is blurred. The resulting red curve is a smoothed version of the original. If you viewed the row of pixels corresponding to this smooth curve, it would appear much less sharp than the pixels for the black curve. So, in essence, the red curve is an unsharp version of the black. Now, subtract the unsharp version from the original and the result is the lower black line in the top graph of Figure 6.32. You could say that this result is just the original curve with its unsharp component masked out.

This is the interpretation of what the Unsharp Mask does, but how does this sharpen the image? The answer is given by the lower graph of Figure 6.32, which shows the original black line representing the row of pixel values. The graph also shows a red curve, which is the original curve and the associated unsharp masked version added to it. As you can see, just before the edge, there is now a dip in pixel value at the low side of the transition and a peak on the high side. Thus, the result is that the edge has been made sharper.

6.4.2 A SIMPLIFIED BUT ILLUSTRATIVE EXAMPLE

So much for the theory of the Unsharp Mask. A simple example brings out the practical effects of this filter. Unsharp Mask can be found in the Image:Filters/Enhance menu. Figure 6.33(a) shows a simple image with just two grayscale regions. Thus, the values along a row of the image resemble the graph of Figure 6.32. Figure 6.33(b) shows the result of applying the Unsharp Mask using the parameters in the filter's dialog shown in Figure 6.33(c). Here a maximum value for the Radius has been chosen to accentuate the effect.

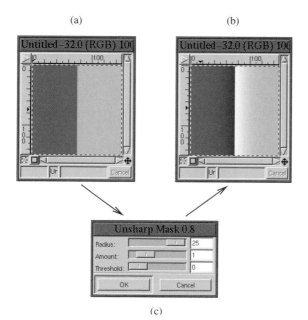

Figure 6.33: Illustrating the Effect of Applying Unsharp Mask

Note that in the sharpened result (see Figure 6.33(b)), there is a light halo on the right side of the edge and a deep shadow on the dark side of the edge. This corresponds to the discussion of the red curve in the lower graph of

Figure 6.32. The effect of the Unsharp Mask is very pronounced, but was chosen to clearly illustrate the effect. In general, the dialog parameters are chosen to produce more subtle results.

The Unsharp Mask dialog has three parameters. Looking at the dialog in Figure 6.33(c), there is Radius, which specifies the relative width of the halo/shadow created by the mask. The parameter named Amount controls the relative magnitude of the dip and the peak created on each side of the edge. Finally, Threshold specifies the difference in pixel values that must exist across the edge for the Unsharp Mask to be applied. Thus, if Threshold is set to 25, adjacent pixels whose difference in pixel value is less than 25 are not sharpened. An important fact is that the Unsharp Mask is applied individually to each color channel, R, G, and B; the results are then combined.

6.4.3 A REPRESENTATIVE EXAMPLE OF APPLYING THE UNSHARP MASK

Figure 6.34 illustrates the application of the Unsharp Mask to a more representative image. Figure 6.34(a) shows the original and Figure 6.34(b) the result of applying the mask. The parameters chosen to perform the sharpening are shown in the Unsharp Mask dialog illustrated in Figure 6.34(c).

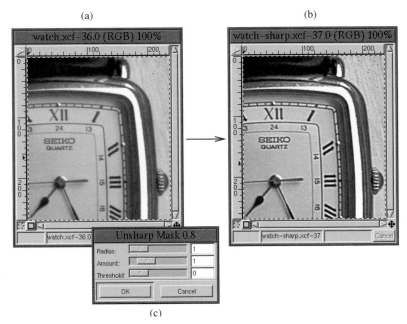

Figure 6.34: An Example of Applying Unsharp Mask

The choice of parameters used to obtain the results in Figure 6.34 was obtained by trial and error. Using Undo (C-z) in conjunction with the keyboard shortcut that recalls the last applied filter (A-S-f), it was possible to apply the Unsharp Mask repeatedly, experimenting with values. In this way, it was possible to obtain the desired effect.

What parameter values should be used with the Unsharp Mask? The answer depends on the image, of course. However, one rule of thumb is the Radius of the mask should be small—2 to 4 pixels wide. This is because the halo and shadow created by the Unsharp Mask should be subtle. On the other hand, the amount should be as much as you can get away with without overly accentuating noise. This is typically in the range of 75% to 150% depending on the pixel values in the image.

6.4.4 UNSHARP MASK PITFALLS

Applying Unsharp Mask can have its problems. For example, this method of sharpening an image can sometimes introduce undesirable color shifts. Figure 6.35 illustrates just such a case. Figure 6.35(a) shows an image with a single edge, with a gray region to the left of the edge and a red region to the right. Figure 6.35(b) shows the result of applying the Unsharp Mask to this image. You can clearly see a cyan colored halo just to the left of the edge even though there is no apparent cyan in the original.

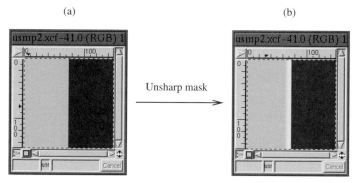

Figure 6.35: Example of Unsharp Mask Provoking a Color Shift

The explanation for this is as follows. Remember that each image is composed of three color channels. Thus, the Unsharp Mask is actually applied to each of the three channels individually and the results are then combined. Imagine, then, that the color on the left side of an edge consists of a low value of red and green but a high value of blue. Furthermore, suppose that the region on the right side of the edge has a high value of red and green but a low value of blue. This situation presents you with an edge that goes from dark to light in the Red and Green channels but from light to dark in the Blue. According to the preceding description, the Unsharp Mask makes a dip for the Red and Green channels on the left side of the edge but a peak for the Blue. Clearly, when adding the Red, Green, and Blue channels, the two dips plus the one peak do not create a color whose relative mix has been maintained. In plain language, this means the hue has been changed.

This is just what has happened in Figure 6.35. The color region to the left side of the edge is a medium gray. Thus, it consists of medium values of red, green, and blue. The right side of the edge is composed uniquely of a high value of red and low (zero) values of green and blue. Thus, the application of the Unsharp Mask creates peaks in the Green and Blue channels of the gray region but a dip in the Red. This explains where the cyan halo comes from, removing red from an image makes it look more cyan.

In most images, the creation of an off-color halo does not occur or is not evident. But when it does happen, don't worry; there is a technique to correct the problem. Figure 6.36 illustrates the procedure. Figure 6.36(a) is identical to Figure 6.35(a). The procedure first decomposes the image into its hue, saturation, and value components. This is done with the HSV option of the Decompose function (found in the Image:Image/Mode menu). The value component of the result is shown in Figure 6.36(b). The Unsharp Mask is then applied uniquely to this value component, the result being shown in Figure 6.36(c). Finally, the hue, saturation, and sharpened value components are recomposed using the HSV option of the Compose function (also found in the Image:Image/Mode menu). Figure 6.36(d) shows the result of the processing sequence. As you can see, the edge has been sharpened without creating a shift in hue at the edge.

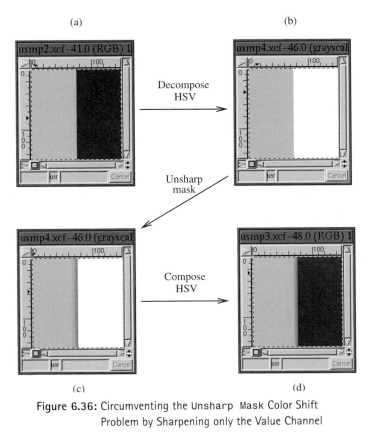

Figure 6.36: Circumventing the Unsharp Mask Color Shift Problem by Sharpening only the Value Channel

Because the value component of the image only contains light and dark information about the image, the sharpening is performed just where it should be and no color shift occurs. Why isn't an HSV decomposition built into the Unsharp Mask? Apparently, a few mysteries of the Unsharp Mask persist...

The other important problem that the Unsharp Mask can create is the amplification of noise. Noise is sharpened just as are the other elements of the image, and if the sharpened noise becomes too apparent, it can become a significant detraction. An approach that can be used to avoid the problem is to set a non-zero value of Threshold in the Unsharp Mask dialog. Setting the threshold diminishes the effect of noise by applying the mask only to edges that have jumps greater than the Threshold value.

6.5   A CASE STUDY

This chapter has covered many elements of photo touchup and enhancement. To put all the elements into perspective, this section presents a case study to illustrate the work flow of a typical sequence of corrections. The photo in Figure 6.37 is the subject of the study; it is a difficult case because it has many defects.

Before we begin, several observations can be made concerning this photo:

- It is dark and clearly underexposed.
- The colors are muddy and there is an overall lack of sharpness.
- The photo has a green tinge or color cast to it.
- There is an unsightly bright green spot on the lefthand side of the photo that will blemish the final product if not removed.
- The subject matter, the cowboy roper with the children, is poorly separated from the background.

In a nutshell, this photo needs a lot of help. It will be significantly enhanced by the steps described in the rest of this section.

The first step, as described in Section 6.1, is to maximize the tonal range of the image. This is done by opening the Levels tool and choosing Auto Levels. Figure 6.38(b) shows the result. Figure 6.38(a) shows the original image for comparison purposes. In addition to selecting Auto Levels, the midtone slider control in the Value channel has been adjusted to lighten the result a bit. Notice that the green color cast has been greatly diminished by the Levels tool adjustment, and the colors seem much clearer.

Figure 6.37: Original Image

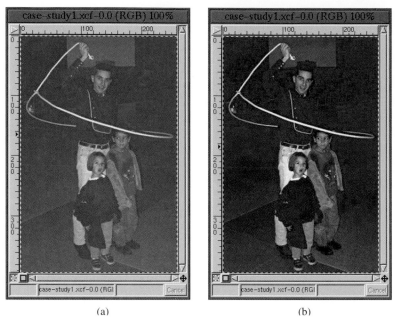

(a)   (b)

Figure 6.38: Tonal Range Maximized and Midtones Adjusted with the `Levels` Tool: (a) Original Image and (b) Result of `Levels` Tool

The second step is to correct for any remaining color casts. As described in Section 6.2.2, this is accomplished using the `Color Picker` to measure neutral colors in the image. The cowboy trick-roper and children are standing on a stone surface that appears to be granite. It is reasonable to guess that this stone should be a neutral gray.

With the `Color Picker`, you can see that there are actually a range of values from shadows to midtones in this stone. Measuring the image colors at several locations yields a representative shadow value of $59^R49^G42^B$ in the dark stone just to the left of the roper's lower legs. Similar measurements made in the lighter stone just beneath the little boy's feet yield a midtone value of 119^R 120^G109^B. From these two measurements, it seems there is a brown/orange cast to the image. As for a representative highlight value, the right rear part of the lasso loop should be neutral but is measured at $177^R183^G167^B$. This is a pale green.

To remove these color casts, the `Curves` tool is used as described in Section 6.2.2. For this case study, the shadow values of red at 59 and green at 49 are both moved to match the blue at 42. The midtone values of green at 120 and blue at 109 are both matched to the red at 119. Finally, the highlight values of green at 183 and blue at 167 are balanced to the red at 177. The result is shown in Figure 6.39(b). In comparing this image to the previous one, shown again in Figure 6.39(a), the stone is now clearly a more neutral gray. Also, you can see that the skin tones had a slight orange tinge, which has been removed.

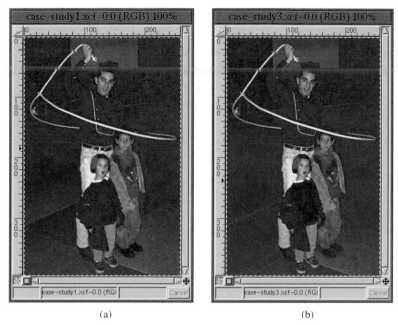

(a)   (b)

Figure 6.39: Color Cast Correction with `Curves`: (a) Previous and (b) Color Corrected Image

The next step is to remove the green glint at the middle left side of the image. This is done as described in Section 6.3 using the `Clone` tool. The image without this blemish is shown in Figure 6.40.

At this point in the sequence of corrections, it should be clear that you cannot get additional subject detail using the methods from Section 6.2.6. The cowboy and children already fill the entire range of tonal values from the darkest shadows in the cowboy's shirt to the brightest highlights in the rope and the little girl's collar. The only way to get more out of this image is to try to separate the subject from the background, which can only be accomplished by making a selection.

Figure 6.41 shows the selection that was made using the `Bezier Path` tool. The selection was made in several stages. The main outline of the subject was made first. Three regions were then removed from this first selection by using the method for subtracting selections described in Section 3.2. These regions are the two enclosures the rope makes with the roper's body and the small hole between the roper's and little girl's leg.

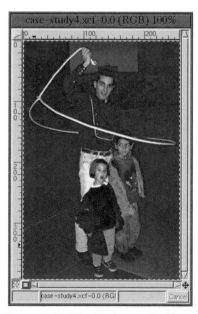

Figure 6.40: Blemish Removed with `Clone` Tool

Figure 6.41: Selection of Background

Inverting the selection by typing c-i in the image window, the background can be lightened by using the perturbation method described in Section 6.2.5 to adjust the Value channel of the Curves tool. As shown in Figure 6.42(b), the result produces a subject that is better defined against the background. This is compared with the image from the previous step, which is shown again in Figure 6.42(a).

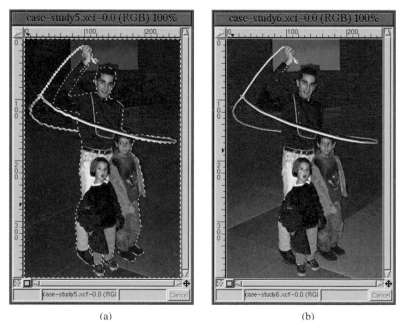

(a)   (b)

Figure 6.42: Background Lightened with Curves: (a) Before and (b) After

The final enhancement to the image is to sharpen the subject a bit. This is done using the Unsharp Mask as described in Section 6.4.1. The Unsharp Mask parameters were chosen to be 3 for Radius and 0.5 for Amount. The final result is shown in Figure 6.43(b), and Figure 6.43(a) shows the initial image from Figure 6.37. The comparison of the two images is dramatic. The original seemed unretrievable, and, although the final result is perhaps unworthy of *National Geographic* magazine, it is, nevertheless, greatly improved.

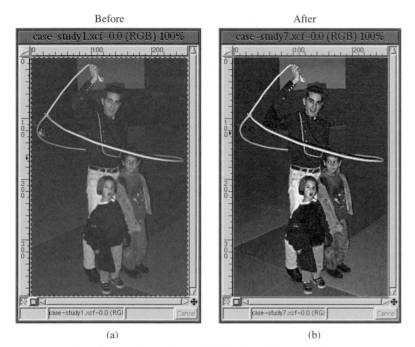

Before   After

(a)   (b)

Figure 6.43: Comparison of Original and Enhanced Photos

The new image has several qualities worth noting. First, the colors of the enhanced image are much sharper and better defined. In comparison, the original image's colors are muddy. This is due primarily to the enhancement of the tonal range. Second, the green tinge seen in the original image has been eliminated; the subject of the enhanced image is also sharper and better defined against the background. This is due to the Unsharp Mask and the reprocessing of the background with the help of selection tools and the Curves tool.

7

COMPOSITING

Compositing means many things to many people. Whole books have been written on this one topic. Broadly speaking, compositing is the technique and the art of piecing together image parts collected from multiple sources to make a new single whole. If the image is intended to be photo-realistic, a scene that could have really existed, the result is called photo-montage. On the other hand, if the objective is to combine images whose juxtaposition communicates a new idea, the result is called collage.

The main differences between the two are that, for photo-montage, lighting and color matching are very important to the success of the composition. Differences of saturation and value between image elements can ruin the illusion of a montage, as can obvious inconsistencies in lighting. It is also important to pay attention to various other visual cues; however, the objective of this chapter is not to provide a complete discussion of these topics. Rather, the goal is to demonstrate the use of the GIMP in several projects and show how the GIMP's tools can be used to solve collage and photo-montage problems.

Regardless of whether a project is photo-montage or collage, the main elements of compositing consist of selections, copy and paste operations, and positioning of image elements. The finer aspects require blending, color matching, and general attention to detail. Thus, most of the GIMP skills needed for compositing have already been discussed in previous chapters. Indeed, this chapter presumes the reader is familiar with concepts presented in earlier chapters. The projects presented here are not described in minute detail. Rather, when techniques that have been described in earlier chapters

are required, the reader is referred to the appropriate section of the book. Although this chapter is mostly project-oriented, some new GIMP tools are also introduced.

7.1   PROJECT 1: FISH ON HOLIDAY!

A primary component of compositing is the assembling of different image elements and the subsequent positioning and scaling required to achieve the final desired composition. Assembling the image components consists of selecting them from their respective images. The selections are made using combinations of techniques from Chapters 3 and 4.

Because I'm often not sure exactly how I'll use selected image components in a project, I first like to assemble all of them into a kind of clip book. A clip book is just a single image consisting of a layer for each image component. This makes an image palette from which the various components can be copied and then pasted into the target composition.

Figure 7.1(a) shows the image clip book used in this project. Each sea creature was obtained from a separate image source using a combination of selection and masking techniques. The Layers dialog in Figure 7.1(b) shows that each of the six separate images is contained in a separate layer. The project goal is to use these reef inhabitants to populate an ecosystem not normally their own. The composition places our denizens of the deep among the palms of a tropical island beach scene. Sometimes even fish need a holiday…

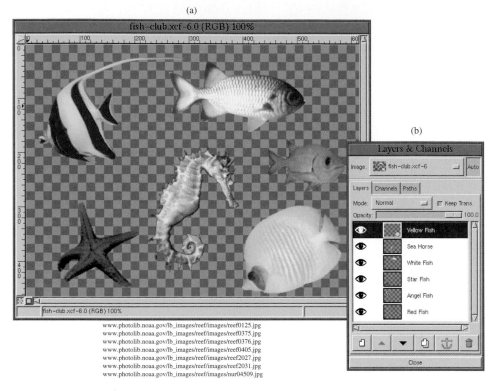

(a)

(b)

www.photolib.noaa.gov/lb_images/reef/images/reef0125.jpg
www.photolib.noaa.gov/lb_images/reef/images/reef0375.jpg
www.photolib.noaa.gov/lb_images/reef/images/reef0376.jpg
www.photolib.noaa.gov/lb_images/reef/images/reef0405.jpg
www.photolib.noaa.gov/lb_images/reef/images/reef2027.jpg
www.photolib.noaa.gov/lb_images/reef/images/reef2031.jpg
www.photolib.noaa.gov/lb_images/reef/images/nur04509.jpg

Figure 7.1: Collection of Selected Sea Creatures

The background image is shown in Figure 7.2(a). This scene will receive all the other image elements. The first element is the angel fish, which has been copied from Figure 7.1 and pasted into this one. The following procedure is used to accomplish this:

1. Make the Angel Fish layer active by clicking on its thumbnail in the Layers dialog shown in Figure 7.1 (see Section 2.1.1 for more on active layers).

2. Copy the Angel Fish layer to the default buffer by typing c-c in the image window shown in Figure 7.1.

3. Paste the Angel Fish layer into the target image by typing c-v in the image window shown in Figure 7.2. This loads the Angel Fish layer into a floating selection.

4. Make the float into a new layer by clicking on the New Layer button in the Layers dialog.

(a)

(b)

Figure 7.2: Pasting an Image Component into the Holiday Scene Background

There are two features worth noting in Figure 7.2. First, the Layers dialog shows that the new layer has been named Angel Fish to more easily identify it later. Second, the Angel Fish layer's boundaries (the yellow and black dashed line) are visible in the image window because it is the active layer in the image. The layer's boundaries can be toggled off by typing c-t in the image window.

With respect to our composition, the first thing you might notice is that the angel fish seems too large for the background. This can be fixed by shrinking the angel fish or by enlarging the background. As already noted in Section 2.6.2, it is almost always preferable to shrink an image element that is too large rather than to enlarge the element that is too small. This is because enlarging an image requires interpolating pixel values, which introduces unpleasant image artifacts. Always avoid this—unless, of course, the artifacts are desirable as an artistic device.

Thus, our first task is to scale the Angel Fish layer to a more fitting size for our scene. This can be done in two ways, either with the Transform tool from the Toolbox, or the Scale Layer command found in the Layers menu. Section 2.6.2 describes both. The Transform tool is used here because it is interactive and gives some visual feedback to the scaling process. The Scaling option of the Transform tool is invoked by double-clicking on the Transform tool icon in the Toolbox, which brings up the Tool Options dialog. The Scaling option can then be selected from the dialog, as shown in Figure 7.3(b). Figure 7.3(a) shows the result of using the Transform tool to scale the Angel Fish layer.

(a)

(b)

(c)

Preserving aspect ratio

Figure 7.3: Scaling the Angel Fish

In scaling the Angel Fish layer, the aspect ratio has been preserved. This prevents the scaled layer from looking distorted. The aspect ratio can be maintained manually by watching the Scaling Information dialog and keeping it manually adjusted during the scaling process. The Scaling Information dialog provides interactive feedback about the X and Y Scale Ratios while the transform is being performed. The aspect ratio is preserved by keeping the X Scale Ratio equal to the Y Scale Ratio. Alternatively, the Scaling option of the Transform tool can be constrained to preserve aspect ratio by pressing the Control and Alt keys while scaling. In this example, the angel fish has been scaled to 60% of her original dimensions. In the compositing process, however, this might be undone and redone several times to achieve the desired effect in the final result.

When the scaling of the angel fish is complete, she can be positioned using the Move tool. Her final location for this project is seen in Figure 7.4. Also seen in this figure is the result of repeating the preceding operations for each of the angel fish's friends. Notice that it is not necessary for the repositioned image elements to be inside the boundaries of the background image window. In fact, having layers that extend partially outside the boundaries can create more interest in their subject elements.

Figure 7.4: The Beginnings of a Composition

The final procedure performed in this project adds an element of depth to our composition. The idea is to make the sea horse's tail look as if it is wrapped around a tree and to make the little red fish appear as if it is peeking out from behind another. This is done with layer masks (see Section 4.2). The elements of the procedure are shown in Figure 7.5. Figure 7.5(a) shows a zoom of the image centered around the sea horse. As you can see from Figure 7.5(b), a layer mask has been added to the Sea Horse layer in the Layers dialog, and the Opacity slider has been set to 50%. This allows the tree in the background image to be seen through the Sea Horse layer. In setting the Opacity slider, the goal is to be able to see the tree's boundaries through the sea horse.

Because the tree's boundaries can be seen, the Paintbrush tool can be used to paint away parts of the Sea Horse mask making the tree fully visible from behind. Figure 7.5(a) shows that this process has been started using a brush from the Brush Selection dialog and shown in Figure 7.5(c). The whole procedure is summarized in the following steps:

1. A layer mask is added to the Sea Horse layer.
2. The layer mask is made active by clicking on its thumbnail in the Layers dialog.
3. The Opacity slider is set so that the tree can be seen through the Sea Horse layer.
4. The Active Foreground Color is set to black by typing d in the image window.

5. An appropriate brush type and size is selected. Here a small hard brush is chosen.

6. Painting tools, such as the Paintbrush and the Airbrush, are used to reveal the tree from behind the sea horse by painting away the appropriate parts of the layer mask.

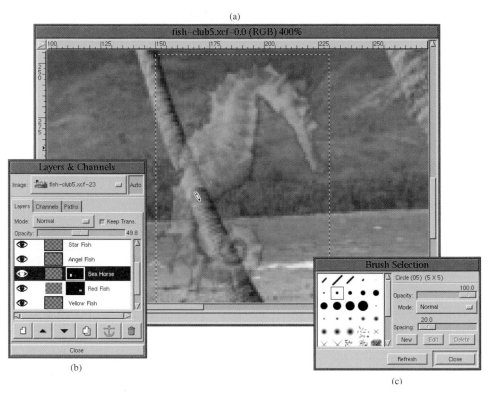

Figure 7.5: Using a Layer Mask to Create the Illusion of Depth

If too much of the layer mask is removed while painting, you can recover it by changing the Active Foreground Color to white by typing x in the image window and by painting over the erroneously removed parts of the mask. Close to the edge of the tree, it is probably worthwhile to work with a smaller brush size in conjunction with the Airbrush tool, which is more effective at applying graded amounts of paint. See Section 4.5.1 for more details.

The result of applying layer masks to both the Sea Horse and the Red Fish layers is shown in Figure 7.6. The sea horse now seems to be well anchored, with its tail securely wrapped around the tree, against unforeseen, rapid air currents. The little red fish, surprisingly coy given its bright coloring, is peeking out from behind another.

Figure 7.6: The Final Composition

The effects obtained with layer masks could have also been accomplished with selections applied in the image window. However, this would have required permanently cutting away parts of the Sea Horse and Red Fish layers. Alternatively, the layer masks used in conjunction with the painting tools simplified the work and produced a more robust solution. Because of the layer masks, nothing has been irrevocably lost in either the Sea Horse or Red Fish layers. Thus, these layers can be repositioned if need be—only the layer masks need be re-edited. This flexibility with positioning adjustments is not possible when using selections because the cut away components are gone.

To summarize, this project reviewed cutting, pasting, scaling, and the positioning of layers for compositing. In addition, a simple application of layer masks was used to give our composition some illusion of depth. The next compositing project is more complicated because it makes use of the blending modes and the Curves tool.

7.2 PROJECT 2: THROUGH THE LOOKING GLASS

Blending modes, discussed in Chapter 5, are very useful tools for compositing. They can be used to give the illusion of one image element not just being delimited by another but of being fused right into it. This is a very powerful device because it allows the artist to convey a message about the relationship of the fused images, which simple juxtaposition does not. The objective of the project in this section is to illustrate this type of effect.

The images shown in Figures 7.7 and 7.8 are the raw materials for this project. They will be fused together to make the tin can seem to reflect the flower and insect. A summary of the procedure used to achieve the effect is as follows:

1. Place the flower image into a new layer above the layer of the tin can image.
2. Position, scale, and orient the flower layer to juxtapose it with the can in the desired manner.
3. Mask the upper layer to the limits of the tin can's borders.
4. Apply an appropriate blending mode to the upper layer.
5. Adjust the upper layer's brightness using the Curves tool.

Figure 7.7: A Tin Can Discarded as Trash

Figure 7.9 illustrates the flower copied and pasted into a layer over the tin can image. As the Layers dialog in Figure 7.9(a) indicates, the flower layer is in a floating selection where it will stay until it is positioned, scaled, and oriented. The Opacity slider in the Layers dialog has been set to 60%, which allows the tin can to be seen through this floating selection.

Figure 7.8: A Flower and a Visiting Friend

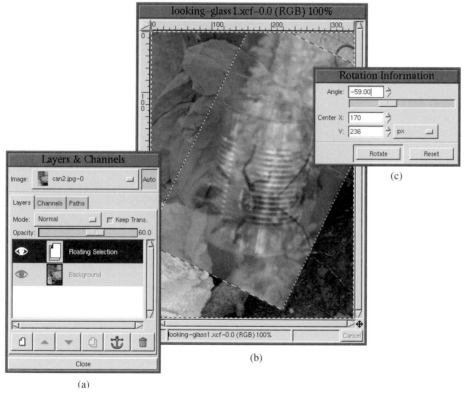

(a)

(b)

(c)

Figure 7.9: The Flower Layer Pasted and Oriented over the Tin Can Layer

The Transform tool is used to rotate the flower layer. The flower image is aligned with the longitudinal axis of the tin can, which requires 59° of rotation. The partial transparency of the floating selection is invaluable, while using the Move tool, for correctly positioning the flower layer over the tin can. This is the stage of the project seen in Figure 7.9(b).

Before moving to the next stage of the project, let's discuss how the rotation value of −59.00, shown in Figure 7.9(c), was determined. This angle was computed using the Measure tool, as is illustrated in Figure 7.10. Figure 7.10(a) shows how the angle of the longitudinal axis of the insect's back is measured, and Figure 7.10(b) does the same for the lateral axis of the tin can. As shown in the two figures, the insect's back measures 68.43° with respect to the horizontal axis, and the tin can measures 9.40°. To make the insect align with the can after rotation requires (9.40°−68.43°) ≈ −59°.

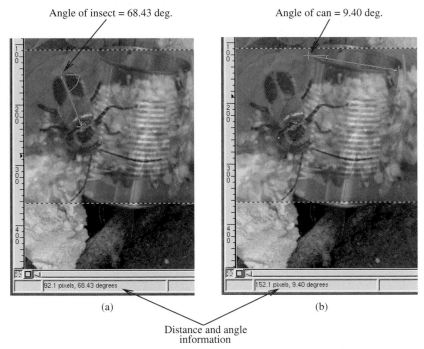

Figure 7.10: Using the Measure Tool to Compute the Correct Angle of Rotation

An alternate technique to using the Measure tool to get an accurate estimate of the amount of rotation needed is to make use of the Path Transform Lock in the Paths dialog (see Section 3.4.1). This feature locks a path to the active layer so that when the layer is transformed with the Transform tool, the path is too. Figures 7.11 and 7.12 illustrate how this helps. Figure 7.11(a) shows a Bezier path outlining the insect, and Figure 7.11(b) shows that the Path Transform Lock for this path is toggled on. In addition, the insect's layer has been made partially transparent, allowing the tin can to be seen through it from behind.

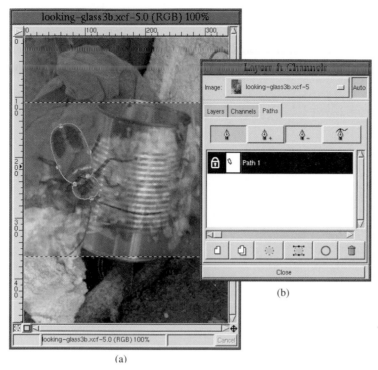

looking-glass3b.xcf-5.0 (RGB) 100%

Layers & Channels

Image: looking-glass3b.xcf-5   Auto

Layers | Channels | Paths

Path 1

Close

(b)

(a)

Figure 7.11: Using a Bezier Path to Delineate the Insect's Outline, and Toggling On the Path Transform Lock

Figure 7.12(a) shows the `Tool Options` window for the `Transform` tool. The Rotation radio button is shown checked, and, take note, the Show Path checkbox is toggled on. This means that the locked Bezier path will be shown with the transform grid lines when the mouse is first clicked in the image window. An accurate transformation of the insect layer can now be performed because the locked path moves visibly with the grid lines as they are transformed by the mouse.

Figure 7.12(b) shows the result of rotating the grid lines, and it can be seen that the insect's outline is also rotated. This is a very powerful technique for getting accurate transforms. In particular, it is the only technique for effectively visualizing how to warp one object to another when using the Perspective option of the `Transform` tool.

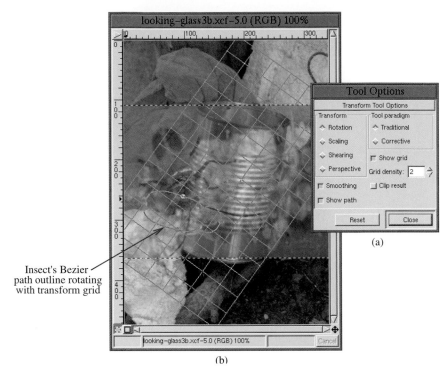

Insect's Bezier path outline rotating with transform grid

(a)

(b)

Figure 7.12: Bezier Path Outline Rotating with Transform Grid

Picking up the project from where we left off, the rotated floating selection is now anchored to a new layer by clicking on the New Layer button in the Layers dialog, and the Opacity slider is set back to 100%. Before the next step, which is to mask the tin can, the flower layer is merged into a transparent layer that has the same size as that of the tin can. This is done as follows:

1. In the Layers dialog, the New Layer button is clicked and the Transparent layer option is chosen in the New Layer Options dialog.
2. The resulting layer is positioned in the layer stack just below the Flower layer.
3. With the Flower layer active, the function Merge Down is selected from the Layers menu (or C-S-m is typed in the Layers dialog window). This merges the flower into the transparent layer.

At this point, it is useful to name the two layers in the Layers dialog. Let's label them Flower and Tin Can.

The next step in the process is to create a mask of the tin can. This is done by making a selection of the can, which is then converted to a layer mask. To facilitate the selection, the visibility of the Flower layer is toggled off. The selection is made using the Bezier Path tool and is illustrated in Figure 7.13.

Figure 7.13: Making a Selection of the Tin Can

After toggling the visibility of the Flower layer back on and making it active, the procedure for creating the layer mask from the selection is performed using these steps:

1. Make the Flower layer active by clicking on its thumbnail in the Layers dialog.
2. Create a layer mask for the Flower layer using the `Add Layer Mask` function from the `Layers` menu, choosing the White (Full Opacity) option.
3. Invert the selection by typing `C-i` in the image window.
4. Make the `Active Background Color` black by typing `d` and then `x` in the image window.
5. Make sure the layer mask is active in the Layers dialog by clicking on its thumbnail, and cut the selection by typing `C-x` in the image window.

Cutting the selection makes the layer mask black outside the tin can's boundaries. Note that although the selection was made in the Tin Can layer, the cut is applied to the layer mask. This illustrates the important rule that regardless of where a selection is made, its effect is only applied to the active layer.

Figure 7.14 shows the result of creating the layer mask. The thumbnail of the mask can be seen in Figure 7.14(a), and its effect can be seen in Figure 7.14(b). Notice that the parts of the Flower layer extending outside the boundaries of the tin can have been masked off.

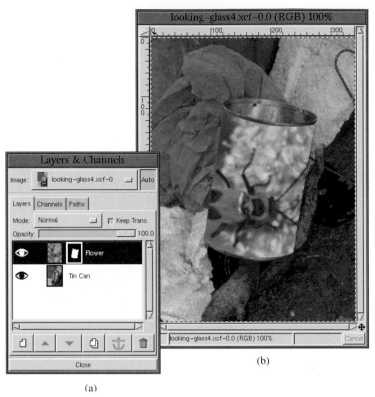

Figure 7.14: Flower Layer Masked by Tin Can

Figure 7.14(b) is almost what we are looking for except that the flower image now looks as if it is pasted onto the outer surface of the can. The effect we are looking for is different. We want to make the flower look fused into the can, as if it is an integral part of it. For example, it would be interesting for the insect and flower to appear as if they were reflected off the can's shiny surface. To achieve this effect, we use a blending mode.

The blending mode used in this example is Multiply (Burn). It is applied by making the Flower layer active and then selecting it from the Mode menu in the Layers dialog. You can see the choice of mode in Figure 7.15(a), and you can see the result on the image in Figure 7.15(b). This mode multiplies the pixel values of the two layers, but only where the Flower layer is not transparent. Thus, the lighting variations of the tin can are impressed onto the flower and insect, making them look as if they are truly a part of the can. The overall result, however, is a little dark.

(a)

(b)

Figure 7.15: Using the `Multiply` Blending Mode on the Flower Layer

The final step, then, is to lighten the dark result in Figure 7.15. This is done by applying the perturbation technique described in Section 6.2.5 to the Flower layer using the Value channel of the `Curves` tool. The Value channel is selected because we do not want to affect the colors, just the lightness of the image. Figure 7.16(a) shows the `Curves` dialog after using the perturbation technique. The resulting effect on the final composition is shown in Figure 7.16(b). Using the perturbation technique, it was determined that it was the highlight part of the value range that needed to be lightened to obtain the best result. Thus, this effect could not have been achieved using the `Levels` or `Brightness-Contrast` tools.

To summarize, this project illustrates the use of blending modes and the `Curves` tool for compositing. Note that the use of the `Multiply` blending mode is not primordial to the technique. Other possibilities could have been `Screen`, `Overlay`, `Lighten Only`, `Darken Only`, and `Color`. It is important to experiment with the different modes and to do so in conjunction with the Opacity slider and the `Curves` tool. The final choice will depend on your aesthetic sensibilities.

Figure 7.16: Final Composition

7.3 PROJECT 3: DESTINATION SATURN

The third project creates a collage that blends together a terrific photo of the planet Saturn with a launch of the space shuttle. This project illustrates a more sophisticated use of layer masks and blend modes.

The raw images for the project are shown in Figures 7.17 and 7.18. The objective is to depict the shuttle lifting off with Saturn sitting majestically in the background…perhaps as a final destination? Although the space shuttle was never conceived for travel to Saturn, the GIMP allows us to imagine, suggest, even portray the inconceivable.

The rough layout of the desired scene is to position the image of Saturn somewhat above and behind the shuttle lift-off. The first step is to get the two images into the same window. For this, a little planning is necessary. The image of Saturn is wider than that of the shuttle. However, the Saturn image has a large black margin that, when cropped, will make the result narrower than the shuttle. Cropping the Saturn image to remove the black margin produces an image that has a width of 527 pixels and a height of 489 pixels. The raw space shuttle launch image has a width of 640 pixels and a height of 636 pixels.

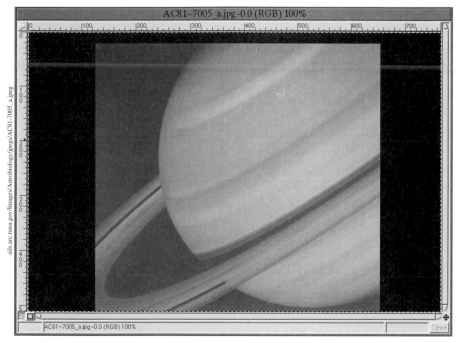

Figure 7.17: Original Image of Saturn

Figure 7.18: Original Image of Shuttle Launch

Considering the rough layout discussed earlier, the width of the shuttle image must be cropped to that of the Saturn image, 527 pixels. Furthermore, I decided that the lower 130 pixels of the shuttle image won't be used, meaning that the height of the shuttle image after cropping will only be 506 pixels. There needs to be some vertical overlap between the two layers in the composited image, so I chose a total vertical height of 750 pixels. The `Crop` tool is used to nicely center the shuttle launch image while producing the desired dimensions.

The two raw images are now ready to be united into a single image. A new window is created by typing `c-n` in the Saturn image window. When the `New Image` dialog appears, the default values for the width and height are those of the Saturn image, 527 by 489. The value of 750 pixels is entered into the height field, and when the new window is created, it has the desired dimensions of 527 by 750.

The shuttle launch image is now copied and pasted into the new image window. This is done by typing `c-c` in the shuttle launch window followed by `c-v` in the new window. The result places the shuttle image into a floating selection that can be seen by opening the Layers dialog (that is, by typing `c-l` in the image window). The `Move` tool is used to position the shuttle to the bottom of the window; it is then anchored to the background by clicking on the `Anchor` button in the Layers dialog.

Creating a new layer by clicking on the New Layer button in the Layers dialog, the image of Saturn is now copied to the new image window, slid to the top of the window using the `Move` tool, and finally anchored into the newly created layer. Double-clicking on each layer in the Layers dialog allows us to name each one. The top layer is named Saturn, and the lower layer is named Shuttle Launch. The result is shown in Figure 7.19(a), which shows the Saturn layer half blocking the Shuttle Launch layer. The Layers dialog is shown in Figure 7.19(b).

Now that the two images are positioned, one approach for blending the two is to use the layer mask and gradient technique described in Section 4.3.3. The idea is to create a layer mask for the Saturn layer and to blend the two layers together by applying a gradient in the layer mask. This produces the image shown in Figure 7.20(a). Figure 7.20(b) shows how a layer mask with a gradient has been added to the Saturn layer.

(a)

Figure 7.19: Assembling the Pieces

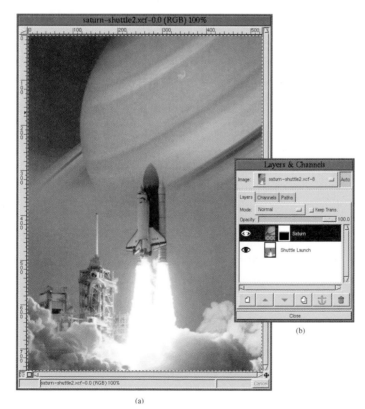

(a)

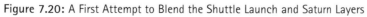

Figure 7.20: A First Attempt to Blend the Shuttle Launch and Saturn Layers

Figure 7.20 is a blend of the two layers, but in many ways it misses the mark. The blend of the two images shows the shuttle against the background of Saturn, however, the lower part of the ringed planet is covered by the blue sky background of the shuttle launch image. This doesn't look natural, and it would be nice to keep the shuttle and launch vehicle equipment well defined while simultaneously blending the background into the Saturn image in a more delicate manner. Fortunately, this can be accomplished using a very clever masking technique.[10]

The idea is to combine two masks into one using a blending mode. The first mask is made from the shuttle and launch equipment, and the second mask is made from a gradient. The two masks are combined using the Darken Only blending mode. Read on!

The implementation of the idea requires a mask of the shuttle equipment. The mask is made using the Decompose and Threshold technique described in

Section 4.5.3. The Decompose function with the HSV option is used to create a hue, saturation, and value decomposition of the Space Shuttle layer. On inspection of the result, the Hue channel seems to have the most potential for a simple separation of the subject from its background. The Threshold tool is used on the Hue channel, and when the best threshold range has been determined and some cleanup has been performed using the Lasso tool, the result is as shown in Figure 7.21. This black and white image is not a perfect mask, but some of the defects will be removed in a moment, and the rest will not matter.

Figure 7.21: Creating a Mask of the Space Shuttle Layer

The next step is to copy and paste the grayscale image from Figure 7.21 into the layer mask of the Saturn layer in Figure 7.20. This is done as follows:

1. The layer mask of the Saturn layer is made active by clicking on its thumbnail in the Layers dialog.

2. The grayscale image in Figure 7.21 is copied into the default buffer by typing C-c in its image window.

3. The contents of the buffer are then pasted into the image of Figure 7.20 by typing C-v in its image window.

4. This creates a floating selection that is then dropped into the layer mask by clicking on the Anchor button in the Layers dialog.

At this point, the layer mask is cleaned up using the Airbrush tool. The technique is described in detail in Section 4.5.1 for a channel mask. Here, the method is applied to a layer mask. To facilitate the cleanup, the opacity of the Saturn layer is adjusted using the Opacity slider in the Layers dialog.

The resulting layer mask allows the shuttle and launch equipment to be seen through the Saturn layer. The state of the project is shown in Figure 7.22(a), and Figure 7.22(b) shows the thumbnail of the resulting layer mask in the Layers dialog.

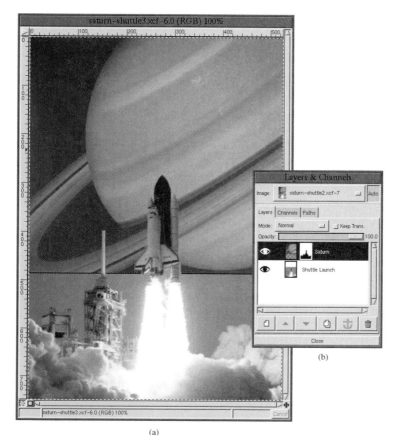

Figure 7.22: Application of the Space Shuttle and Launch Equipment Layer Mask

Figure 7.22(a) is almost what we're looking for. To finish, the boundary between the two layers should be blended with a gradient similar to the one in Figure 7.20(a), but without disturbing any part of the masked shuttle and launch equipment.

This final touch is achieved by applying a gradient to the layer mask using the Darken Only blending mode. As described in Section 5.6.4, this mode combines foreground and background pixels by retaining the darker of the two. Thus, a gradient applied using the Darken Only mode only changes the layer mask where the gradient is darker than the mask. This is just what we are looking for. The shuttle and launch equipment will not be affected by the gradient because these parts of the mask are already black…can't get any darker than that!

Let's see how it works. To apply the gradient to the layer mask, the following steps are used:

1. The layer mask of the Saturn layer is made active by clicking on its thumbnail in the Layers dialog.
2. A linear FG to BG (RGB) gradient is chosen from the Gradient tool options dialog.
3. The Active Foreground Color is set to black, and the Active Background Color is set to white by typing d in the image window.
4. The blending mode is set to Darken Only in the Brush Selection dialog.
5. A gradient is applied to the layer mask by clicking in the image window just above the lower edge of the Saturn layer and dragging vertically to a point just a little higher up than the shuttle's wings, before releasing the mouse button.

The result of this new mask is shown in Figure 7.23(a). Figure 7.23(b) shows the corresponding Layers dialog, Figure 7.23(c) shows the Gradient tool's Tool Options dialog, and Figure 7.23(d) shows the Brush Selection dialog (notice the choice of the Darken Only blending mode). This produces a lovely collage of the two original images.

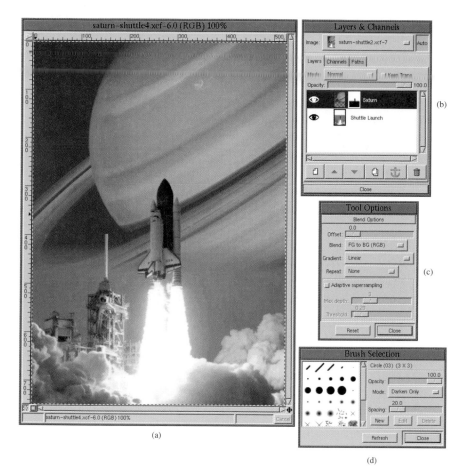

(a)

(b)

(c)

(d)

Figure 7.23: The Final Blended Image

7.4 PROJECT 4: THE CALL OF THE MERMAID

The fourth project is a bit more complicated than the third. It uses many of the techniques of the first three projects and adds several more. The objective is to actually combine image elements from two disparate sources, a young woman and a fish, to create a realistic and alluring mythological creature—the mermaid.

The raw image materials used to create the mermaid are shown in Figure 7.24. The first step of this project is to fuse together parts of the young woman and fish in a realistic way to create the mermaid. The second step is to place the mermaid composite into an appropriate underwater background scene.

To create the mermaid, the woman and the fish must be selected and united into a single image but on separate layers. The woman is selected using the Decompose and Threshold technique described in Section 4.5.3. The HSV option of the Decompose function is chosen, and Threshold is applied to the resulting value component. The result is shown in Figure 7.25(a). The range of values used with the Threshold dialog is shown in Figure 7.25(b).

Figure 7.24: Original Images of the Young Woman and the Fish

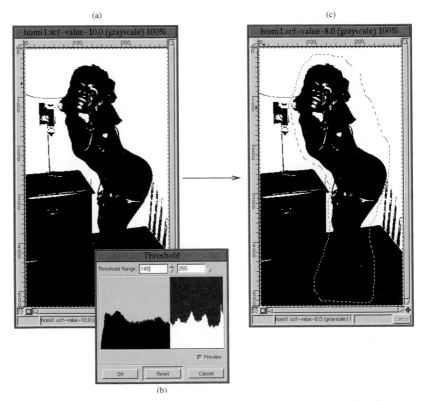

Figure 7.25: Using `Threshold` and the `Lasso` to Create a Mask for the Woman

The image shown in Figure 7.25(a) has separated a large part of the subject from the background but requires a little more work to achieve the desired result. First, there are elements of the background that must be removed, and second, there are holes in the subject that must be filled. Both tasks are relatively easy to accomplish. The background is removed by following these steps:

1. Draw a rough selection around the woman's silhouette using the Lasso tool. Make sure the path of the Lasso separates the background from the woman.

2. Invert the resulting selection by typing C-i in the image window. This phase is shown in Figure 7.25(c).

3. Choose white as the Active Background Color by typing d and then x in the image window.

4. Cut the selection by typing C-x in the image window.

Figure 7.26(a) shows the result of having cut away the unwanted background. The remaining work is to fill in the holes seen in Figure 7.26(a) using the Paintbrush tool. As shown in Figure 7.26(b), a medium hard brush is chosen for this. Figure 7.26(c) shows the final mask. Although the lower portion of the woman's legs are not cleanly separated from the background, this is remedied shortly.

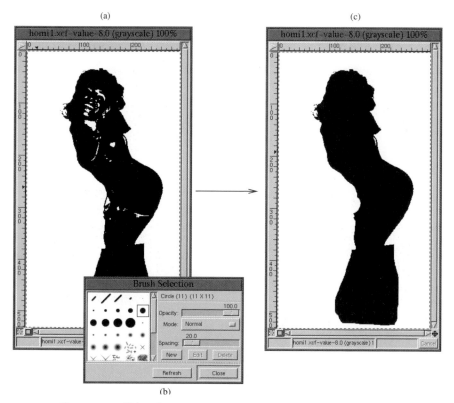

Figure 7.26: Using the Paintbrush to Finish the Mask of the Woman

The next task is to create a layer mask for the image in Figure 7.24(a) and to paste into it the grayscale image shown in Figure 7.26(b). This is done in the following steps:

1. Invert the black and white regions of the image in Figure 7.26(b) using `Invert` from the `Image:Image/Colors` menu.

2. Copy the resulting grayscale image to the default buffer by typing `C-c` in the image window.

3. Create a layer mask for the image in Figure 7.24(a) by opening the Layers dialog and choosing `Add Layer Mask` from the `Layers` menu.

4. Paste the default buffer's contents into Figure 7.24(a) by typing `C-v` in the image window.

5. Drop the resulting float into the layer mask by clicking on the `Anchor` button in the Layers dialog.

The effect of the layer mask on the image is shown in Figure 7.27(a), and the thumbnail of the mask can be seen in the Layers dialog shown in Figure 7.27(b).

Figure 7.27: Applying a Layer Mask to the Woman

Now that the layer mask is in place, the remaining parts of the background around the woman's lower legs are removed by painting away the offending parts of the layer mask with black paint using the `Paintbrush` tool.

The `Decompose` and `Threshold` technique is the easiest method for selecting the woman. She presents a relatively difficult selection using any other tool. In particular, the outline of her hair would have been an especially thorny problem. In comparison, the parts of the fish that are needed for the project present a simple outline that can easily be selected using the Bezier Path tool. This step is not illustrated here, but the Bezier Path tool is described in detail in Section 3.1.1.

The selection of the woman and the fish are now united into a single image, as shown in Figure 7.28(a). Figure 7.28(b), which shows the Layers dialog, indicates that the woman and the fish each reside in separate layers. Note that both images have been rotated 90° with respect to their original orientations. This properly orients our mermaid in preparation for inserting her into her final underwater setting.

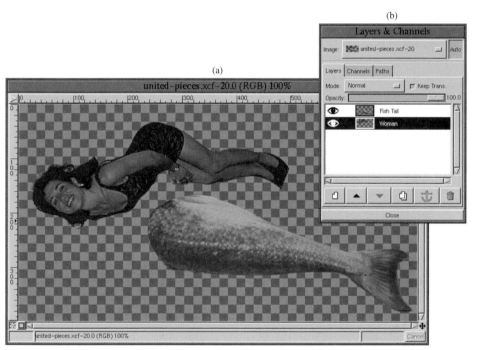

Figure 7.28: Uniting the Pieces

At this stage, we are ready to begin melding the two image components together. The strategy is to take pieces of the fish's tail and appropriately fuse them onto the woman's body. The fish's tail is too large to superimpose in one piece; thus, it is cut into two parts using the Lasso tool. Using the Move tool, the bottom part, the tail fin, is repositioned over the lower part of the woman's legs. This is shown in Figure 7.29.

Notice that I vertically flipped the tail fin (using the Flip tool) because that orientation looked better to me. The positioning of the tail fin over the woman's legs was facilitated by using the Opacity slider in the Layers dialog.

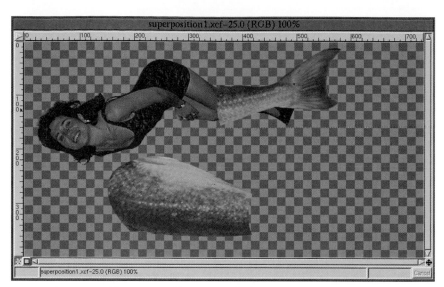

Figure 7.29: Flipping and Positioning the Tail Fin

To convincingly fuse the tail fin to the woman's lower legs, a layer mask is needed. The layer mask, which is applied to the Tail Fin layer, is used to mask off the parts that extend beyond the boundaries of the woman's legs. Figure 7.30(a) shows that the Tail Fin layer has been made partially transparent to allow the woman's legs to be seen through it. Figure 7.30(b) shows the corresponding Layers dialog. The Tail Fin layer mask is highlighted in the Layers dialog and the Opacity slider is set to 56%.

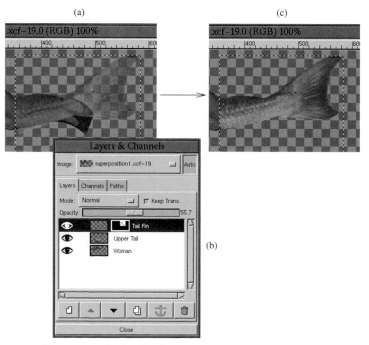

Figure 7.30: Fusing the Tail Fin to the Woman's Lower Legs

The Paintbrush and Airbrush tools were used to mask off parts of the tail fin in Figure 7.30(a). The Eraser tool was used to remove the parts of the woman's feet that extend out beyond the tail fin. The result, after returning the Opacity slider to 100% in the Layers dialog, is shown in Figure 7.30(c). The tail fin now seems to be fused onto the woman's legs.

Figure 7.31 shows the image after performing a similar sequence of fusing the upper part of the fish's tail to the woman's body between her waist and her knees. As before, a layer mask is used to perform the fusion. Also, in order to better align the highlight in the scales of the tail with the axis of the woman's upper legs, the Rotation option from the Transform tool is used.

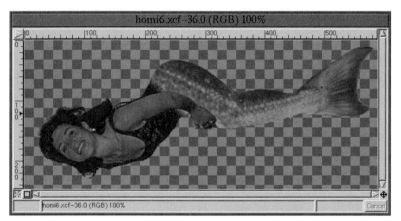

Figure 7.31: Fusing the Remainder of the Tail and Correcting for Image Inconsistencies

In addition to fusing the tail to the woman's body, Figure 7.31 also shows that her wristwatch has been removed with the Clone tool. Let's hope she wasn't too attached to it. The Clone tool was also used to remove some overly bright highlights in her face (for more on how to use the Clone tool, see Section 6.3). Finally, the image was cropped to the dimensions seen in Figure 7.31.

It is now time to insert our siren of the sea into a scene reflecting her natural habitat, swimming with her faithful fishy companions along a reef, undoubtably somewhere in the south Pacific. The insertion of the mermaid into the scene was accomplished by first merging all the layers used to create Figure 7.31, applying the layer mask, and then copying and pasting the result into the underwater image. As usual, the paste gives rise to a floating selection, which is then dropped into a new layer using the New Layer button in the Layers dialog. The Move tool is used to position the Mermaid layer and the result is shown in Figure 7.32.

Figure 7.32: The Mermaid Placed into an Underwater Scene

Actually, the result in Figure 7.32 also displays an additional finesse. The obvious sunburn of our underwater beauty, as seen in Figure 7.31, has been color corrected to a tint more in keeping with her new environment. This is accomplished using the perturbation technique for the `Curves` tool, as described in Section 6.2.5. The result is that her skin color has been changed to a mild bluish-green tint.

Looking at Figure 7.32, the edge between the mermaid's upper body and the blue of the background waters seems fine. However, the edge of her yellow tail seems a little too abrupt, too sharp. It looks as if this part of her body were cut out of another image and pasted into this one. Indeed, it was. So, as a final attention to detail, it would be nice to diminish the abruptness of this edge. You can do this using a clever technique based on the `Border` function found in the `Image:Select` menu (see Section 3.3.9).

The idea is to blur together the background and the mermaid in a narrow region around the mermaid's edge. To do this, follow these steps while referring to Figure 7.33:

1. Activate the Mermaid layer by clicking on her thumbnail in the Layers dialog (shown in Figure 7.33(b)).
2. Create a selection of the mermaid using `Alpha to Selection` from the `Layers` menu.
3. Use the selection to make a border 3 pixels wide using `Border` (Figure 7.33(c) shows the `Border` tool's dialog, and Figure 7.33(a) illustrates the selection result).
4. Merge the Mermaid layer into the background by typing `C-m` in the Layers dialog or the image window.

5. Apply `Gaussian Blur (IIR)` with a radius of 3 pixels (Figure 7.33(d) shows the dialog for this filter).

6. Remove the selection by typing C-S-a in the image window.

The final result gives a much softer edge between the mermaid and the background. This is shown in Figure 7.34.

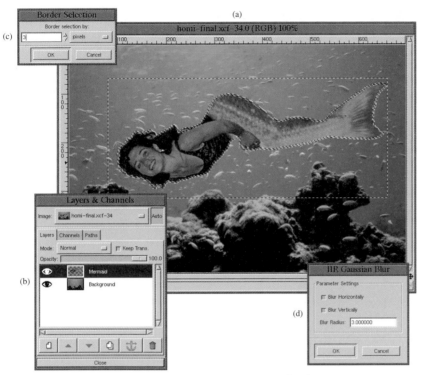

Figure 7.33: Using `Border` and `Gaussian Blur (IIR)` to Soften the Cut-Out Look of the Mermaid's Edge

Figure 7.34: The Final Mermaid Composition

To summarize, this project illustrates how layer masks, in conjunction with many other tools, can be used to literally fuse together image elements. This project also shows how the Border tool can be used to finesse the edges of composited images.

7.5 PROJECT 5: PANORAMAS

By piecing together a series of normal photographs, panoramic and wide angle views can be created in the GIMP. The approach of piecing together a group of images to create a panorama instead of using special purpose camera lenses gives rise to a number of photo inconsistencies among the individual pieces of the image. Nevertheless, the GIMP is perfectly capable of correcting these problems and creating a well integrated whole. This chapter describes the problems involved in creating panoramas from collections of individual images and how to overcome them in the GIMP.

To create a panorama from a collection of photos, the steps are well defined. First, the photos have to be grouped together into a single image, each placed into a separate layer. The procedure for this has been explained many times already in this book. In particular, Section 2.4 describes the copying and pasting of images into layers, and Section 2.6.1 explains how to position layers within an image.

Figure 7.35(a) illustrates a set of images, each taken with about 50% overlap, using a digital camera. They were stored in JPEG file format and then individually loaded into the GIMP. Each was then copied and pasted into a separate layer in a single image. Each layer was then positioned using the Move tool. The Opacity slider in the Layers dialog was used to facilitate the positioning of each layer.

Figure 7.35(a) shows the result after positioning the layers as well as possible, and Figure 7.35(b) shows the organization of the layers in the Layers dialog. The layers are named with the letters of the alphabet, A through E, where A corresponds to the rightmost layer and E to the leftmost.

Figure 7.35 illustrates the primary problems that must be overcome to achieve a consistent looking panorama. As shown, these problems are geometric distortion, color matching, and brightness matching. Each of these is addressed in the following sections.

7.5.1 Correcting Geometric Distortions

The first step after the initial positioning of the individual layers is to remove, as much as possible, the geometric distortions. Figure 7.35(a) has distortions that can be seen in several places. The two most flagrant problems are the molding around the ceiling of the room and the alignment of the grain in the hardwood floor, especially on the left side of the image. However, there are also many other small details in the image that are slightly off kilter. Also, there are several places where elements of the images do not line up properly.

The first step is to correct for the misalignment problems. Using the Scale option of the Transform tool, some of the layers are squeezed in an effort to make them more consistent with the others. A very important guideline, however, is that there are limits to what can be done without introducing other serious mismatches. The goal is to adjust, but with a light hand.

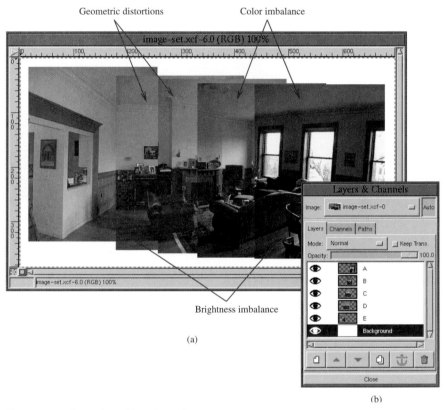

Figure 7.35: Collection of Positioned Images

Referring again to Figure 7.35(a), perhaps the biggest inconsistency is that the vertical scale of the image in layer C seems to be larger than the others. This explains the lack of registration of the ceiling molding and the fireplace mantle for this layer. The remaining details might be acceptable defects. This will be reevaluated after the most important corrections are made.

Before you begin, it is worthwhile to point out that, of all the Transform tool options, Scaling introduces the fewest artifacts. This is especially true when care is taken to maintain the aspect ratio between the horizontal and vertical dimensions. The Scaling option of the Transform tool can be constrained to preserve aspect ratio by pressing the Control and Alt keys together while scaling.

Figure 7.36(a) illustrates the result of using the `Transform` tool to adjust layer C. As shown in Figure 7.36(b), the tool is used with the `Scaling` option. The upper-right corner of layer C was adjusted until both the X and Y Scale Ratios shown in the `Scaling Information` dialog became 0.95.

(a)

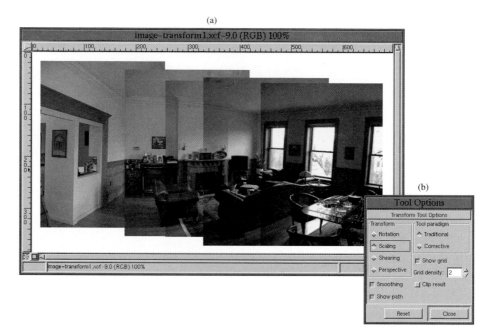

Figure 7.36: Initial Geometric Distortion Corrections

How was the value 0.95 determined? The answer depends on whether you are challenged by ratios. If not, the swiftest way is to use the `Measure` tool to determine that the height of the molding at the left edge of layer C is 271 pixels from layer C's bottom edge, and that the height of the molding in layer D at layer C's left edge is 258 pixels. This makes the ratio 258/271 = 0.95. If you don't like ratios, a simple trial-and-error approach does not take much more time. Just choose a scaling factor and use `C-z` to perform an undo if the scale isn't correct. The result of the scaling operation aligns the molding on the ceiling between layers C and D.

As already noted, the upper-right corner of layer C was used to perform the scale. Thus, layer C has shrunk horizontally by 5%, shifting its right edge to the left. This means that to properly register with layer C, layers A and B must now be repositioned to the left.

7.5.2 COLOR AND BRIGHTNESS MATCHING

You can see that there is significant brightness variation from layer to layer in Figure 7.35. This is normal for photos taken with most consumer digital and regular film cameras. These cameras typically auto-expose scenes according to average lighting conditions and do not offer user controls for exposure. For the image in layer A of Figure 7.35, the light coming from the windows is very bright which, due to the average light metering of the camera, causes the features of the room's interior to be underexposed. Thus, the room features in this layer are quite a bit darker than in the other layers. Otherwise, the bright ness of the other layers are more or less consistent with each other.

In addition to the brightness mismatch between layers, you can also see from Figure 7.35 that there is a color balance mismatch from layer to layer. The combination of color and brightness variations means that the layer boundaries are plainly visible instead of presenting a smooth and imperceptible transition across the panorama.

The strategy for correcting the differences in brightness and color is to use the Curves tool. The idea is to match color at boundaries between layers using a method similar to that described in Section 6.2.2. The method measures pixel values on both sides of a layer boundary using the Color Picker tool. The Curves tool is then used to match the values. This procedure corrects for both color and brightness mismatch simultaneously.

Matching the color and brightness of two layers has a chain reaction effect in a panorama project. Matching layer B to its neighbor A means that subsequently layer C must be matched to B, and so on. Thus, some care must be taken to avoid blowing out the available tonal range. Typically, the wisest decision is to choose the layer of average brightness and to match the other layers working away from this one. However, for this panorama project, it is layer E that is chosen as the reference because its lighting for the room seems the most natural. The work flow, then, is from the leftmost layer to the rightmost, from layer E to layer A.

Starting with the boundary between layers E and D, a pixel value was measured on the white wall just above the wood wainscoting. The measured values are $177^R183^G194^B$ to the left of the boundary and $153^R156^G171^B$ to the right. Using this information, the Curves tool is used on layer D to match the pixel values measured in D to those of layer E. Representative pixels are then measured across the boundary between layer D and layer C. Here, the measured pixel values are located at the midway point between the hanging picture and the ceiling molding. The values are found to be $179^R175^G185^B$ to the left of the boundary and $112^R119^G139^B$ to the right. The Curves tool is employed again, this time on layer C, matching C's pixel values to those of D's.

Continuing with the boundary between layers C and B, the measured pixel values at a point midway between the mantle and the molding are 201^R197^G 211^B to the left and $101^R99^G112^B$ to the right. The final boundary is between layers B and A. Here the pixels are measured at the midpoint between the plant and the molding. The values found are $199^R198^G208^B$ and $86^R75^G81^B$. The Curves tool is applied for each of these boundaries, as it was for the first two.

The results of the color and brightness matching operations are shown in Figure 7.37. The overall color and brightness of the images in the layers are now much more consistent. However, there continues to be a sufficient mismatch between the layers to perceive the layer boundaries. Fortunately, this visual defect can be corrected using a layer mask blending technique described in the next section.

Figure 7.37: Initial Color and Brightness Matching

7.5.3 BLENDING

The remaining color mismatches at layer edges can be corrected using layer masks. The idea is to blend the edges by using a gradient in a layer mask. The technique of layer blending using a gradient in a layer mask is discussed in Section 4.3.3.

Figure 7.38(a) shows the remaining color mismatch at the edge between layers A and B. Figure 7.38(b) shows a layer mask created for layer A. This mask is a black-to-white gradient where the black point is placed at the left edge of the mask and the white point slightly to the right of this. This layer mask has the effect of making the left side of layer A's boundary semi-transparent, letting layer B show through. The end result is the two layers are blended in this small band removing the visibility of the boundary. Figure 7.38(c) illustrates the Layers dialog showing that four of the five layers have had layer masks added. This makes one layer mask for each boundary.

Figure 7.39(a) shows, again, the boundary between layers A and B before blending. Figure 7.39(b) shows the result after blending. As you can see, the technique is very effective. However, some experimentation was necessary to find the correct width for the gradient blend.

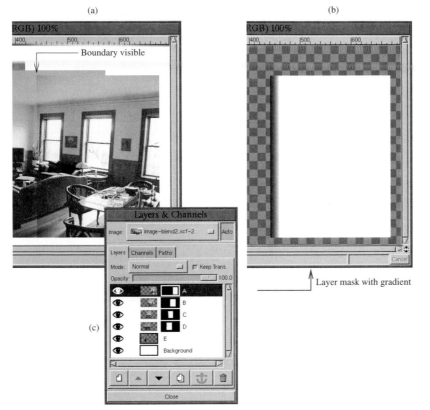

Figure 7.38: Construction of a Gradient in a Layer Mask to Blend
Away the Boundary Between Two Layers

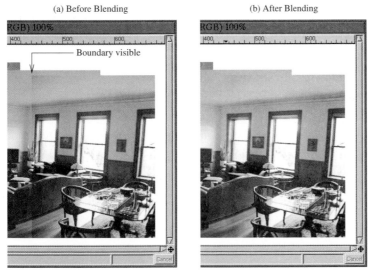

Figure 7.39: The Result of Blending Two Layers

Although the gradient blending trick works well in most cases, there are times when it is not appropriate for the entire boundary to be between two layers. In this case, parts of the boundary can be targeted for a blending gradient by using the Rectangle Select tool. This is necessary, for example, for the blend of layers D and E. Here, separate selections are made at layer D's left edge for the regions corresponding to the hardwood floor, the wainscoting, and upper wall areas. Separate gradient blends are produced for each one.

The layer mask produced by these separate gradients is shown in Figure 7.40(a). Figure 7.40(b) shows the associated Layers dialog.

(a)

(b)

Figure 7.40: Using the `Rectangle Select` Tool to Create a Custom Gradient Mask

7.5.4 FINAL TOUCHES

At this point in the creation of the panorama, the image can be cropped and the various layers merged. Using the `Crop` tool to retain only the regions corresponding to a complete rectangular image produces Figure 7.41. In addition to the crop, the layers are also merged by typing `c-m` in either the Layers dialog or the image window.

Figure 7.41: The Cropped and Layer Merged Panorama

There is a remaining defect that still seems important in the image: the molding along the ceiling in what was layer E before the merge. This piece of molding is not properly aligned with that of what was layer D. The `Clone` tool described in Section 6.3 can be used to repair this defect. You can repair the molding by cloning the lower edge of the old layer E's visible molding to the top edge. This makes it vertically align with the molding in the segment from the old layer D. After the top edge has been reconstructed in this way, you can eliminate the lower edge by cloning the unadorned part of the wall just below it and using this to cover it up. The resulting final panorama is shown in Figure 7.42, ready for an online version of *Better Homes and Gardens* magazine.

Figure 7.42: The Molding Corrected and Final Panorama

8

RENDERING TECHNIQUES

Most of this book is about manipulating and combining existing image materials. However, the GIMP is also an excellent tool for creating and enhancing image materials. In particular, there are many tools in the GIMP that can be used to render image objects. By this, I mean that image objects can be made to look more three-dimensional by dotting them with textures, shadings, lighting effects, and shadows. Many intriguing effects can be created in this way, and that is the subject of this chapter.

The first half of this chapter covers some basic GIMP tools useful for rendering. These include the `Bucket Fill` tool, the `Gradient` tool, the `Emboss` filter, and the `Bump map` filter. The second half of the chapter describes techniques for creating shadows and for combining these with several other image rendering techniques.

8.1 THE BUCKET FILL TOOL

`Bucket Fill` is a very useful tool for rendering. It is found in the Toolbox window and is represented by the bucket icon shown in Figure 8.1(a). The `Bucket Fill` tool is used for filling regions, in whole layers or selections, with a specified color or image pattern. The `Tool Options` dialog, shown in Figure 8.1(b), indicates that the choice between color and image pattern is specified by clicking the appropriate radio button. For color fills, either the `Active Foreground Color` or `Active Background Color` can be used. The choice of color is specified with the `Color Selection` dialog shown in Figure 8.1(c). For pattern fills, the image pattern is chosen from the `Pattern Selection` dialog, shown in Figure 8.1(d). The `Pattern Selection` dialog is found in `Image:Dialogs/Patterns`, and can also be invoked by typing `C-S-p` in the image or Toolbox windows, or by clicking on the `Active Pattern` icon in the Toolbox window.

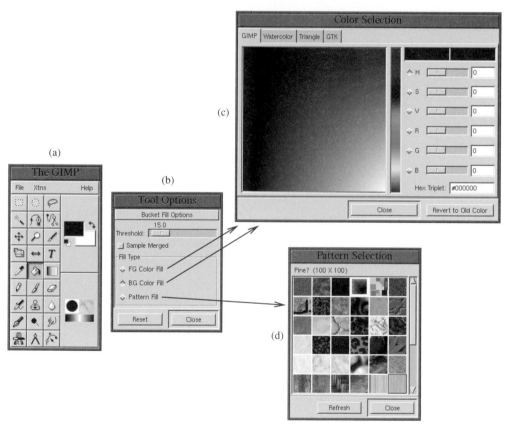

Figure 8.1: Using the `Bucket Fill` Tool

The `Bucket Fill` tool fills the image with a color or a pattern in a manner similar to the way the `Magic Wand` makes selections (see Section 3.1.1). Clicking in an image specifies a seed pixel. The color value of the seed is then compared against the color of the seed's neighboring pixels; if the difference between their color values and the seed's is less than a threshold, they are filled. This process repeats for the neighbors' neighboring pixels, and so on, until all the contiguous pixels whose color values differ from the seed's by less than the threshold are filled. The `Bucket Fill`'s threshold value is set using the Threshold slider found in the `Bucker Fill`'s `Tool Options` dialog (see Figure 8.1(b)).

There are several controls found in the `Brush Selection` dialog that affect the way `Bucket Fill` applies paint or patterns to an image canvas. In particular, there is the Opacity slider, which controls the alpha channel of the applied color or pattern (see Chapter 4 for more on alpha channels), and there is the `Mode` menu which selects the blending mode to be used (blending modes are described in Section 5.6).

Figure 8.2 illustrates the effects of the Threshold and Opacity settings. Figure 8.2(a) shows the location of a seed pixel selected in an image containing a radial gradient. The color of the gradient varies gradually from the center of the image to its edge. This allows you to see how the `Bucket Fill` tool affects a region of the image depending on the placement of the seed and the value of the Threshold. Figure 8.2(b) shows how much of the original gradient is filled with blue when the Threshold is set to 15. Setting the Threshold to 255 would have resulted in completely filling the image with blue. Figure 8.2(c) shows the result when the Opacity slider in the `Brush Selection` dialog is set to 40%. Here, the applied blue fill mixes with the red gradient behind it in a ratio of 40% to 60%.

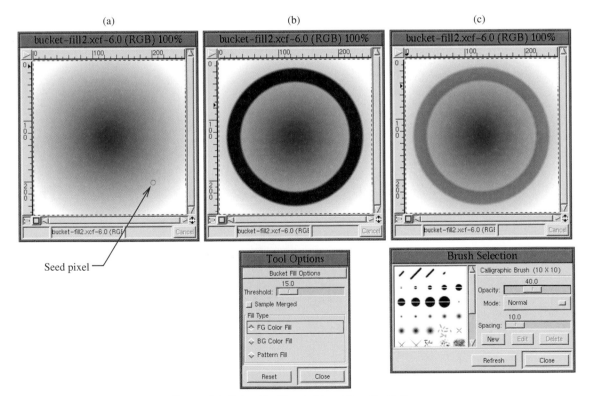

Figure 8.2: Using the Threshold and Opacity Options

Figure 8.3 illustrates filling a part of an image with patterns. Figures 8.3(a) and (b) show that the image consists of two layers, a white background and some blue text on an otherwise transparent layer (shown in the Balcony Angels font). Figure 8.3(c) shows the result of filling each letter in the text with a different pattern, and Figure 8.3(d) shows that the Threshold for these fills is set to 255. This is necessary to get a complete fill. A lower value of Threshold would fail at some text edge pixels because the text there is antialiased (see Section 3.1.2).

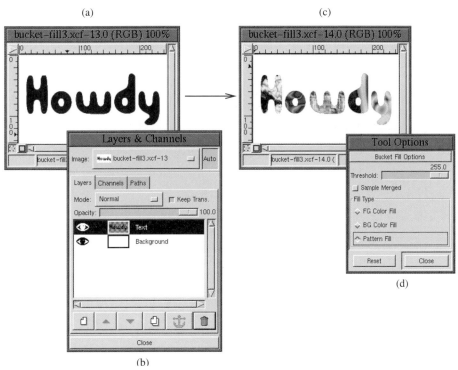

Figure 8.3: Filling with Image Patterns

8.2 GRADIENT RENDERING TECHNIQUES

In Section 4.3.3, gradients were discussed as tools for making masks. However, they are also very useful for rendering.

Figure 8.4 shows the Tool Options dialog for the Gradient tool. As shown in the Blend menu, there are a total of 11 different gradient types. The Conical (symmetric), Shapeburst, and Bi-Linear options are of particular interest for rendering effects.

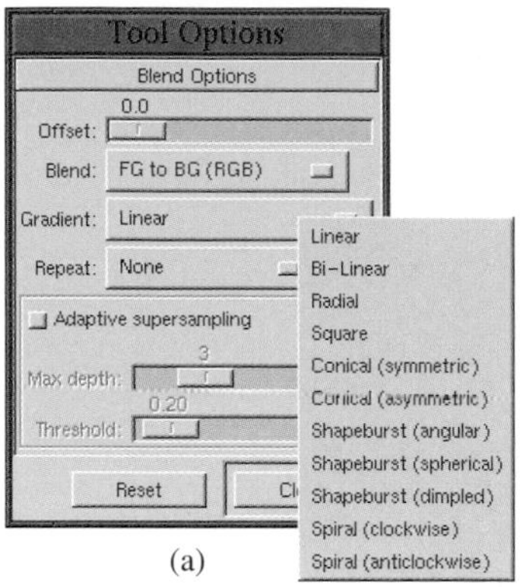

Figure 8.5 illustrates examples of conical, bi-linear, and shapeburst gradients. As shown in Figure 8.5(a), conical gradients produce a dimpled effect. As illustrated in Figure 8.5(b), bi-linear gradients create the illusion of the specular sheen that would be created from a metallic or glassy cylindrical surface. As displayed in Figure 8.5(c), shapeburst gradients produce a beveled effect. Thus, each of these gradients produces an illusion of a 3D surface.

(a)

(b)

Figure 8.4: The Different Gradient Types

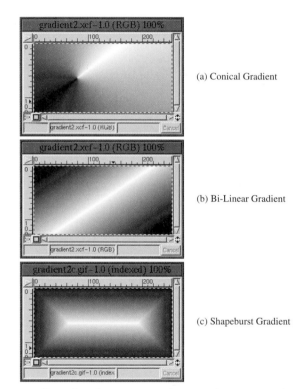

(a) Conical Gradient

(b) Bi-Linear Gradient

(c) Shapeburst Gradient

Figure 8.5: Examples of Conical, Bi-Linear, and Shapeburst Gradients

As an example of using a gradient to render a 3D effect, a beveled look is created for some text using a shapeburst gradient. Figure 8.6(a) displays the text, created using the Baltar font at a height of 175 pixels. This is a thick, blocky type that is perfect for a bevel effect. The Layers dialog, displayed in Figure 8.6(b), shows that the image consists of three layers. There is the white background and a transparent layer, both created before invoking the Text tool, and a floating selection containing the text. The floating selection is created automatically by the Text tool and must be anchored before being able to work on other layers in the image.

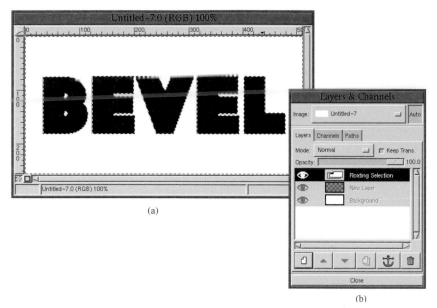

(a)

(b)

Figure 8.6: Creating Text to be Used in Gradient Rendering Example

Before anchoring, however, the text is centered. This is accomplished by typing C-x and then C-v in the image window. This trick cuts and then re-pastes the floating selection, perfectly centered in the window. After the floating selection is anchored into the transparent layer below it, the text is selected using the Alpha to Selection function found in the Layers menu. The selected text can be seen in Figure 8.6(a).

Figure 8.7(a) shows the application of a gradient to the selected text (note that for clarity, the visibility of the Marching Ants has been toggled off). Figure 8.7(b) shows that the Shapeburst (angular) gradient has been chosen, and Figure 8.7(a) displays the resulting beveled effect that this creates with the text.

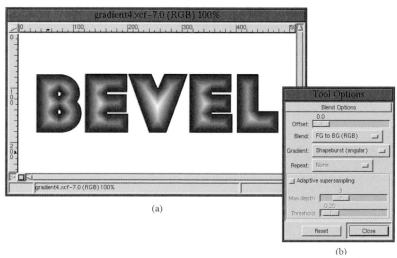

(a)

(b)

Figure 8.7: Rendering a Beveled Look

Normally, gradients are applied to images by clicking and dragging in the image window. The two points defined by where the mouse was clicked and where it was released specify the orientation and the extent of the applied gradient. The curious thing about Shapeburst gradients, however, is that the result does not depend on where the mouse is clicked, nor on where it is released. It just fills the active region with a shapeburst, regardless of how the mouse is used.

The way in which a shapeburst gradient transitions from the foreground to background color can be controlled by the type of shapeburst. As shown in Figure 8.4, there are three different shapeburst types: angular, spherical, and dimpled. Shapeburst (spherical) produces the roundest bevel and Shapeburst (dimpled) the sharpest. Shapeburst (angular) is a compromise between the two.

The result in Figure 8.7 can be made to look a lot jazzier by applying another shapeburst gradient to the Background layer. The result of applying the Shapeburst (spherical) gradient to the Background layer is shown in Figure 8.8(a). The gradient's foreground color is red and the background color is black. Figure 8.8(b) shows the corresponding Layers dialog.

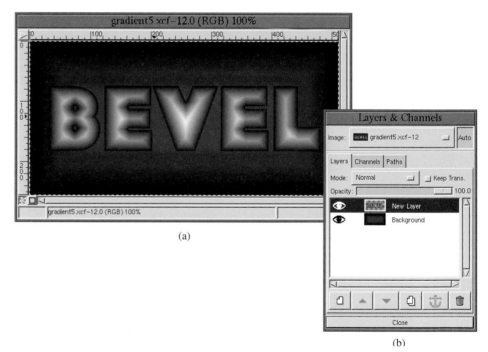

(a)

(b)

Figure 8.8: The Beveled Text on a Rendered Background

8.3 THE EMBOSS AND BUMP MAP FILTERS

There are two filters that are particularly useful for rendering. These are Emboss and Bump map.

The Emboss filter, found in `Image:Filters/Distorts`, creates the effect that an image is embossed into a thin metal plate. Figure 8.9 illustrates the use of the filter for a very simple case. Figure 8.9(a) shows an image that was created using a radial gradient, and Figure 8.9(b) shows the corresponding dialog for the Emboss filter. The dialog consists of a preview, two radio buttons labeled Emboss and Bumpmap, and three sliders called Azimuth, Elevation, and Depth.

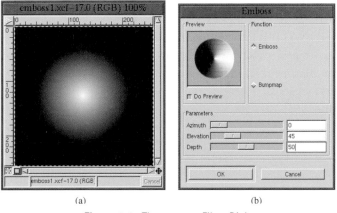

(a)   (b)

Figure 8.9: The Emboss Filter Dialog

The three sliders in the filter dialog control the embossing effect, and Figure 8.10 shows a 3D scene that defines the effect of each one. In the scene there is a pyramid object illuminated by a light source. Two angles, the Azimuth and Elevation, define the position of the light with respect to the pyramid. The Azimuth describes the light source's angular position in the horizontal plane, similar to a compass bearing. The Elevation is the angular measure of the source above the plane.

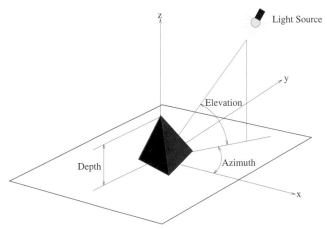

Figure 8.10: Geometric View of the Emboss Filter Options

When the light source is on one side of the object, the other side must be in shadow, as shown in Figure 8.10. When the Elevation is 90°, the light source is positioned vertically over the object, and all faces are equally well illuminated, which eliminates the shadow. There is, however, more reflected light coming from surfaces that are perpendicular to the rays of light than from those that are oblique. Thus, Azimuth and Elevation control the direction of light and shadow.

"Wait a minute! That's fine for a 3D object," you might say. "But we are working with flat images…how does Emboss determine the relative angles for something that, in reality, is completely flat?" I was hoping you would ask. Figure 8.11 shows the radial gradient from Figure 8.9(a) in a 3D context. That is, the image is 2D, but an imaginary light source is positioned over it at some azimuth and elevation. The little red arrows shown in the image plane explain how the filter embosses the image.

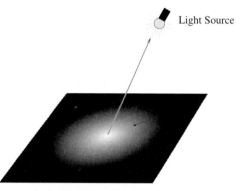
Light Source

Figure 8.11: How Emboss is Applied to a 2D Image: Magnitudes of the Gradient Vectors

The red arrows, called gradient vectors, are computed for each pixel in the image (only three are shown in Figure 8.11). For each pixel, the gradient is drawn in the direction that pixel values decrease the fastest, and the length of the arrow is determined by the amplitude of that change. Thus, in Figure 8.11, there are two arrows each pointing from their pixels in the direction of greatest change, and one is longer than the other because its slope of change is greater. The third arrow is just a dot because it is located in a region where there is no change in pixel value. Its length is zero.

The Emboss filter works by computing the amount each pixel's gradient vector projects along the vector from the pixel to the light source. You can see that the gradient vector labeled *a* in Figure 8.12 has a positive projection onto the vector pointing towards the light source. Alternatively, the gradient vector labeled *b* has a negative projection because it points away from the light source. Finally, the gradient vector labeled *c* has no component along the direction to the light source. Its projection is zero.

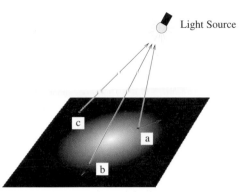

Light Source

Figure 8.12: How Emboss is Applied to a 2D Image: Directions of the Gradient Vectors

Gradient arrows that have a large positive projection in the light source direction are mapped to lighter grays up to the maximum projection, which is mapped to white. Gradient arrows that have negative projections are mapped to darker grays up to the maximum negative projection, which is mapped to black. Pixels whose gradient arrows have no component in the light source direction are mapped to the midtone gray, $127^R127^G127^B$. Exactly how much light or dark is used in the map depends on the third slider control, labeled Depth in the Emboss dialog (see Figures 8.9(b) and 8.10). A Depth value of zero produces no shadow, and a large value produces a deep, well-defined one.

Referring back to Figure 8.9(a), the Azimuth slider is set to zero. This means that the light source is positioned to the right of the image. Furthermore, the Elevation slider is set to 45°, meaning that the left side of the image is in the shadow zone. This agrees with the vector analysis given earlier. The pixels on the left side of Figure 8.9(a) have gradient vectors that point away from the light source, and so these pixels are mapped to darker values. The pixel values on the right side have gradient vectors pointing towards the light source, so their pixels are mapped to lighter values. The result is the embossed image looks like a cone, which can be seen in the image preview area in Figure 8.9(b).

So much for the theory. How about an example? Figure 8.13(a) illustrates the photo of a daisy, and Figure 8.13(c) shows the result of applying the Emboss filter to it. The filter options are shown in Figure 8.13(b). The result is impressive. Figure 8.13(c) shows a version of the daisy that appears to be embossed into a thin sheet of metal.

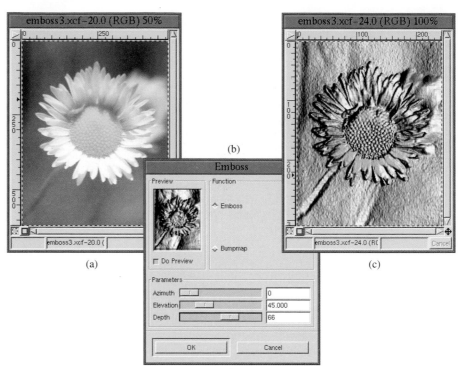

Figure 8.13: Example of Using the Emboss Filter

You should note that, although the result of the Emboss filter is a grayscale, it is still an RGB image. Furthermore, it is important to know that Emboss does not work on images with an Alpha channel. The Alpha channel must be removed by choosing Flatten Image from the Layers menu before the image can be embossed. Flatten Image is described in more detail in Section 2.7.2.

A filter that works in a manner similar to Emboss is Bump map, which is located in the Image:Filters/Map menu. The Bump map filter is more versatile than Emboss, and it is very useful for rendering (see Sections 8.6 and 8.7 for two interesting applications of bumpmapping).

The Bump map filter works by embossing one image and then multiplying the result with another image. This creates the effect of embedding the texture of the first image into the second. The filter's dialog has many options that control the final effect.

Figures 8.14 and 8.15 illustrate an example of using Bump map. Figure 8.14(a) shows a photo from space of Cape Cod in the great state of Massachusetts, and Figure 8.14(b) shows a small image created by filling with a pattern selected from the Pattern Selection dialog. These two images are the raw materials used by Bump map in what follows.

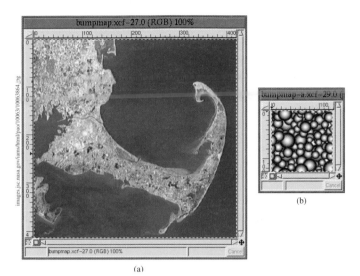

Figure 8.14: Cape Cod from Space and a Pattern Texture

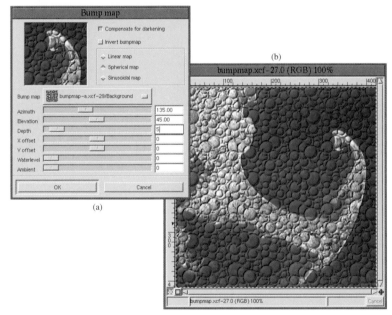

Figure 8.15: Applying the Bump map Filter to Cape Cod

Figure 8.15(a) shows the Bump map dialog, and Figure 8.15(b) shows the result of applying the filter to Figure 8.14(a) using the image in Figure 8.14(b) as the embossing map. As you can see in Figure 8.15(a), the Bump map filter dialog has a few more options than the Emboss filter. The most important is the menu labeled Bump map (not to be confused with the filter name). Clicking on this menu provides a list of all the layers in all open images, and the image layer chosen in this menu is the one that is used as the embossing map. However, unlike the restriction of the Emboss filter, Bump map allows any layer, with or without an Alpha channel, to be used. The Bump map dialog also has all the usual options for embossing: Azimuth, Elevation, and Depth.

`Bump map` also has a number of additional options. There are X Offset and Y Offset, which are useful for positioning the embossing image with respect to the embossed one. There is also the Waterlevel option, which is only useful if the embossing image has an Alpha channel. In this case, the embossing is applied as a function of the alpha and Waterlevel values. Low values of alpha diminish the embossing effect, and high values increase it. This is modulated by the value of Waterlevel. High values of Waterlevel accentuate the Alpha channel effect, and low values proportionally diminish it.

The Ambient option in the `Bump map` dialog controls the relative strength of the directional light source (refer back to Figure 8.10). An ambient light source is one that shines equally from all directions. This is the kind of illumination that is useful in a photography studio, where all shadows on a subject must be eliminated. A strong ambient light source cancels the effect of a directional one. A directional light source creates shadows because it illuminates a scene from a single direction, but the more ambient light there is, the weaker the shadow-making effect of the directional light becomes. Thus, you can use the Ambient option in the `Bump map` dialog to control the relative amount of directional light and, in so doing, control the strength of the shadows.

Multiplying an embossing map with an image produces a result that is darker than either of the first two. This is a natural result of image multiplication (see the description of the `Multiply` blending mode in Section 5.6). The Compensate for Darkening checkbox reduces this effect. The Invert Bumpmap checkbox simply inverts the relationship of shadow and light in the embossing map.

Finally, there are three radio buttons that control the multiplication process. These are labeled Linear Map, Spherical Map, and Sinusoidal Map. The Linear Map option does a straight multiply of the embossing map with the image. The Sinusoidal and Spherical Map options, however, act somewhat like the `Curves` tool (see Section 6.2.1). That is, the effect of the embossing map is warped according to a curve. The sinusoidal curve provides more contrast to the midtone embossing values and the spherical curve more to the shadow and highlight values. This may sound a little complicated, but it isn't. Just play around with them, and you'll see right away what they do.

8.4 SHADOWS

A shadow is just a dark silhouette of an object, but with a somewhat fuzzy edge to account for the diffraction of the illuminating light source. Furthermore, depending on the location of the source of light, a shadow is somewhat displaced with respect to the object. You can construct very convincing shadows in the GIMP. These are surprisingly useful rendering tools in image manipulation, and this section explains how to make them.

To make a shadow for an image object you must have a selection of it. The following describes the steps needed to create the selected region's shadow:

1. Cut the selected region by typing C-x in the image window. This places the selection into the default buffer.

2. Create a new transparent layer by clicking on the New Layer button in the Layers dialog and choosing the Transparent option.

3. Paste the contents of the default buffer by typing C-v in the image window. This places the paste into a floating selection. Anchor the float to the new layer by clicking on the Anchor button in the Layers dialog.

4. Duplicate the new layer by clicking on the Duplicate Layer button in the Layers dialog. The duplicated layer is placed above the original layer in the layer stack.

5. Name the duplicated layer Object and the original layer Shadow.

6. Make the Shadow layer active by clicking on its thumbnail in the Layers dialog, toggle on the Keep Trans. checkbox in the Layers dialog, and use the Bucket Fill tool with its Threshold set to 255 to fill the image object with black or some other appropriate, dark color.

7. Toggle off the Keep Trans. checkbox in the Layers dialog, use Gaussian Blur (IIR) found in the Image:Filters/Blur menu to blur the Shadow layer, and use Offset from the Image:Image/Transforms menu to shift it.

8. Use the Opacity slider in the Layers dialog to give the shadow an appropriate degree of transparency.

This procedure is often referred to as making a drop shadow.

An example of creating a drop shadow is now presented using the preceding recipe. Figure 8.16(a) illustrates a photo of a daisy. Using techniques from Chapters 3 and 4 a selection of the daisy is made and, as shown in Figure 8.16(b), this is used to cut away the daisy's background. (Note: the cut produces a transparent background only if the original image layer has an Alpha channel. For more on Alpha channels see Section 4.2.1.) The Layers dialog in Figure 8.16(c) shows that the Daisy layer has been duplicated and that the lower layer has been labeled Daisy Silhouette.

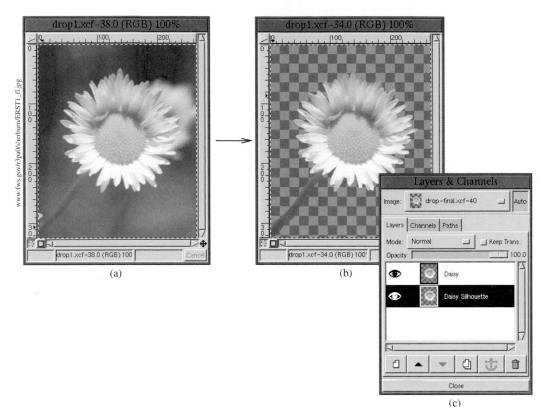

Figure 8.16: A Daisy Selection

The remaining steps in the creation of the shadow are now easy. The Daisy Silhouette layer is filled with black using the `Bucket Fill` tool (don't forget to set Threshold to 255 in the `Bucket Fill` dialog). The blurring can be performed with any of the blur functions from the `Image:Filters/Blur` menu (but make sure that the Keep Trans. button in the Layers dialog is toggled off before applying one). Here, `Gaussian Blur (IIR)` is used with a radius of 20.* This is followed by using `Offset`, which can be applied by typing C-S-o in the image window. The offset parameters are set to 15 for both the X and Y components, and the Wrap-Around radio button is toggled off. The result is shown in Figure 8.17(a). Figure 8.17(b) and (c) show the dialogs for the `Gaussian Blur` `(IIR)` and `Offset` filters used in this example.

---

* Gaussian Blur (IIR) and Gaussian Blur (RLE) produce exactly the same results. However, Gaussian Blur (RLE) runs faster on images that have broad, constant-valued pixel regions because it exploits a compression technique known as *run length encoding*. For photographs of real world scenes, Gaussian Blur (RLE) provides no advantage and might even run slower than Gaussian Blur (IIR).

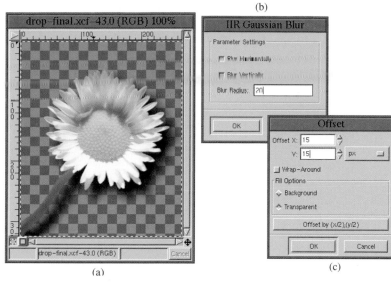

Figure 8.17: Filling, Blurring, and Offsetting Creates the Shadow

All that remains is to place the flower and shadow over an appropriate background. This could be anything: a solid color, an image pattern, or a photograph. Figure 8.18(a) illustrates the daisy on a light blue background. The Layers dialog in Figure 8.18(b) shows the placement of the blue layer at the bottom of the image stack. This layer was created by clicking on the New Layer button in the Layers dialog, positioning it to the bottom of the layer stack, and using the Bucket Fill tool to give it the desired color.

Figure 8.18: The Final Drop Shadow

By the way, the shadow produced using this technique can be made to look more diffuse by making it more transparent. Simply make the shadow layer active in the Layers dialog and set the desired value of transparency using the Opacity slider.

A technique very similar to making drop shadows is that of making punchouts. A drop shadow creates the illusion of an image object floating above a background. The punchout is also a shadow technique but gives the illusion that part of the background has been cut away, casting a shadow on yet another background behind. This is the effect you would see by holding a stencil slightly in front of a wall. The light shining through the stencil casts a shadow that can be seen through the stencil's hole against the wall.

Just like drop shadows, to make a punchout for an image object you must have a selection of it. The procedure for making a punchout is similar to that for making a drop shadow, but with a couple of twists. To make a punchout in the shape of a selected image region follow these steps:

1. Set the default colors by typing d in the image window.
2. Create a new layer by clicking on the New Layer button in the Layers dialog, and select Foreground as the Layer Fill Type in the New Layer Options dialog. This fills the new layer with black.
3. Make sure that the new layer is active in the Layers dialog, and fill the selected region with white using the Bucket Fill tool. Label this layer Shadow.
4. Cancel the selection by typing C-S-a in the image window, and create a layer mask for the Shadow layer by choosing Add Layer Mask from the Layers menu.
5. Make the Shadow layer active by clicking on its thumbnail in the Layers dialog, and copy it to the default buffer by typing C-c in the image window.
6. Make the layer mask of the Shadow layer active by clicking on the layer mask's thumbnail in the Layers dialog, paste the default buffer's contents by typing C-v in the image window, and anchor the resulting float to the layer mask by typing C-h in the image window.
7. Make the Shadow layer active, blur it with Gaussian Blur (IIR), and shift it with Offset.

This creates the punchout effect.

An example of making a punchout is now presented. The example deviates slightly from the steps described in the preceding list. Figure 8.19 shows an impressive flash of lightning across a deep purple sky. You can just imagine the powerful clap of thunder that's coming. But in case you can't, we're going to drive the message home by punching it out of the photo.

Figure 8.19: Lightning Strike!

We begin by setting the default colors by typing d and then switching the background and foreground colors by typing x in the image window. A new layer is created by opening the Layers dialog and clicking on the New Layer button. The Background radio button is selected from the New Layer Options dialog. This sets the new layer to black. For this example the new layer is labeled Inverse Text.

The Text tool is now invoked by clicking on its icon in the Toolbox and then clicking in the image window. This brings up the Text tool dialog shown in Figure 8.20(c). The Brushstroke font has been chosen with a height of 100 pixels, and, because the goal of choosing this font is to get a rough punchout effect, the Antialiasing option has been turned off, as shown in the Text tool's Tool Options dialog (Figure 8.20(d)). Clicking on the OK button in the Text tool dialog places the text into a floating selection. Because the Active Foreground Color is white, so is the newly created text.

Cutting the floating selection with C-x and then pasting it back with C-v centers the text before it is anchored into the layer below by clicking on the Anchor button in the Layers dialog. This makes a layer with white text on a black background. Figure 8.20(a) shows the image window, and Figure 8.20(b) shows the corresponding Layers dialog at this stage in the example.

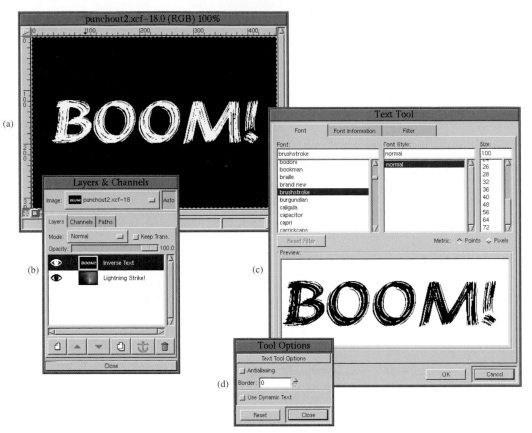

Figure 8.20: Placing Some Text

The procedure is almost complete. If we were making a drop shadow, the new layer would be blurred and offset. However, for the punchout, we first copy the Inverse Text layer into its own layer mask. This is done in the following steps:

1. Make the Inverse Text layer active by clicking on its thumbnail in the Layers dialog.
2. Copy the Inverse Text image contents to the default buffer by typing c-c in the image window.
3. Create a layer mask by choosing Add Layer Mask from the Layers menu.
4. Paste the default buffer contents by typing c-v in the image window.
5. Anchor the resulting floating selection to the layer mask by clicking on the Anchor button in the Layers dialog.

The result is shown in Figure 8.21(a). Figure 8.21(b) shows the corresponding Layers dialog.

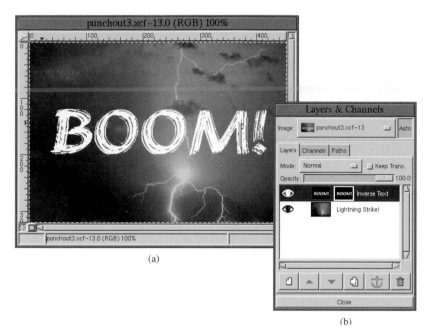

Figure 8.21: Creating the Layer Mask

The final step is to blur and offset the text in the Inverse Text layer. To do this, the Inverse Text layer is made active by clicking on its thumbnail in the Layers dialog. This layer is then blurred using the `Gaussian Blur (IIR)` filter with a radius of 8, and shifted using `Offset` with values of 4 for both X and Y. The result is shown in Figure 8.22(a). The blurred and offset inverted text now appears as a shadow seen through a stencil punched out of the photo. Figures 8.22(b) and (c) show the dialogs for the `Gaussian Blur (IIR)` and `Offset` filters used in this example.

Figure 8.22: The Final Punchout

8.5 RENDERING PROJECT I: DROP SHADOW AND PUNCHOUT

To illustrate some of the techniques discussed in this chapter, let's apply them to a project using the image shown in Figure 8.23(a). The astronaut in this image is selected from its background using various methods from Chapters 3 and 4. After the selection, methods described in Section 6.1 are used to improve the tonal range, and the result is shown in Figure 8.23(b).

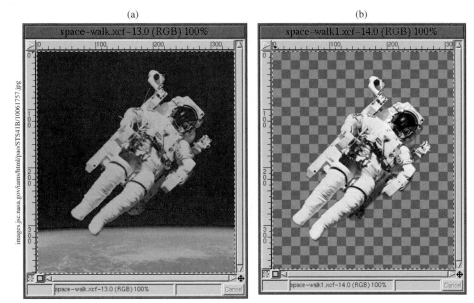

Figure 8.23: Original Image and Color Corrected Selection of Astronaut

This project uses a drop shadow and a punchout to create a composition with our astronaut. The goal is to create the effect that he has extracted himself from the 2D plane and is wandering off on his own. To start, the selected astronaut is placed over a blue-gray layer. The result of this is shown in Figure 8.24(a), and the associated Layers dialog is shown in Figure 8.24(b).

The most important element of the project is the outline of the astronaut because this is used to create both the shadow and the punchout effects. Thus, the next step is to save the outline as a channel mask. This is done by making the Astronaut layer active, applying the `Alpha to Selection` function found in the `Layers` menu, and then using `Save to Channel` from the `Image:Select` menu. This creates the channel mask shown in Figure 8.24(c). After the save-to-channel operation, it is important to cancel the selection by typing `C-S-a` in the image window.

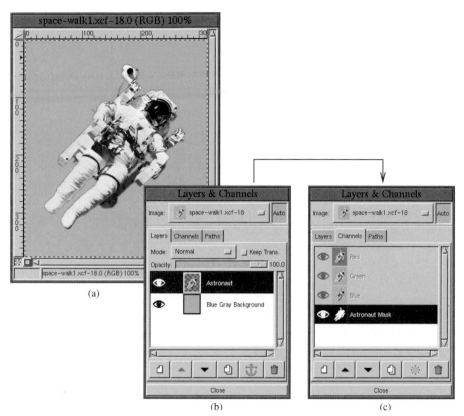

(a)

(b)   (c)

Figure 8.24: Making a Gray-Blue Background Layer and Creating a Channel Mask from the Astronaut's Alpha Channel

The punchout is made first. This is begun by copying the astronaut mask and pasting it into a new layer. This new layer, labeled Punchout, is positioned between the Blue Gray Background layer and the Astronaut layer as shown in Figure 8.25(a). To create the punchout, this new layer is copied into its own layer mask as shown in Figure 8.25(b).

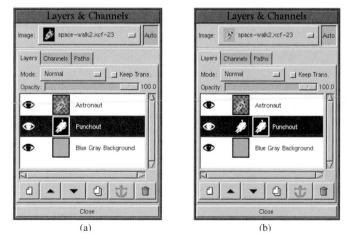

(a)   (b)

Figure 8.25: Starting the Punchout

All that remains to finish the punchout effect is to blur the image in the Punchout layer and to offset it. Figure 8.26(a) shows that a value of 20 is chosen in the Gaussian Blur (IIR) dialog, and Figure 8.26(b) shows that values of 8 and 4 have been chosen in the Offset dialog. The result is shown in Figure 8.26(c). Note that, for the punchout to be seen in Figure 8.26(c), the visibility of the Astronaut layer has been toggled off, as shown in Figure 8.26(d).

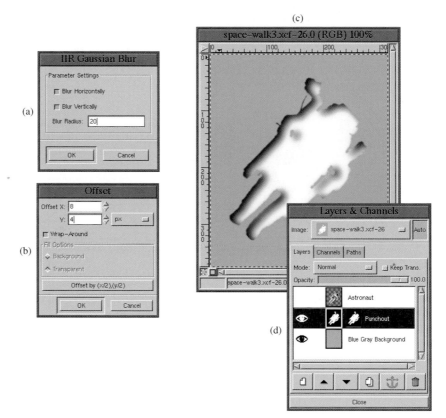

Figure 8.26: Finishing the Punchout

Before moving to the next stage of the project, let's give the punchout a bit more pizzazz by inserting an interesting image pattern. To do this, the Punchout layer is duplicated by first clicking on its thumbnail in the Layers dialog, and then clicking on the Duplicate Layer button. This creates a layer called Punchout Copy just above the original. The image part of the Punchout layer is made active by clicking on its thumbnail. This layer is now filled with the pink marble pattern from the Pattern Selection dialog (see Figure 8.27(c)). This is done using the Bucket Fill tool, where the fill type is set to Pattern Fill and the Threshold is set to 255. Finally, the Mode menu for the Punchout Copy layer is set to Multiply, as shown in Figure 8.27(b). This produces the result shown in Figure 8.27(a), which makes it appear as if the wall behind the Background layer is made of pink marble.

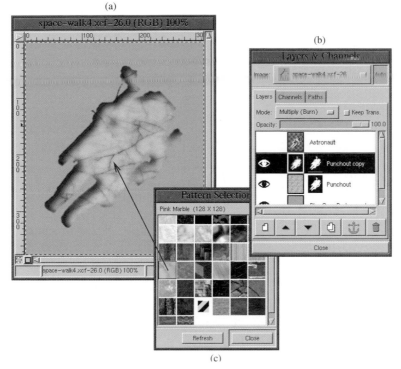

(a)

Figure 8.27: Jazzing Up the Punchout with a Pattern Image Background

The final step of this project is to rotate the astronaut, reposition him, and give him a drop shadow. To do this, he is first made visible by clicking on the Eye icon of the Astronaut layer in the Layers dialog. The rest is detailed in the following steps:

1. Rotate the astronaut using the Transform tool.
2. Move the astronaut to a new position using the Move tool.
3. Duplicate the Astronaut layer, creating a layer labeled Astronaut Copy.
4. Set the threshold of the Bucket Fill tool to 255 and use it to fill the Astronaut layer with black.
5. Blur the Astronaut layer with Gaussian Blur (IIR).
6. Offset the Astronaut layer an appropriate amount.

The final result is shown in Figure 8.28(a). The resulting Layers dialog is shown in Figure 8.28(b).

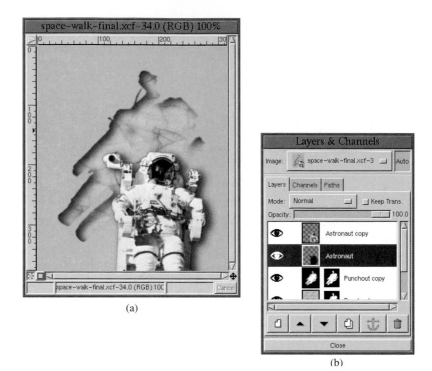

(a)

(b)

Figure 8.28: The Final Rendered Image

8.6 RENDERING PROJECT II: A CARVED STENCIL

This project describes a rendering effect that looks like carving into wood. It makes use of bumpmapping and shadows.

The technique creates the carved effect using two layers. Figure 8.29(a) shows the first layer, a bit-mapped image of a boat. Figure 8.29(b) shows the second layer, a background inserted under the bitmap and filled, using the `Bucket Fill` tool, with a wood pattern from the `Pattern Selection` dialog. The visibility of the boat layer has been toggled off so the pattern can be seen. Figure 8.29(c) illustrates the disposition of the two layers in the Layers dialog.

The first step in creating the carved effect is to obtain a selection of the boat's outline. Since the bitmap of the boat consists of only two colors, black and white, this is most easily done with the `By Color` selection tool found in the `Image:Select` menu (see Section 3.3.11). The resulting selection is used to create an inset for the carved effect.

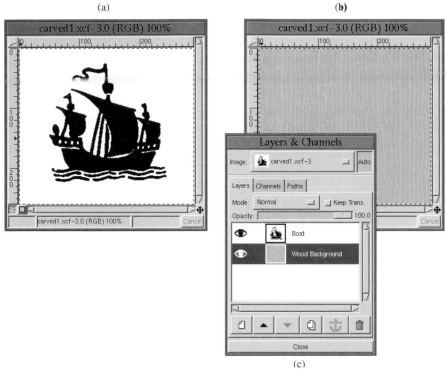

(a) (b)

(c)

Figure 8.29: The Two Layers Used to Create the Carved Rendering Effect

What is an inset? It is just the Wood Background layer darkened slightly within the perimeter of the boat selection. This helps create the illusion that this part of the image is recessed, or inset, into the wood. Figure 8.30(a) shows the Marching Ants of the selection. The selection is seen floating over the Wood Background layer because the Eye icon in the Boat layer has been toggled off as shown in Figure 8.30(b). Notice that the color of the wood seems a little darker inside the selection. This darkening was created by sliding the middle Input Slider control of the Levels tool slightly to the right in the Value channel. After this step, the selection is canceled by typing C-S-a in the image window.

The next step is to apply the Bump map filter to the Wood Background layer using the bitmap of the Boat layer as the embossing map. Before doing this, the bitmap of the boat is blurred slightly because it improves the effect of the bumpmapping. Figure 8.31(a) shows the result of applying Gaussian Blur (IIR) with a radius of 3 pixels to the bitmap of the Boat layer, and Figure 8.31(b) shows the Bump map dialog. As already stated, the bitmap of the Boat layer has been chosen as the embossing map. The other Bump map filter parameters are as shown in Figure 8.31(b). Note that the Compensate for darkening checkbox has been toggled on. The result of the Bump map filter is shown in Figure 8.31(c).

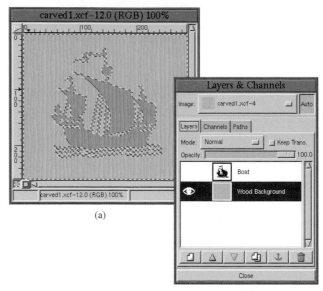

(a)

(b)

Figure 8.30: Creating an Inset

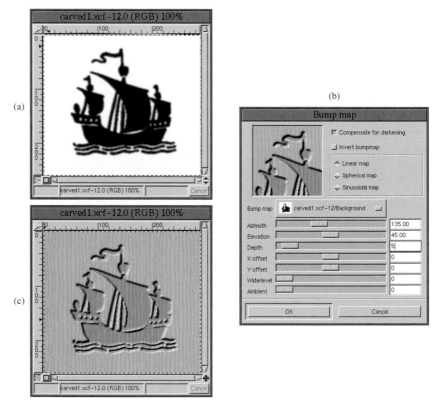

(a)

(b)

(c)

Figure 8.31: Creating the Carved Effect Using `Bump map`

At this point, the result shown in Figure 8.31(c) already looks carved. However, the effect can be accentuated by making clever use of a punchout. The idea is that the perimeter of the carving should cast a punchout–like shadow onto the inset. To achieve the effect, the colors of the Boat layer need to be inverted, the layer must be copied into its own layer mask, and the layer must be blurred and offset. The following list summarizes these steps:

1. Invert the colors of the Boat layer using `Invert` from the `Image:Image/Colors` menu.

2. Copy the Boat layer to the default buffer by typing `C-c` in the image window.

3. Create a layer mask for the Boat layer.

4. Paste the contents of the default buffer by typing `C-v` in the image window.

5. Anchor the resulting floating selection into the layer mask by clicking on the `Anchor` button in the Layers dialog.

6. Make the Boat layer active by clicking on its thumbnail in the Layers dialog.

7. Blur and offset the Boat layer using `Gaussian Blur (IIR)` with a radius of 5, and `Offset` the layer by 5 in X and Y.

These steps produce the image shown in Figure 8.32(a). Figure 8.32(b) shows the associated Layers dialog.

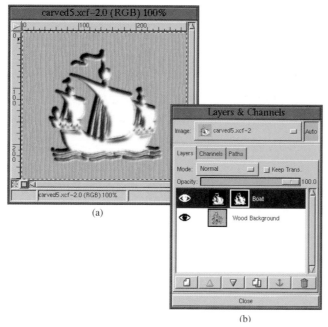

Figure 8.32: Making the Punchout Effect

Notice that the creation of the punchout has turned the inset white. To recover the dark colored wood of the inset the Boat layer is made active and the `Multiply` mode is selected from the `Mode` menu in the Layers dialog. As a final finesse, the shadow from the punchout is made a bit more diffuse by setting the Opacity slider, in the Layers dialog, to 65%. The final carved result is shown in Figure 8.33(a). Figure 8.33(b) shows the associated Layers dialog.

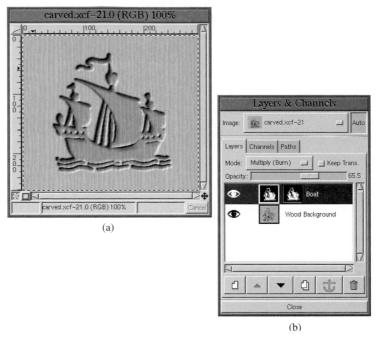

(a)

(b)

Figure 8.33: Using the Multiply Mode and the Opacity Slider to Obtain the Final Carved Effect

8.7 RENDERING PROJECT III: CHISELED TEXT

This project describes a nice rendering effect that creates the illusion of chiseling into stone. The example is illustrated using text, however, it can be applied to any shape. The chiseling effect is created using gradients, bumpmapping, and shadows—basically all the rendering tools discussed in this chapter.

The finished project will consist of three layers. The background layer will contain an image pattern, in this case pink marble. The top layer will contain text filled with the same image pattern and bumpmapped to make it look chiseled. The middle layer will be a drop shadow for the text.

To begin, a new image of dimensions 600×100 pixels is created. It is then filled, using the Bucket Fill tool, with the pink marble pattern from the Pattern Selection dialog. This layer is labeled Marble Background in the Layers dialog and is shown in Figure 8.34(a). The next step is to create some black text on a transparent layer above the Marble Background layer.

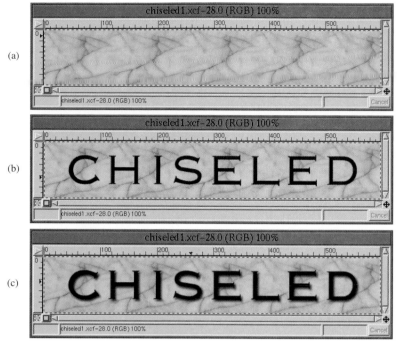

Figure 8.34: Creating the Background, Text, and Drop Shadow for the Chiseled Effect

The transparent layer is made by clicking on the New Layer button in the Layers dialog, and the text is created by first selecting black as the `Active Foreground Color`, and then invoking the `Text` tool. The `Text` tool is used to place the word CHISELED, in the Engraver font at a size of 72 pixels, into a floating selection. Cutting and repasting the float perfectly centers the text in the image window. It is then anchored to the transparent layer beneath it by clicking on the `Anchor` button in the Layers dialog. This layer is labeled Text in the Layers dialog, and the resulting image is illustrated in Figure 8.34(b).

The drop shadow is created by duplicating the Text layer, blurring it with `Gaussian Blur (IIR)` using a radius of 5 pixels, and then applying `Offset` with the values of 3 pixels for both the X and Y directions. This layer is then positioned between the Text and Marble Background layers using the positioning buttons in the Layers dialog button bar. This layer is labeled Text Shadow in the Layers dialog. The result is shown in Figure 8.34(c).

The next step is to fill the text in the Text layer with a shapeburst gradient. For this, the layer is made active by clicking on its thumbnail in the Layers dialog, and the text is selected using the `Alpha to Selection` function from the `Layers` menu. Setting the `Active Foreground Color` and the `Active Background Color` to white and black, respectively, the `Gradient` tool is used to fill the text with a `Shapeburst (angular)` gradient. The selection is then canceled by typing `C-S-a` in the image window, and the result is shown in Figure 8.35(a). The associated Layers dialog is shown in Figure 8.35(b).

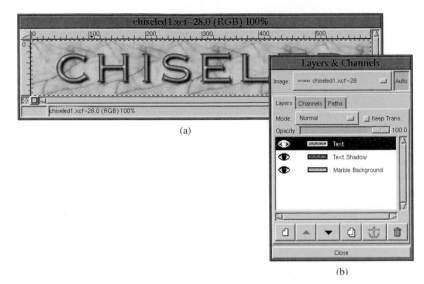

(a)

(b)

Figure 8.35: Using the Shapeburst Gradient on the Text Layer

The project is now almost complete. What remains is the application of the shapeburst filled text as an embossing map to the marble background layer. This is done, of course, using Bump map. The Marble Background layer is made active by clicking on its thumbnail in the Layers dialog and the Bump map filter is invoked. The filter dialog illustrated in Figure 8.36(b) shows the parameters used and Figure 8.36(a) shows the resulting effect on the Marble Background layer. Note that the visibility of the Text and Text Shadow layers has been toggled off so the chiseled text can be seen in the figure.

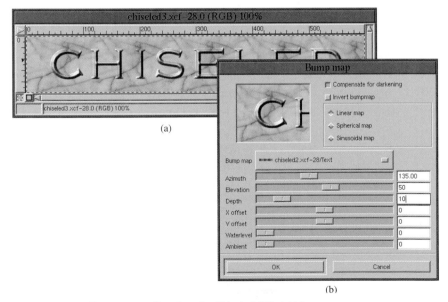

(a)

(b)

Figure 8.36: Creating the Chiseled Effect Using Bump map

All that remains to complete this project is to move the chiseled text to the top layer of the stack. This is done in the following steps:

1. Make the Text layer active by clicking on its thumbnail in the Layers dialog.

2. Select the text using the `Alpha to Selection` function from the `Layers` menu.

3. Make the Marble Background layer active by clicking on its thumbnail in the Layers dialog, and copy the chiseled text into a buffer by typing `c-c` in the image window. Due to the selection obtained in step 2, only the chiseled text is copied to the buffer.

4. Cancel the selection by typing `c-s-a` in the image window.

5. Make the Text layer active by clicking on its thumbnail in the Layers dialog, and paste the buffer contents to a floating selection by typing `c-v` in the image window.

6. Anchor the float to the Text layer by clicking on the `Anchor` button in the Layers dialog.

The result is shown in Figure 8.37(a), and the Layers dialog is shown in Figure 8.37(b).

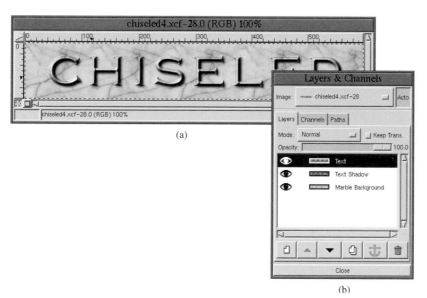

Figure 8.37: Copying and Pasting the Chiseled Text to the Top Layer

As a final flourish, the chiseled text is lightened somewhat to make it more prominent against the marble background. This is done by making the Text layer active and, as shown in Figure 8.38(b), by adjusting the middle control of the input slider of the Levels tool dialog. Figure 8.38(b) shows the resulting settings in the Levels dialog, and Figure 8.38(a) shows the final effect.

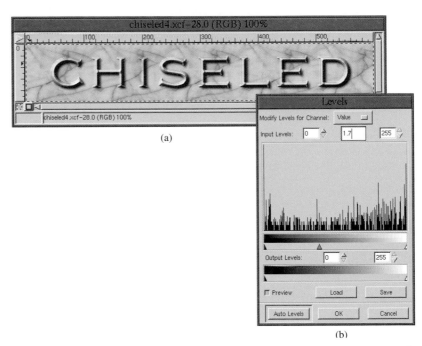

(a)

(b)

Figure 8.38: Lightening the Text with the Levels Tool to Produce the Final Chiseled Effect

9

WEB-CENTRIC GIMP

The GIMP has many powerful tools for creating interesting and useful graphic components for Web pages. In this chapter, you will learn how the GIMP can be used to create animated GIFs, clickable image maps, fancy type styles, and tileable backgrounds, all of which are important features for dynamic, exciting Web pages. The chapter finishes with a discussion on how to best prepare color images to be viewed on the Web using a standard Web browser.

9.1 WEB ANIMATIONS

A graphic tool often seen on Web pages is the ubiquitous, animated GIF. This is an image file format that can contain a sequence of frames combining text, images, and timing information to create a flip-book-like movie. As you will see in this chapter animated GIFs are easy to create, edit, and view in the GIMP.

9.1.1 USING GIF FILES FOR ANIMATION

The GIMP can save animations to several different file formats, but when making animations for the Web, the choice is limited to GIFs. GIF stands for Graphics Interchange Format, and GIF format files support a number of features that are particularly useful for Web graphics.

First, GIF is an 8-bit-per-pixel format, which means that with careful planning a GIF can be almost always properly displayed on systems providing only 8 bits of color (see Section 9.5). Second, GIFs allow for transparency, a feature not supported by JPEG (Joint Photographic Experts Group), the other principle file format for images on the Web. Third, GIFs support

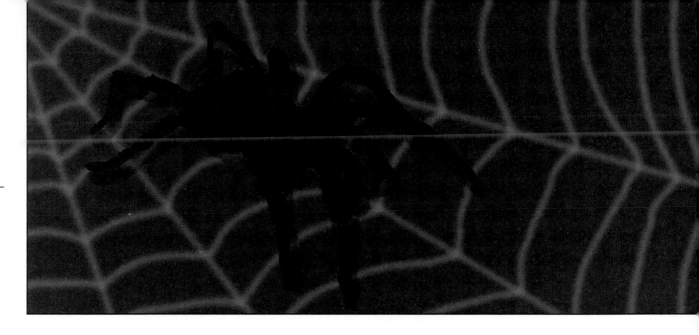

interlacing which may be of interest for the transmission of images over low bandwidth networks. Finally, the GIF format supports layers and attached layer timing information. This last feature is the one exploited for GIF animations.

9.1.2 GIMP Layers Can Behave Like Animation Frames

Animations are sequences of images that can be played according to timing information attached to each frame. The GIMP has built-in support for animations because each layer in an image can be treated as an animation frame by the GIMP. The GIMP supports this equivalence by allowing timing information to be attached to layers, by providing a tool for playing layered images as animations, and by supporting the conversion of layered images to Indexed format and output as GIF files.

Figure 9.1 illustrates some of the GIMP's built in animation features. Figure 9.1(a) shows an image that consists of five layers. The organization of the layers is seen in the Layers dialog shown in Figure 9.1(b). This image is constructed by creating an image with a white background, and then adding four new layers, each one containing, in sequence, one of the four letters G, I, M, and P. The letters were colored using the `Bucket Fill` tool.

Notice that each layer is named and that the names contain timing information used for the frame animation. The timing information is indicated by the text in the format (*XXXX*ms), where *XXXX* is a 1 to 4 digit number, and ms indicates that the units of the number are in milliseconds. The parentheses are a required part of the format. Thus, for this example, the Background layer appears empty for 1 second (1000ms) followed by the four letters appearing at intervals of 100ms, 400ms, 600ms, and 800ms. Name and timing information is added to each layer by double-clicking the layer title area to the right of the thumbnail as described in Section 2.1.1.

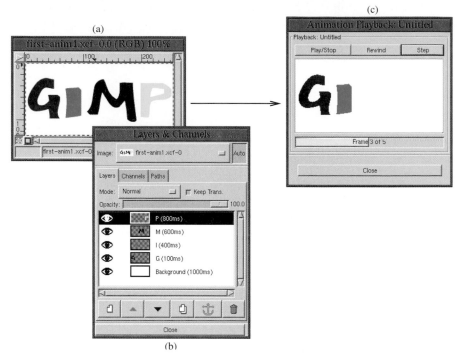

Figure 9.1: Example of Some GIMP Animation Features

The animation in Figure 9.1(a) can be viewed in the GIMP using the `Animation Playback` tool found in the `Image:Filters/Animation` menu. As you can see in Figure 9.1(c), the tool consists of a Play/Stop button, a Step button, which allows the animation to be stepped along a frame at a time, and a Rewind button, which can be used to set the animation back to the first frame. This last button is particularly useful if the animation consists of a very large number of frames. The `Animation Playback` tool plays the animation associated to the image using the timing information as specified in the name of each layer. Note that there is also a progress bar that shows the animation's current frame number.

By default, GIMP animations sequentially present frames using the Combine mode. This means that as each new frame is displayed, it is stacked on the previous one. Thus, if a new frame is partially transparent the previous frame can be seen through its transparent parts. This is not the traditional movie paradigm for animation, which, instead of combining frames, replaces each frame with a new one. Consequently, although the frames in Figure 9.1 all consist of single letters on a transparent field, the animation spells out the word GIMP a letter at a time on the white background of the first layer.

Figure 9.2 illustrates the same example as in Figure 9.1, except now each layer uses Replace mode instead of Combine mode in the animation sequence. The Layers dialog in Figure 9.2(b) shows that the Replace mode is specified by typing the text (replace) in the title field of each layer. The `Animation Playback` tool shown in Figure 9.2(c) shows the animation at the same point in the sequence as before. However, now, due to Replace mode being used, the white background and the red letter G are not visible. There is only the green letter I on a transparent background. This is the traditional movie paradigm for animation.

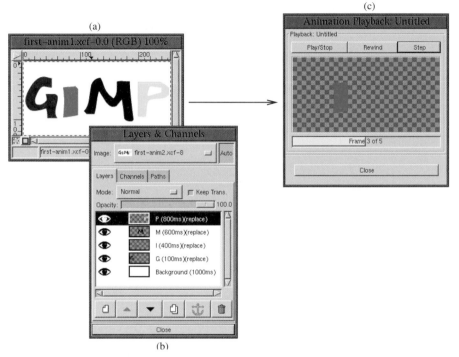

Figure 9.2: Example of Replace Mode

The explicit use of Combine mode can be made by typing the text (combine) instead of (replace) in a layer title. The two modes can be used together in an animation with some frames replacing and others combining.

9.1.3 SAVING ANIMATIONS TO GIF

The GIMP allows animations to be made in RGB and Grayscale formats, but an animation must be converted to Indexed format before it can be saved as a GIF. Trying to save to GIF without being in Indexed format generates an Export File dialog message that provides the user with information and options to correctly save the image.

Properly converting an image to Indexed format is accomplished with the function Indexed found in the Image:Image/Mode menu. This brings up the Indexed Color Conversion dialog shown in Figure 9.3(b). This dialog has two main option areas. The first covers the Palette options and the second covers the Dither options. The default options usually work fine, but if a particular conversion to Indexed format has problems, refer to Section 9.5, which discusses Web-safe color palettes and covers these dialog options in detail.

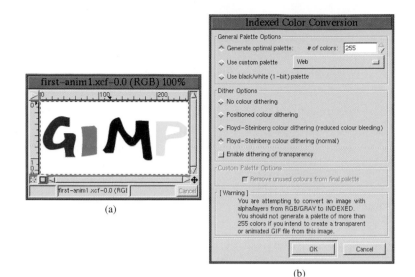

(a)

(b)

Figure 9.3: Converting to Indexed

After an image has been converted to Indexed, it can be saved in GIF format. This is accomplished by choosing `Image:File/Save As` which brings up the `Save Image` dialog shown in Figure 9.4(a). The GIMP automatically saves the file in GIF format if the name entered into the entry box at the bottom of the dialog ends with the `.gif` extension. Alternatively, GIF can be selected from the `Save Options` menu. This automatically attaches the `.gif` extension to whatever name has been typed into the entry box.

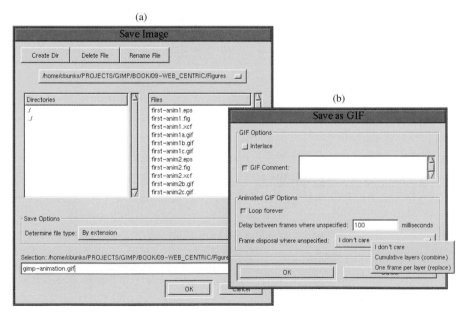

Figure 9.4: Saving an Animation as a GIF File

Clicking the OK button in the `Save Image` dialog brings up the `Save as GIF` options dialog shown in Figure 9.4(b). Because the image to be saved is multi-layered, the Animated GIF Options are available. These are not enabled for single layer images. The first option specifies whether the animation will loop continuously or not. Looping is the default. The next option is an entry box that specifies the time per frame for frames that have not been explicitly specified. The default is 100ms. For the examples in Figures 9.1 and 9.2, the timing information is given for each layer, so this option is irrelevant for these layers. Finally, the animation mode, either Replace or Combine, can be selected for all frames that have not been explicitly specified. The I Don't Care option defaults to Combine mode.

9.1.4 A SECOND EXAMPLE OF CREATING A GIF ANIMATION

The compositing techniques discussed in Chapter 7 provide you with many tools for creating animated GIFs. In this section, an example of creating an animation illustrates how you can use some simple techniques to generate sophisticated animations.

The animation scenario has the space shuttle flying from an earth orbit to a distant landing on the planet's surface. The animation is created by compositing the four separate images shown in Figure 9.5 on the background image shown in Figure 9.6.

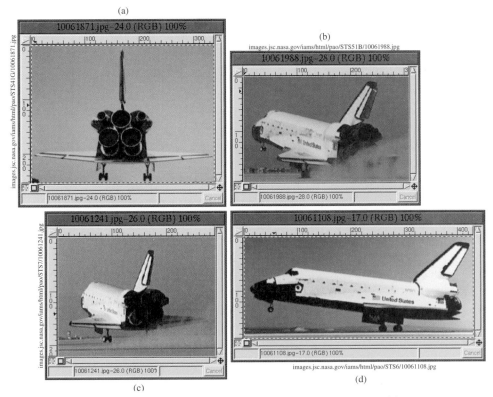

Figure 9.5: Clockwise from the Top Left, Four Views of the Space Shuttle: (a) Rear, (b) 2/3 Profile, (c) 1/3 Profile, and (d) Full Profile

Figure 9.6: Image to Be Used as Background to Shuttle Landing

The first step is to prepare the images in Figures 9.5 and 9.6. The image in Figure 9.6 is cropped to the desired size, and each of the shuttle images in Figure 9.5 are selected from their backgrounds and placed into individual layers of a single image, as shown in Figure 9.7. Placing the shuttle images into a single clip book is a technique also used in Section 7.1, and it is a convenient tool for organizing, using, and re-using a collection of images that are to be composited together.

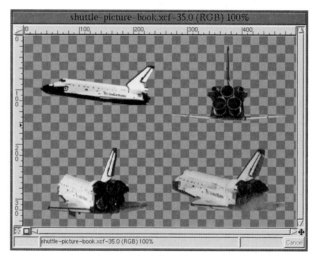

Figure 9.7: Preparation of the Raw Shuttle Images and Creation of the Shuttle Image Clip Book

The next step composites the shuttle images from Figure 9.7 into the cropped background image from Figure 9.6. The goal is to do this in a way that makes the shuttle look as if it is flying on a trajectory from its orbit in space to a landing point on the surface of the earth. The approach is to show the shuttle at various aspects while it distances itself from the viewer.

The primary tools used to achieve the desired result are the Transform tool and the Move tool. Figure 9.8 shows how the shuttle images from Figure 9.7 are composited onto the background image. Each of the seven shuttle images is obtained by copying and pasting from the shuttle picture clip book. Each shuttle image is scaled to the appropriate size using the Transform tool and positioned with the Move tool. In some cases, the Transform tool is also used to rotate the shuttle. These operations are repeated until the desired composition is achieved. Because each shuttle image is on a separate layer, I was able to fine-tune the positioning and scaling operations to my satisfaction.

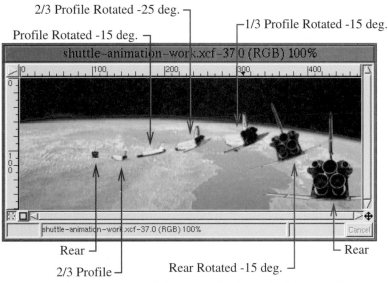

Figure 9.8: Sequence of Shuttle Layers Used to Make the Animation Sequence

To give the shuttle landing a final special effect, an additional layer showing a reflected glint of light is created. This is intended to represent the shuttle entering the earth's atmosphere. The effect is created by duplicating the background layer of the earth and running the SuperNova filter found in the Image:Filters/Light Effects menu. The dialog for this filter is shown in Figure 9.9(b). The dialog allows the choice of color for the SuperNova effect, which is set by entering numeric values for the red, green, and blue components. The values shown in Figure 9.9(b) produce a white flash with a radius of 5 pixels and 20 spokes, or rays. The filter allows the position of the effect to be interactively chosen, which is done by clicking and dragging the cross hairs in the image thumbnail to the desired location. Alternatively, you can enter the position numerically in the X and Y entry boxes. The result of using the filter is shown in Figure 9.9(a).

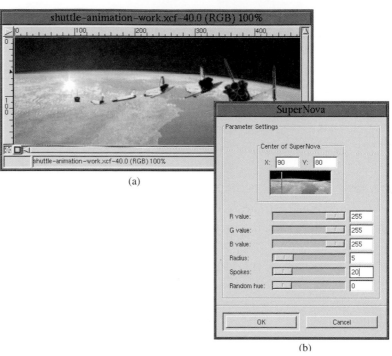

Figure 9.9: Adding the SuperNova Light Effect

The animation is now almost complete. One more step is necessary before it can be saved as a GIF file. The current state of the animation consists of the background, a duplicate background with the SuperNova effect, and seven transparent layers with various shuttle images. This is shown in Figure 9.10(a).

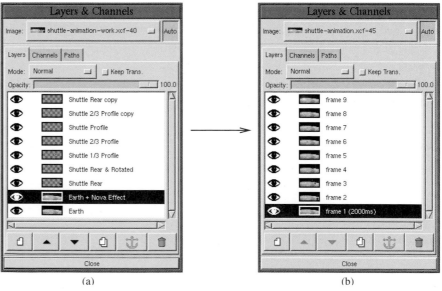

Figure 9.10: Merging Each Shuttle Frame with a Background

The problem with Figure 9.10(a) is that neither the Replace nor Combine modes will create the desired animation with the layer frames as shown. In Replace mode, the animation would show a frame of the earth, then a frame with the earth showing the SuperNova effect, and then seven frames, each empty except for the shuttle. Alternatively, the animation obtained by using the Combine mode would show the earth, then a SuperNova effect on the earth, followed by a sequence of shuttles that appear one at a time but that only disappear at the end of the animation sequence. Neither of these is what we want.

To produce an animation that runs correctly, it is necessary to give each layer frame a copy of the Earth layer. This is done by duplicating the Earth layer seven times and then merging each copy with a shuttle frame. Section 2.7.1 describes how to do this using the Merge Down function. The result of merging the seven background layers with the seven shuttle frames is shown in the Layers dialog illustrated in Figure 9.10(b). Also shown, the layer with the SuperNova effect has been moved to the top of the layer stack (the final animation frame), and the timing information of the layer at the bottom of the stack (the first animation frame) has been set to 2000ms. Thus, the final animation sequence remains in the bottom layer for 2 seconds, followed by a sequence of 8 frames showing the shuttle's trajectory into the atmosphere, and, finally, showing the top frame, which displays the burst of light from the SuperNova effect.

9.1.5 ANIMATION OPTIMIZATION

Saving an animation to GIF format can create large files, especially if the animation has many frames. For example, the space shuttle animation discussed in the previous section consists of an image whose dimensions are 476 × 182 pixels and has 9 frames. This is an image consisting of 780 thousand pixels. Due to compression built into the GIF image format, this saves to a 389 kilobyte file. However, the file size can still be significantly reduced by taking advantage of the high degree of redundancy in the image.

The redundancy is due to this animation changing very little from frame to frame. In fact, the background is always the same, and only the position and shape of the shuttle is changing. The function Animation Optimize in the Image:Filters/Animation menu takes advantage of this and can greatly reduce the size of the resulting file. It does this by differencing frames and only saving the non-zero values. The original animation is reconstructed by adding the differenced frames back into the background.

For the space shuttle animation, the file is reduced from 389 to 163 kilobytes if the Animation Optimize option is applied after conversion to Indexed format. If it is applied to the image in RGB mode, before conversion to Indexed format, an additional savings is realized and the resulting file only occupies 106 kilobytes on the disk. This improvement might not be general, and for projects where file size is important (as it is for low bandwidth network connections), it is advisable to experiment with the two methods.

9.1.6   IWarp

The `IWarp` filter, found in the `Image:Filters/Distorts` menu, can interactively warp parts of an image and then automatically generate an animation that morphs from the original image to the warped one. This can be useful for creating certain types of animations.

Figure 9.11(a) illustrates an image of Canadian geese, and Figure 9.11(b) shows the dialog for the `IWarp` filter. The dialog opens in the Settings tab, which offers a number of options. The Deform Radius and Deform Amount sliders control the size and intensity of the warping effect, and the type of warping is selected using one of the Move, Remove, Grow, Shrink, Swirl CCW, or Swirl CW radio buttons. The warping is applied by clicking and dragging in the thumbnail of the image. The selected warping mode is applied in the region around the mouse cursor; the size of the region of application is specified by the Radius slider. In this example, the Move warping function is applied, and the mouse is clicked in the middle of the head of the central goose. Dragging the mouse vertically upwards creates the distortion shown in the dialog's thumbnail in Figure 9.11(b).

(a)

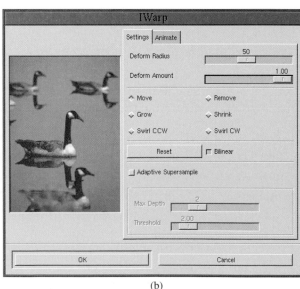

(b)

Figure 9.11: The IWarp Filter

To automatically convert the distortion into an animation, click on the Animate tab in the dialog. The dialog corresponding to this tab is shown in Figure 9.12. The animation is created by clicking the Animate checkbox and then using the slider to choose the number of frames to use. This creates a sequence that morphs from the original image to the distorted one. If the Reverse radio button is clicked, the animation goes from the distorted image to the original. If the Ping Pong radio button is chosen, the animation starts with the original image, animates to the distorted, and then returns to the original. This last option generates twice the number of frames selected by the Number of Frames slider. Choosing the Ping Pong animation option for the example with the Canadian goose produces an animation where the goose stretches its neck up, perhaps to get a better look around, before returning to its original state.

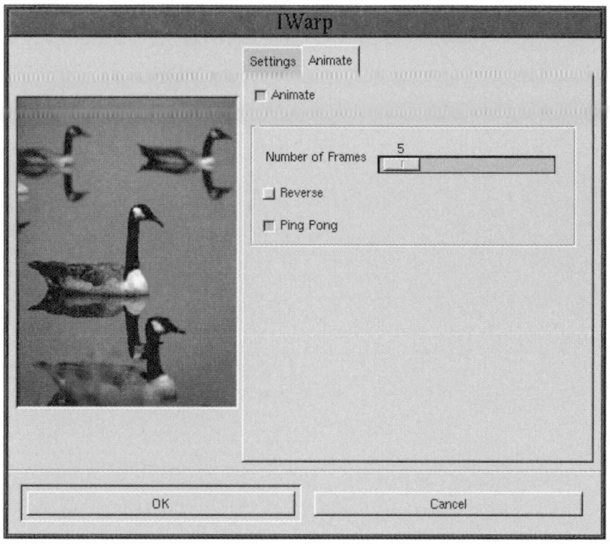

Figure 9.12: Using the IWarp Automated Animation Feature

9.2   CLICKABLE IMAGE MAPS

A common graphical device on the Web is the clickable image map. A clickable image map is a graphic that has multiple hyperlinks, and, perhaps, Java scripts, associated to a single image. Such an image allows the Web designer to associate links and dynamic actions to graphical cues.

As an example, one use of a clickable image map might be for a travel agency offering vacation packages to different exotic locations around the world. A clickable image map of the world could be constructed to contain hyperlinks cued to the location of a mouse click on the map. For example, clicking on France might send the user to another Web page giving details of vacation packages, sites to see, places to stay, and restaurants to try when visiting Paris. Clicking on Venezuela would send the user to pages on Caracas, and so on.

Clickable image maps are very useful devices for the Web because they represent an alternate, graphical means of navigating to other pages. One problem, however, is that they can be difficult to construct. For each hyperlink, a region of the image must be defined that activates the link when the mouse is clicked in it. This region is defined by a polygon, which in turn is specified by a set of pairs of coordinates giving the locations of the polygon's vertices. The difficulty comes from trying to determine the coordinate values. For an image map containing many hyperlinks associated to complicated regions, the task of assembling these points can be quite arduous.

Fortunately, the `ImageMap` plug-in, found in the `Image:Filters/Web` menu, allows you to graphically input the vertices of polygonal regions by drawing directly on the image. The plug-in also allows you to easily assign hyperlinks and Java scripts to the regions. When finished, the plug-in automatically writes the HTML file that displays the newly created image map. All the positional information about vertices for the map regions is written into this file along with the hyperlinks and references to the Java scripts associated with the regions.

The initial description of how the `ImageMap` plug-in works is based on the blank image shown in Figure 9.13(a). A blank image is not terribly useful as a practical image map but is great for illustrating how the `ImageMap` plug-in works. Figure 9.13(b) illustrates the `ImageMap` dialog, which consists of three main areas. There is the Drawing Canvas, where the image that the map is being created for is shown. Because the image in Figure 9.13(a) is blank, the canvas area shows a white background. To the left of the Drawing Canvas, is the toolbar containing the selection and editing function icons. These are used to draw the outlines of regions in the image that will become the clickable zones. Finally, there is the Region List, which is located to the right of the Drawing Canvas area. This is used to organize and edit the list of drawn regions.

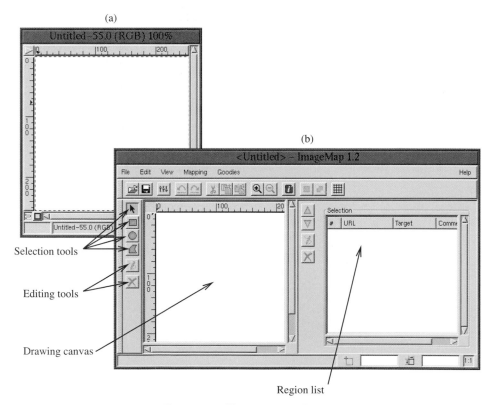

Figure 9.13: The `ImageMap` Plug-in

The `ImageMap` selection tools are used to define the clickable regions. The selection tool choices are rectangular, circular, and polygonal. Of the three, the polygon tool is the most general because it allows for the most complex shapes to be selected. Figure 9.14(a) illustrates an irregular shape made with the polygon selection tool. The shape is made by clicking on the polygon selection tool button and then by clicking on points in the Drawing Canvas area. Each point becomes a new vertex of the polygon. The selection is terminated, and the polygon fully defined when the left mouse button is double-clicked.

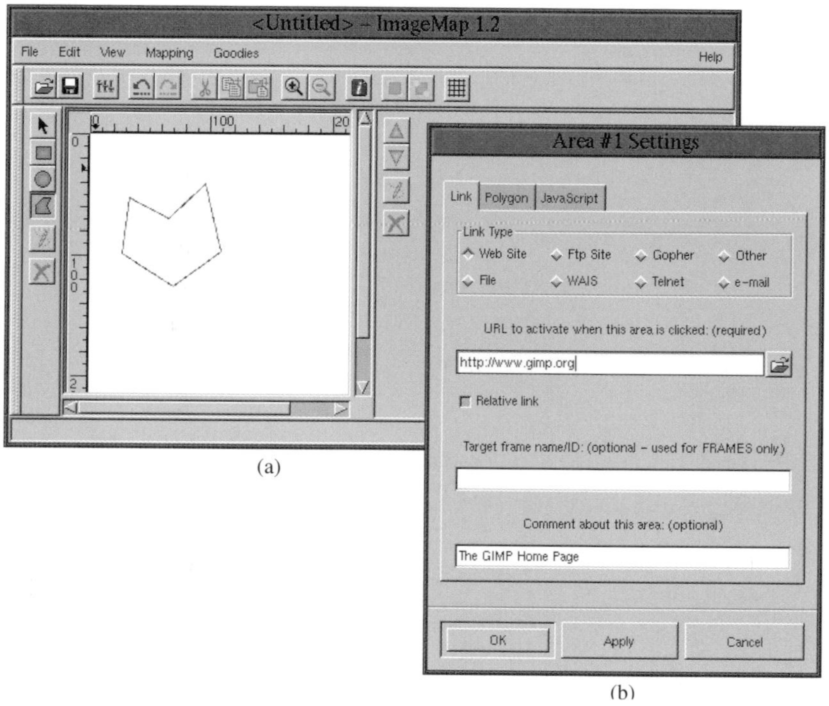

Figure 9.14: Selecting a Polygon Region

As soon as an area like the polygon in Figure 9.14(a) has been defined, the `Settings` dialog appears as shown in Figure 9.14(b). This is used to specify the hyperlink associated to the selected area. As you can see from the dialog, any valid Web link can be specified. In this example, the text `http://www.gimp.org` has been entered as the link. In addition, informational text has been added to the Comment field at the bottom of the dialog. The `Settings` dialog allows the polygon to be edited and Java scripts to be associated with the selected area. These functionalities are accessed by clicking on the relevant tabs shown in the dialog.

Figure 9.15(a) shows the `ImageMap` dialog after several areas have been selected. The three areas are each shown in the Region List, and the active one is high-lighted in blue. The editing tools can be used to modify any of the areas in the Region List. You can make a particular area active by clicking on it, you can delete the active area by clicking on the button displaying the red, X icon, and you can bring up the area's Settings dialog by clicking on the button showing the pencil icon.

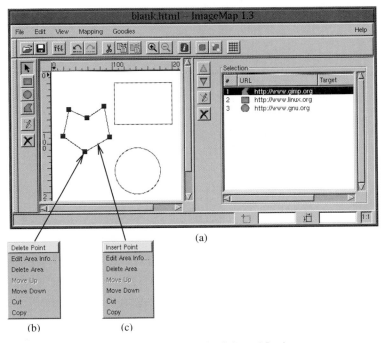

Figure 9.15: Managing the Selected Regions

As seen in Figure 9.15(a), the points of the active region are displayed as red squares. It is possible to insert, delete, or move these points. Choosing the Arrow icon from the selection tools, any point can be moved by clicking and dragging it. A point can be deleted by right-clicking it, which brings up the menu shown in Figure 9.15(b). A point can be added to a line segment by right-clicking it, which brings up the menu shown in Figure 9.15(c).

After all the desired areas have been selected and hyperlinks defined, you can save the work by clicking on the floppy disk icon or selecting the Save As function from the File menu. This brings up a dialog that allows a file name to be entered. This should be a file whose extension ends in .html or .htm.

A more realistic example of the ImageMap plug-in's use is illustrated with the image shown in Figure 9.16(a). This image is a map of the southeastern United States. Each of the ten states is designated by its two-letter abbreviation: FL for Florida, GA for Georgia, AL for Alabama, and so on. The goal is to create an image map having a separate hyperlink for each state. Figure 9.16(b) shows the ImageMap dialog with the image from Figure 9.16(a) loaded into the Drawing Canvas area. The outline of each state can easily be made using the polygon selection tool. When all the states have been delineated, and when the final result is saved it produces the following file:

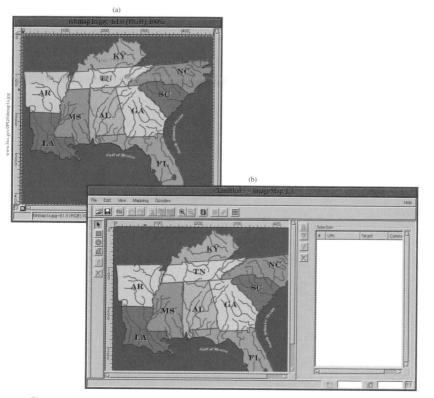

Figure 9.16: Map of the Southeast United States and the `ImageMap` Dialog

```
<IMG
SRC="/home/cbunks/PROJECTS/GIMP/BOOK/08-WEB_CENTRIC/Figures/southeast-usa.gif"
WIDTH=482 HEIGHT=428 BORDER=0 USEMAP="#">

<MAP NAME="">
<!-- #$-:Image Map file created by GIMP Imagemap Plugin -->
<!-- #$-:GIMP Imagemap Plugin by Maurits Rijk -->
<!-- #$-:Please do not edit lines starting with "#$" -->
<!-- #$VERSION:1.1 -->
<!-- #$AUTHOR:Carey Bunks -->

<AREA SHAPE="POLY" COORDS="6,91,10,178,21,183,21,195,98,195,113,144,128,
107,113,104,120,92" HREF="http://www.good-travel.com/arkansas.html">

<AREA SHAPE="POLY" COORDS="21,197,21,234,32,252,22,291,49,292,69,299,75,
295,101,312,117,307,131,308,150,312,142,298,120,281,138,276,130,255,83,253,
100,197" HREF="http://www.good-travel.com/louisiana.html">

<AREA SHAPE="POLY" COORDS="119,136,172,135,174,276,140,277,132,255,85,253"
HREF="http://www.good-travel.com/missouri.html">

<AREA SHAPE="POLY" COORDS="119,136,269,127,288,106,334,74,168,83,170,88,
136,93" HREF="http://www.good-travel.com/tennessee">

<AREA SHAPE="POLY" COORDS="139,91,170,90,170,81,285,75,319,43,295,28,293,12,
274,18,251,4,243,4,243,12,232,18,218,39,209,33,186,48,171,46,157,65,145,68"
HREF="http://www.good-travel.com/kentucky.html">

<AREA SHAPE="POLY" COORDS="173,272,200,271,190,248,261,247,261,208,235,130,
170,133" HREF="http://www.good-travel.com/alabama.html">
```

```
<AREA SHAPE="POLY" COORDS="237,132,263,213,266,254,342,255,342,245,357,247,
367,207,305,139,292,135,296,126" HREF="http://www.good-travel.com/georgia.html">

<AREA SHAPE="POLY" COORDS="300,127,296,133,365,205,420,146,388,120,357,122,351,
113,317,117" HREF="http://www.good-travel.com/south-carolina.html">

<AREA SHAPE="POLY" COORDS="333,74,270,124,304,124,314,117,354,112,360,120,386,
120,423,145,433,145,440,127,465,111,459,97,479,78,468,60"
HREF="http://www.good-travel.com/north-carolina.html">

<AREA SHAPE="POLY" COORDS="195,253,198,271,227,271,257,288,284,275,318,303,
328,303,329,345,347,365,360,395,388,416,404,410,408,367,385,317,355,249,342,
248,342,259,335,259,335,255,266,256,259,249"
HREF="http://www.good-travel.com/florida.html">

</MAP>
```

As you can see, each of the areas defined in the ImageMap dialog is specified by an AREA hypertext markup tag. This tag contains the coordinates of the polygon region and the text of the associated hyperlink.

HTML files created with ImageMap can be reloaded and edited by the plug-in. Normally, this is done by reloading the original image into the GIMP, running the ImageMap plug-in on the image, and then loading the saved imagemap file using the Open command from the plug-in's File menu. Figure 9.17 shows the result of doing this with the HTML file created for Figure 9.16. However, instead of running the ImageMap plug-in on the original map image, it is done on a blank image having the same dimensions as the map. This allows you to clearly see the loaded imagemap regions against the white background. Doing this has no practical application, but it is a nice way of illustrating the results of the example. Note that the Region List area shows that each of the 10 states has an entry. Clicking on an entry in this list highlights the region in the Drawing Canvas, as is illustrated for the state of Alabama in Figure 9.17.

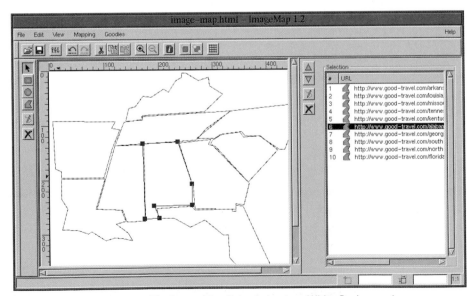

Figure 9.17: The Image Map Reloaded onto a White Background

As a final note, with a Web browser, you can open the HTML file created by `ImageMap` to verify that it is working correctly. If necessary, you can edit the HTML file directly with a text editor. Figure 9.18 shows how the clickable image map for the preceding example displays in the Netscape Navigator Web browser. Notice that the mouse cursor, represented by the small left-pointing hand, is located at the lower tip of the state of Florida. The fact that the mouse cursor appears as a hand means that it is over an active HTML link, and at the bottom of the browser window you can see the associated hyperlink in the link information field.

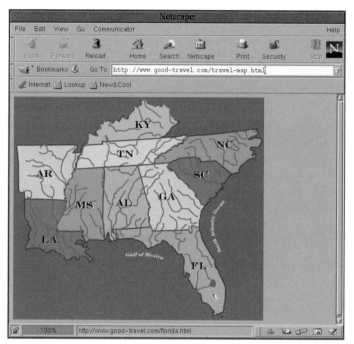

Figure 9.18: Map of the Southeast United States Seen in Netscape

The `ImageMap` plug-in has many other features. This book is not the appropriate place to cover this plug-in in detail. However, most of the features are not difficult to discover, and you should be able to determine their use with a little experimentation.

9.3 TYPE EFFECTS

Type effects can give a Web page character. They are a great way to make Web page logos and titles, and they introduce stylistic elements that say something about the content of your page. The GIMP can produce great type effects, and the best news is that many effects have been automated with scripts, using a scripting language called Script-Fu.

Figure 9.19 shows that the scripts for creating type effects are contained in the `Toolbox:Xtns/Script-Fu/Logos` menu. There are 27 different effects in the `Logos` menu. This section presents one of them.

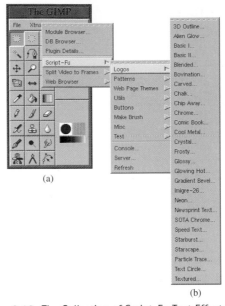

(a)

(b)

Figure 9.19: The Collection of Script-Fu Text Effect Scripts

Figure 9.20(a) shows the dialog for the `3D Outline` script. In this dialog, you can specify the text to be rendered, the font and size (in pixels) of the text, and an image pattern that is used to create the 3D outline. The dialog contains defaults for each of these. For this example, the text string default is The Gimp.

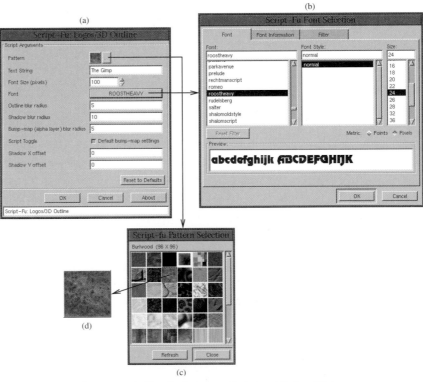

Figure 9.20: The `3D Outline` Script and Helper Dialogs

Figure 9.20 shows how the defaults can be changed. For example, the default font used in this example is Rootsheavy but other fonts can be chosen using the Text tool. As shown in Figure 9.20(b) the Text tool can be invoked directly from the 3D Outline dialog by clicking on the Font menu button. The image pattern can also be changed interactively by clicking on the Pattern menu button (the button with the three dots). This brings up the Pattern Selection dialog shown in Figure 9.20(c). The small image squares in the dialog are thumbnails of each available pattern. To get a larger view of a pattern, use the mouse to click and hold on the pattern of interest. This displays a larger thumbnail of the pattern, as shown in Figure 9.20(d).

The result of running the 3D Outline script is shown in Figure 9.21. Note that caution is required when using the Script-Fu scripts to generate text effects. Typically, text effects are constructed of multiple layers, many with layer masks (for example, see Section 8.7). Before using a result obtained using the auto-mated logo scripts, it is usually necessary to flatten the image before saving it to a JPEG or GIF file format. This can be done by choosing Flatten Image from the Layers menu.

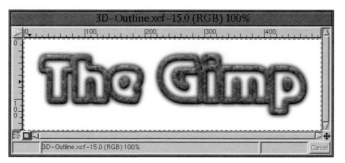

Figure 9.21: Result of Running the 3D Outline Script-Fu Script

9.4 TILEABLE BACKGROUNDS

Most Web browsers can use a small image to construct a tiled background for Web pages. Normally the background image should be subtle enough to avoid interfering with text and other graphics, and this usually means that the image should be seamlessly tileable. Seamless means that you should not be able to see the edges between adjacent copies of the image.

Any image can be made to tile seamlessly in the GIMP. The Make Seamless plug-in found in the Image:Filters/Map menu does the trick. Figure 9.22 illus-trates the use of this plug-in. Figure 9.22(a) shows a small image of a fish, and Figure 9.22(b) shows the result of using the Make Seamless plug-in on it. The effect of tiling with the modified image can be tested by running the Tile plug-in (the Tile plug-in is also found in the Image:Filters/Map menu). The Tile plug-in tiles an image horizontally and vertically a specified numbers of times. The result of using `Tile` on the image in Figure 9.22(b) is shown in Figure 9.22(c). The image is displayed as a 2 × 2 tiled array with some white text placed over it. The text was made using the Beta Dance font at a size of 150 pixels.

(a)   (b)

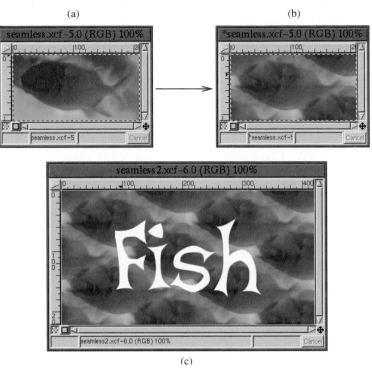

(c)

Figure 9.22   Using the Plug-in Make Seamless

9.5   WEB-SAFE COLOR

A problem with the exchange of images on the Internet is that not all computers have the capability of displaying a large number of colors simultaneously. For example, a computer using a display resolution of 1024 × 768 and using 1 byte (8 bits) of color per pixel requires at least 0.786MB of RAM on the video adapter card. Such a system is capable of displaying only $2^8 = 256$ colors simultaneously.

Alternatively, a system that is using 2 bytes (16 bits) per pixel can display $2^{16} = 65,536$ colors, and 3 bytes (24 bits) per pixel can display $2^{24} = 16,777,216$ colors. Thus, the available color palette grows significantly on a 16 bits-per-pixel (bpp) system. A 24 bpp system is known as a true or high color system. However, the demands on the video adapter for these systems also grows. A 16 bpp system on a 1024 × 768 pixel display requires about 1.6MB of video RAM and a 24 bpp system requires 2.4MB.

Many video adapter cards have only 1MB or less of RAM. Although this is less and less common with current computers being delivered with up to 32MB of video RAM, there are still many legacy machines that have smaller quantities. The consequence is that an image containing more than 256 colors cannot be faithfully displayed on machines with only an 8 bpp color depth. Some of the original colors in the image will have to be replaced because of the lack of a sufficient number of available colors on the displaying system. This replacement creates color distortion in the displayed image.

The GIMP uses 24 bits per pixel to represent color, 8 bits for each of the R, G, and B channels. Thus, the GIMP can easily generate images that have color distortion when displayed on low color systems. This is a concern for the Web designer who wants to ensure an accurate representation of color for his or her graphics. This section discusses the issues of preparing Web-safe color graphics and how to achieve this in the GIMP.

9.5.1 TYPES OF COLOR DISTORTION

Color distortion occurs when the monitor is already displaying all the colors it can, and a request for a new color is made. The least sophisticated way of handling this request is by color clipping. This approach displays new colors using the closest color from the palette already being displayed. For images with subtle color shading, this can give rise to banding, which is also called posterization. An example of this type of color distortion is shown in Figure 9.23. Figure 9.23(a) shows the original image and Figure 9.23(b) the same image on a system with insufficient colors. You can plainly see the banding of colors in this image.

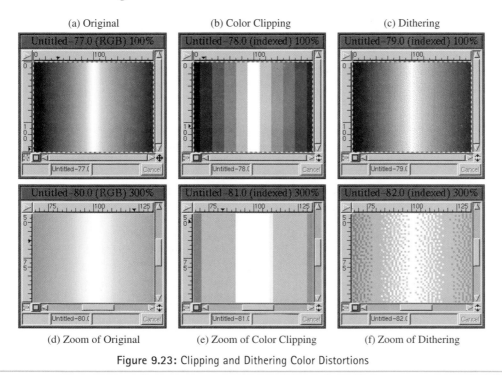

Figure 9.23: Clipping and Dithering Color Distortions

The other type of color distortion is called dithering. Although dithering is a color distortion, this is not a bug, it's a feature! Dithering is a technique used to simulate unavailable colors by spatially mixing the available ones as a mesh of small dots. The idea is that color dithering is more visually acceptable than color banding. Figure 9.23(c) illustrates the effect of dithering. Figure 9.23(f) shows a zoomed version of Figure 9.23(c) so that you can see the mix of small dots used to simulate unavailable colors. Compare this zoomed image with the zooms of the original and color clipped images shown in Figure 9.23(d) and (e), respectively.

Figure 9.23 shows that dithering is a much more sophisticated approach to the problem of color distortion than is banding. For continuous gradients of color, the rule seems to be that the dithering approach is superior. However, there are caveats to this rule. To see why, you need to understand how dithering works. A simple illustration is shown in Figure 9.24, where a crude dithering scheme is employed using the `Checkerboard` plug-in (found in `Image:Filters/Render/Pattern` menu). The `Checkerboard` dialog is shown in Figure 9.24(b). This plug-in creates a checkerboard pattern in the active layer using the colors specified by the `Active Foreground Color` and the `Active Background Color`. Figure 9.24(a) shows that these colors have been set to red and green.

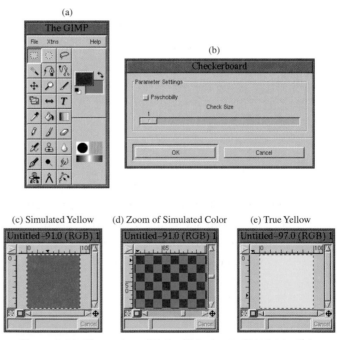

Figure 9.24: Illustration of Using Dithering to Simulate a Color

Figure 9.24(b) shows that a 1-pixel check size is being used by the `Checkerboard` plug-in. The result is a simulated dither of the color yellow, as you can see in Figure 9.24(c). That the resulting dithered color is yellow follows from the discussions of the RGB colorspace in Section 5.1. The vector sum of red and green in the RGB cube yields yellow.

A zoomed version of Figure 9.24(c) is shown in Figure 9.24(d). This plainly shows the red and green checks. For comparison purposes, a pure yellow is shown in Figure 9.24(e). The example shown in Figure 9.24 is exaggerated because it is never necessary to dither two colors as distant from each other in the color cube as are red and green. However, it nicely illustrates how dithering works.

The dithering algorithms used in the GIMP are far more sophisticated than that illustrated in our checkerboard example. In the GIMP, several dithering algorithms are available including the Floyd-Steinberg algorithm. The main feature of Floyd-Steinberg dithering is that it uses a pseudo-random spatial distribution of up to three colors to simulate an unavailable color. Figure 9.23(f) clearly shows the pseudo-random nature of Floyd-Steinberg dithering. In many cases, it is this pseudo-random aspect of Floyd-Steinberg dithering that improves the overall perception of a dithered color image…but not always. See Section 9.5.4 for more on this subject.

9.5.2   LOW-COLOR SYSTEMS AND WEB BROWSER COLOR PALETTES

A low color system provides only 8 bits of color per pixel, which allows only 256 colors to be simultaneously displayed. When used on low-color systems, Web browsers must choose how to represent unavailable colors. Browsers such as Netscape Navigator and Internet Explorer use color palette systems that are similar but not identical. The colors that these two browsers have in common are known as the Web-safe color palette.[12] Any designer that is concerned with avoiding color distortion must be aware of this special palette and how to use it.

The Web-safe color palette consists of combinations of the six values 0, 51, 102, 153, 204, 255 in each of the three colors red, green, and blue. Thus, using notation introduced in Section 5.1, $51^R204^G153^B$ is a color from the Web-safe color palette, and $52^R204^G153^B$ is not. The total number of colors in the palette is $6^3=216$. The reason six values are used is because seven would create too many colors for a low-color system (that is, $7^3=343$). What happens to the remaining 40 colors available on a low color system? They are used for system specific colors, and these uses differ for Mac and PC and for Netscape Navigator and Internet Explorer. The bottom line is you can't rely on them.

If you are using the GIMP's drawing and painting tools to create graphics from scratch and you desire the result to be Web-safe, it would be useful to have a palette of the 216 Web-safe colors to work with. You could use this palette to select the colors for your graphics, knowing that the result will be the same on most all systems, low color or not. The GIMP has a variety of pre-defined color palettes available in the `Color Palette` dialog found in the `Image:Dialogs/Palette` menu or obtained by typing `C-p` in the image or Toolbox windows.

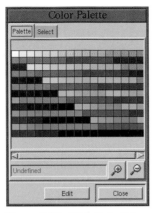

Figure 9.25: Web-Safe Color Palette

Of interest is the GIMP's Web color palette shown in Figure 9.25. The Web palette illustrates the 216 Web-safe colors that can be used on low color systems without fear of color distortion. However, because the colors are disorganized in this palette, it is of limited use as a tool for creative design. A palette that organizes colors by hue, saturation, and value would be much more useful.

The VisiBone palettes at `http://www.visibone.com/swatches` are just such tools. The VisiBone2 palette is illustrated in Figure 9.26. The VisiBone2 palette has exactly the same Web-safe colors as the GIMP's Web palette, but the advantage is that its colors are organized into a logical color wheel. It is much easier to pick out colors of common hue, saturation, and value with the VisiBone2 palette than it is for the Web palette.

9.5.3 CONVERTING TO INDEXED COLOR

For display on 8-bit (low-color) systems, the best way to control the color in an image is to convert it to Indexed format. Figure 9.27(a) illustrates the `Indexed Color Conversion` dialog which is invoked by the `Indexed` function found in the `Image:Image/Mode` menu.

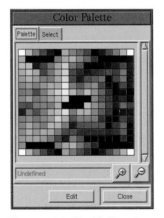

Figure 9.26: The VisiBone2 Web-Safe Color Palette

The dialog allows the choice of three types of palettes. The first option, Generate Optimal Palette, is based on the colors actually in the image. The number of colors used in this palette can be specified up to a maximum of 256.

The second option, Use Custom Palette, allows you to select from a large collection of palettes including user-defined ones. The names of the GIMP's standard palettes are shown in Figure 9.27(b) and (c). The default custom palette, Web, is optimized for display on low-color systems using browsers such as Netscape Navigator or Internet Explorer. This consists of the 216 color, Web-safe color palette illustrated in Figure 9.25. Choosing this option guarantees that the resulting indexed image will display with the same colors on almost all systems.

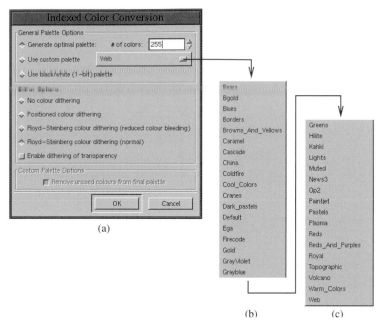

Figure 9.27: The Indexed Color Conversion Dialog

The final palette option choice, shown in Figure 9.27, is the Use Black/White (1-bit) Palette. This option converts the image to a true black and white (no grays) Indexed format.

The second area in the `Indexed Color Conversion` dialog is for dithering options. The following are the choices:

- No colour dithering
- Positioned colour dithering
- Floyd-Steinberg colour dithering (reduced colour bleeding)
- Floyd-Steinberg colour dithering (normal)

Normal Floyd-Steinberg dithering is the default. Some experimentation might be necessary to find the best conversion to Indexed, especially if the image consists of smooth color variations and large, solid color regions. Read on!

9.5.4 WHAT IS THE BEST CHOICE?

Given that the designer chooses to limit the color palette to one that is Web-safe, converting to Indexed format still requires making choices about the type of color distortion that is acceptable when it can't be avoided. Usually the choice depends on the type of image to be displayed.

If the image is a photograph, or one that has smooth color variations, chances are good that there are more than 256 colors in the image, and many will not be from the Web-safe palette. Normally, the color distortion to photos on an

8-bit display is not noticeable, and it could be argued that it is fruitless to convert the image to an Indexed format under these conditions. However, when photographs are mixed with other graphic materials the argument is no longer valid. Under these circumstances, the best choice is to dither. This is illustrated in Figure 9.28.

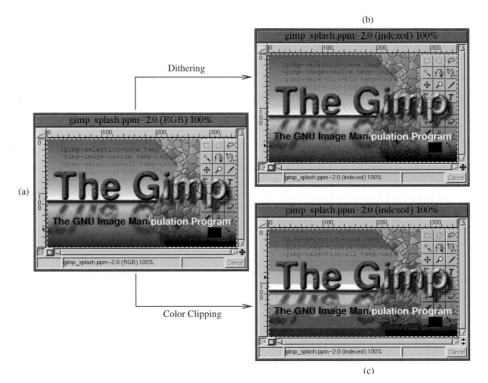

Figure 9.28: Choosing the Type of Color Distortion for Images with Smooth Color Variations

Figure 9.28(a) shows a splash screen used with version 1.0.4 of the GIMP. A dithered version of the splash screen, obtained using the Web-safe color palette, is shown in Figure 9.28(b). A color clipped version of the splash screen using the same palette is shown in Figure 9.28(c). Due to the heavy banding seen in Figure 9.28(c), the color distortion due to dithering, seen in Figure 9.28(b), seems much more acceptable. This example shows that for images with smoothly varying color, the dithered solution is better because clipping gives rise to a strongly objectionable color distortion.

If the image is not a photograph and does not have smoothly varying variations in color but rather large regions of constant color, the strategy is completely different. This is illustrated in Figure 9.29. Figure 9.29(a) shows a graphic design celebrating the 150th anniversary of the creation of the U.S. Department of the Interior. This design is constructed of four main colors: black, white, a blue consisting of $46^R 110^G 207^B$, and a yellow consisting of $241^R 214^G 47^B$. There are other colors in the image, but they are there for antialiasing (see Section 3.1.2) and sharpness (see Section 6.4.1). From the previous discussion, you can see that the blue and the yellow are not from the Web-safe palette, which only take RGB components from the set of values [0, 51, 102, 153, 204, 255]. This means that some color distortion will be introduced if the image is saved to Indexed format with the Web-safe palette. Indeed, Figure 9.29(b) shows the result of applying Floyd Steinberg dithering, and Figure 9.29(c) shows the result of color clipping.

The dithering in Figure 9.29(b) produces a very undesirable effect. The blue and yellow regions both suffer from unsightly color speckle. On the other hand, the color clipped version in Figure 9.29(c) produces a blue and a yellow that are slightly different than those of the original. Nevertheless, it is likely that this result is preferable because it preserves the homogeneity of the large, uniform color regions.

In conclusion, images that have a lot of detail and subtle color variations are better served by dithering than color clipping. Alternatively, images that have broad uniform color regions should avoid dithering and use color clipping. For images that consist of a mix of the two conditions, some experimentation is necessary. Unfortunately there are sometimes no easy choices.

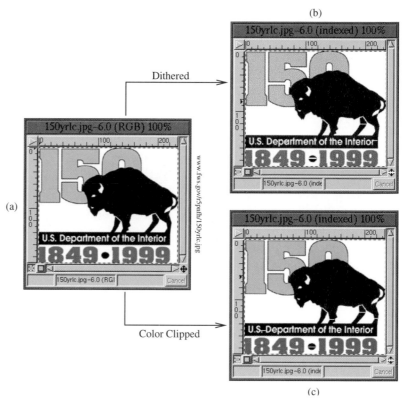

Figure 9.29: Choosing for Images with Large Uniform Color Regions

9.6 SEMI-TRANSPARENCY AND INDEXED IMAGES

Semi-transparency presents a particularly knotty problem when converting an image to Indexed format. This is a problem for indexed images because they only support alpha values of 0 (fully transparent) and 255 (fully opaque). When converting to Indexed format, partially transparent pixels (that is, with alpha values in the range 1 to 254) have their alpha values forced to 0 or 255. This is a problem for antialiasing (see Section 3.1.2) and for the general use of transparency in indexed images.

Fortunately, there is a solution. The `Semi-Flatten` plug-in is a work-around for the problem of semi-transparency in indexed images. This filter, found in the `Image:Filters/Colors` menu, requires knowing the background color that will be used beneath the semi-transparent image. If you can't determine the background color in advance, the `Semi-Flatten` filter cannot help you.

To use the `Semi-Flatten` filter, you must determine the color that will be behind the semi-transparent image, and you must specify it in the `Active Background Color` patch in the Toolbox window. The `Color Picker` tool can be useful for determining colors, and although the `Color Picker` automatically sets the `Active Foreground Color`, you can easily toggle this color to the background by clicking on the `Switch Colors` icon (the two-headed arrow above the foreground/background color patches in the Toolbox). The semi-flattening process combines the `Active Background Color` with the layer colors in proportion to the layer's alpha values.

As an example, Figure 9.30 illustrates how a conversion to Indexed format ruins the antialiasing of some text. Figure 9.30(a) shows a transparent layer containing the letter K from the Comicscartoon font at a size of 275 pixels. Antialiasing was turned on when the text was created; however, when this image is converted to indexed format the antialiasing is lost, as can be more plainly seen when the letter is placed over a yellow background. This is shown in Figure 9.30(b). The jagged staircase effect is clearly visible at the edges of the letter. Figure 9.30(c) shows the disposition of the two layers in the Layers dialog.

Figure 9.31 shows how using `Semi-Flatten` resolves the antialiasing problem. Figure 9.31(a) displays the Toolbox window, which shows that the `Active Background Color` patch has been set to the yellow color seen in Figure 9.30(b). Figure 9.31(b) shows a zoomed version of the result after applying `Semi-Flatten` to Figure 9.30(a). The edges of the letter K now show that the semi-transparent pixels that were used for antialiasing have taken on color values between the black of the letter and the yellow of the `Active Background Color`. Pixels that were fully transparent have remained so. The result of placing this layer over a yellow background layer is shown in Figure 9.31(c). You can see that the antialiasing effect has been conserved.

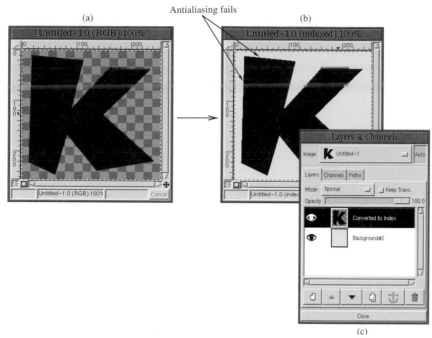

Figure 9.30: Antialiased Text After Conversion to Indexed...Yeeeks!

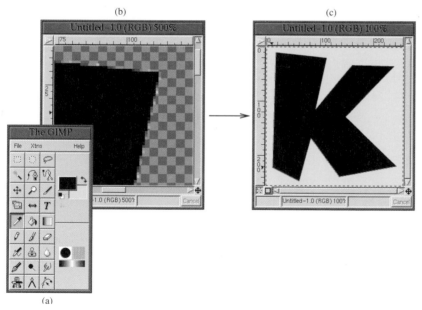

Figure 9.31: Using Semi-Flatten to Preserve the Effect of Semi-Transparency

9.7 Which Format: GIF or JPEG?

There are two image file formats that can be interpreted by all major Web browsers: GIF and JPEG. The question is which one is better? The answer is *it depends*. For Web-safe color, the answer is clear. Only GIF images can guarantee that almost every monitor will be able to display your image as you composed it on your own computer. This should be taken with a small grain of salt because the color balance of every monitor is a little different. However, within limits, GIF can provide pretty uniform access to your Web images if you follow the advice given in this chapter.

JPEG, on the other hand, is an image format that has two major features. The first is it saves images in 24-bit color. For photographs where there are typically subtle variations in color, 24 bits are required to get a high fidelity representation of the image. Of course, out on the Internet, only those who have high-color (16 or 24 bpp) systems can see the image as it was originally composed. The image is dithered for those with low-color (8 bpp) systems.

Alternatively, using only 8 bits of color for a photo is almost certainly insufficient to represent all its color variation. Thus, converting the image to GIF requires dithering anyway. The conclusion is that for most images having a high degree of color variation, which includes most photographs of real world scenes, the use of JPEG is clearly preferable. It allows those with high-color systems to view the image as it was originally prepared; whereas the degradation in image quality for those with low color systems is similar, whether the image is in GIF or JPEG format.

The second major feature of JPEG files is that they can provide a high degree of perceptually optimized image compression. This is useful especially for Web site designers concerned about the overall bandwidth required to view their site. JPEG image files can achieve much greater levels of compression than GIF files can. Furthermore, the degree to which an image is compressed using JPEG can be specified by the user. Thus, for any particular image, it is possible, by making several tries, to find just the right balance between minimizing the file size and maintaining the visual integrity of the image.

The conclusion is that for images with subtle variations, such as most photographs of real world scenes, use JPEG. For images that contain only a small number of colors, such as those created using the GIMP's painting or rendering tools, use a Web-safe color palette and save as a GIF.

REFERENCES

[1] Eric S. Raymond, *The New Hacker's Dictionary, 3rd Edition*, MIT Press, 1996.

[2] Karin and Olof S. Kylander, *The GIMP User Manual*, `http://manual.gimp.org`.

[3] Olof Kylander and Karin Kylander, *GIMP: The Official Handbook*, The Coriolis Group, 1999.

[4] Charles A. Poynton, *Frequently Asked Questions about Color*, `ftp://ftp.inforamp.net/pub/users/poynton/doc/colour/ColorFAQ.pdf`.

[5] William K. Pratt, *Digital Image Processing*, John Wiley & Sons, New York, 1991.

[6] Dan Margulis, *Professional Photoshop 5: The Classic Guide to Color Correction*, John Wiley & Sons, 1998.

[7] Ansel Adams, Robert Baker (Contributor), *The Negative (Ansel Adams Photography, Book 2)*, Little Brown & Co, Reprint 1995.

[8] Ansel Adams, Robert Baker (Contributor), *The Print (Ansel Adams Photography, Book 3)*, Little Brown & Co, Reprint 1995.

[9] Gregory Cosmo Haun, *Photoshop Collage Techniques*, Hayden Books, Indianapolis, Indiana, 1997.

[10] Barry Haynes and Wendy Crumpler, *Photoshop 4 Artistry*, New Riders Publishing, Indianapolis, Indiana, 1997.

[11] David Lai and Greg Simsic, *Photoshop 4 Type Magic*, Hayden Books, 1997.

[12] Lynda Weinman and Bruce Heavin and Ali Karp, *Coloring Web Graphics*, New Riders Publishing, 1996.

A

GIMP RESOURCES

There are many online resources that can be used to get additional information about the GIMP. The best place is the GIMP's home page, which can be found at

`http://www.gimp.org`

This Web site is full of information and resources for the GIMP. It contains FAQs, information about GIMP internals, installation help, and developer information. It is also a source for downloading both the current stable and developer's versions of the GIMP, as well as the archive of patterns, palettes, brushes, gradients, fonts, and scripts. Finally, this site also points to other sites displaying GIMP art, and to other important links.

There are two other sites related to `www.gimp.org`:

`http://registry.gimp.org`

`http://manual.gimp.org`

The first site is the repository for GIMP plug-in filters. This is where the latest versions of new and old filters can be found. The second site is the online reference manual written by Olof and Karin Kylander. This manual is also available as a printed book.[3]

A great place to ask questions about the GIMP is on the newsgroup:

`Comp.graphics.apps.gimp`

This is the place to look for answers to questions about the GIMP. As usual with newsgroups, it is considered polite to look through older postings for an answer before blindly posting your question, which might have already come up three times this week.

As for news and developments about the GIMP, there is no better place than GIMP News:

```
http://www.xach.com/gimp/news/index.html
```

This page will keep you abreast of everything going on in the GIMP world. It's a great place for us GIMP junkies. ;-)

Finally, more useful information is probably available right on your machine as man pages. Try checking out

```
% man gimp
```

for plenty of additional information.

B

KEYBOARD SHORTCUTS

The GIMP has a set of default keyboard shortcuts that are documented here. All the defaults are contained in a file in the directory ~/.gimp found in the user's home directory. The first time the GIMP is run this file is created and named menurc. You can modify the keyboard shortcuts by adding new ones or changing default entries to suit personal tastes. There are two ways to change the defaults. The first is by editing the file menurc. This is a good method when you want a major reorganization of the default keystrokes. The second method is interactive and produces a single addition or change while working in the GIMP. You do this by placing the mouse cursor over the menu item and then typing the desired keystrokes. As you type the keystrokes they appear to the right of the menu entry. The next time the function is to be used, it can be invoked by the new shortcut.

In the following tables, all the keyboard shortcuts are executed by typing them in the image window. A shortcut consists of a keystroke, perhaps in conjuction with the Shift, Control, or Alt modifier keys. The modifier keys are designated by S for Shift, C for Control, and A for Alt. Thus, the shortcut C-S-i, which produces the Info Window, is composed by simultaneously holding down the Control and Shift keys and then typing the letter i.

TABLE B.1: THE TOOLBOX FUNCTIONS

Tool Name	Keystroke	Full Path
Airbrush	a	Image:Tools/Airbrush
Bezier Select	b	Image:Tools/Bezier Select
Blend	l	Image:Tools/Blend
Bucket Fill	S-b	Image:Tools/Bucket Fill
Clone	c	Image:Tools/Clone
Color Picker	o	Image:Tools/Color Picker

Tool Name	Keystroke	Full Path
Convolve	v	Image:Tools/Convolve
Crop & Resize	S-c	Image:Tools/Crop & Resize
Default Colors	d	Image:Tools/Default Colors
Dodge & Burn	S-d	Image:Tools/DodgeBurn
Ellipse Select	e	Image:Tools/Ellipse Select
Eraser	S-e	Image:Tools/Eraser
Flip	S-f	Image:Tools/Flip
Free Select (Lasso)	f	Image:Tools/Free Select
Fuzzy Select (Magic Wand)	z	Image:Tools/Fuzzy Select
Ink	k	Image:Tools/Ink
Intelligent Scissors	i	Image:Tools/Intelligent Scissors
Magnify	S-m	Image:Tools/Magnify
Move	m	Image:Tools/Move
Paintbrush	p	Image:Tools/Paintbrush
Pencil	S-p	Image:Tools/Pencil
Rectangle Select	r	Image:Tools/Rect Select
Smudge	S-s	Image:Tools/Smudge
Swap Colors	x	Image:Tools/Swap Colors
Text	t	Image:Tools/Text
Transform	S-t	Image:Tools/Transform
XinputAirbrush	S-a	Image:Tools/XinputAirbrush

TABLE B.2: VIEW MENU FUNCTIONS

Function Name	Keystroke	Full Path
Info Window	C–S–i	Image:View/Info Window
Nav. Window	C–S–n	Image:View/Nav. Window
Shrink Wrap	C–e	Image:View/Shrink Wrap
Toggle Guides	C–S–t	Image:View/Toggle Guides
Toggle Rulers	C–S–r	Image:View/Toggle Rulers
Toggle Selection	C–t	Image:View/Toggle Selection
Toggle Statusbar	C–S–s	Image:View/Toggle Statusbar
Zoom In	=	Image:View/Zoom In
Zoom Out	–	Image:View/Zoom Out
1:1	1	Image:View/Zoom/1:1

TABLE B.3: SELECT MENU FUNCTIONS

Function Name	Keystroke	Full Path
All	C–a	Image:Select/All
Feather	C–S–f	Image:Select/Feather
Float	C–S–l	Image:Select/Float
Invert	C–i	Image:Select/Invert
None	C–S–a	Image:Select/None
Sharpen	C–S–h	Image:Select/Sharpen

TABLE B.4: FILE MENU FUNCTIONS

Function Name	Keystroke	Full Path
Close	C–w	Image:File/Close
New	C–n	Image:File/New
Open	C–o	Image:File/Open
Quit	C–q	Image:File/Quit
Save	C–s	Image:File/Save

TABLE B.5: EDIT MENU FUNCTIONS

Function Name	Keystroke	Full Path
Clear	C–k	Image:Edit/Clear
Copy	C–c	Image:Edit/Copy
Copy Named	C–S–c	Image:Edit/Copy Named
Cut	C–x	Image:Edit/Cut
Cut Named	C–S–x	Image:Edit/Cut Named

Function Name	Keystroke	Full Path
Fill	C-.	Image:Edit/Fill
Paste	C-v	Image:Edit/Paste
Paste Named	C-S-v	Image:Edit/Paste Named
Redo	C-r	Image:Edit/Redo
Undo	C-z	Image:Edit/Undo

TABLE B.6: LAYERS MENU FUNCTIONS

Function Name	Keystroke	Full Path
Anchor Layer	C-h	Image:Layers/Anchor Layer
Merge Visible Layers	C-m	Image:Layers/Merge Visible Layers

TABLE B.7: IMAGE MENU FUNCTIONS

Function Name	Keystroke	Full Path
Duplicate	C-d	Image:Image/Duplicate
Offset	C-S-o	Image:Image/Transforms/ Offset
Grayscale	A-g	Image:Image/Mode/ Grayscale
Indexed	A-i	Image:Image/Mode/Indexed
RGB	A-r	Image:Image/Mode/RGB

TABLE B.8: DIALOGS

Dialog Name	Keystroke	Full Path
Brushes	C-S-b	Image:Dialogs/Brushes
Gradients	C-g	Image:Dialogs/Gradients
Layers & Channels	C-l	Image:Dialogs/Layers & Channels
Palette	C-p	Image:Dialogs/Palette
Patterns	C-S-p	Image:Dialogs/Patterns

TABLE B.9: FILTER MENU FUNCTIONS

Function Name	Keystroke	Full Path
Re-show last	A-S-f	Image:Filters/Re-show last
Repeat last	A-f	Image:Filters/Repeat last

INDEX

Layers Palette, 37-38
legal issues, copyright of digital images, 11-12
Levels tool, 187-190
Lighten Only blending mode, 124-125, 170
lights
ambient, 276
Bump map filter. *See* Bump map filter
Emboss filter, 271-274
shadows, 276-288
Load Image dialog, 23-24
loading images, 23-24
low-color systems, Web-safe color palette, 321-322
Lower Layer function, 42
lowering layers, 42
luminance, 152-153

M-N

Magic Wand tool, 7, 72-73, 82, 97, 141-142, 335
Magnify tool, 335
Make Seamless plug-in, 317-318
man pages (GIMP), 333
Marching Ants (selections), 44, 70, 101
Mask To Selection function, 117
masks, 102-103. *See also* selections
channel masks. *See* channel masks
converting to selections/alpha channels, 131
layer masks. *See* layer masks
natural mask, finding, 136-143
refining selections, 132-135
tools, 117-130
troubleshooting, 143-144
Measure tool, 7, 56, 63, 234
memory management, 8-10
menus, opening as separate windows, 19
Merge Down function, 66
Merge Visible Layers function, 66, 337
merging layers, 66
Mermaid project, 247-256
midtones, finding, 199-200
Mode menu, 38, 122-125, 161
mouse cursor position, 19
Move tool, 7, 44, 48-50, 335
moving
layers, 48-49
selection boundaries, 85
selections, 47
moving dashes (Marching Ants), 44
multiple files, loading, 24
Multiply blending mode, 123-124, 166-168

name completion feature (Load Image dialog), 24
named buffers, 29
natural mask, finding, 136-143
Navigation Window, 31, 99, 336
neutral axis, 149
neutrals, balancing, 195-199
New function, 25, 336
New Image dialog, 25
New Layer function, 41, 44
New Point mode button (Bezier paths), 94
New View function, 32
newsgroups (GIMP), 332
noise, amplification, 219
None function, 86, 336
Normal blending mode, 162

O-P

Offset function, 277, 337
online resources for the GIMP, 332
opacity, 174-176. *See also* transparency
channel masks, setting, 107
editing layer masks, 125-127

Opacity slider, 38-39
Open function, 23, 336
opening menus as separate windows, 19
optimizing performance, 8
animations, 307-308
cache requirements, 8-10
color depth, 11
fonts, 10-11
RAM requirements, 8
video RAM requirements, 8
ordering. *See* lowering; raising
output value range, 191
Overlay blending mode, 169

paint tools, blending modes, 161
Paintbrush tool, 7, 118, 335
painting tools, masks, 118-119
Palette dialog, 337
palettes
Channels Palette, 104
Color Palette dialog, 22-23
Layers Palette, 37-38
Paths, 92-94
VisiBone2, 322
Web-safe color palette, 321-322
panner window, 19
panning in zoomed images, 31
panoramas, creating, 256-257
color and brightness corrections, 258-260
cropping and merging layers, 262-263
geometric distortion correction, 257-258
gradient blends, 260-262
repairing with Clone tool, 263
partially selected pixels. *See also* antialiasing
channel masks, 112
feathering selections, 81-82, 86
sharpening, 86
Paste As New function, 29
Paste function, 28, 43, 91, 337
Paste Into function, 28
Paste Named function, 29, 337
Paste Path function, 95
pasting, 28-30
layers, 226-227
selections, 91
PAT file format, 25
Path Transform Lock, 56, 65, 92-93
paths. *See* Bezier paths
Paths dialog, 19-20, 91-92
button bar, 96
Control Point Mode Buttons, 94-95
Paths menu, 95-96
Paths Palette, 92-94
Paths menu, 95-96
Paths Palette, 92-94
Pattern Selection dialog, 21, 264, 317, 337
Pencil tool, 7, 118, 335
performance optimization. *See* optimizing performance
Perspective option (Transform tool), 64-65
Perspective Transform dialog, 65
perturbation technique
Call of the Mermaid project, 254
case study, 222
removing color casts, 201-204
Through the Looking Glass project (reflective tin can), 239-240
photo touchup, 184
case study, 219-223
Clone tool, 210-213
removing color casts. *See* color casts, removing
sharpening images, 213-219
tonal range, 185-190
photo-montage, 224
photos. *See* digital images; panoramas

pixels, 34
interpolation, 56
partially selected. *See* partially selected pixels
remapping value ranges, 194
plug-ins
Checkerboard, 320
filters, troubleshooting, 33
Glass Tile, 129
ImageMap, 310-315
Make Seamless, 317-318
Semi-Flatten, 326-327
Spread, 129
Tile, 317
Waves, 129
positioning
layers, 48-51, 228-229
selections, 100
posterization (color distortion), 319
Preferences dialog, 26
primary colors, 146
problems. *See* troubleshooting
projects
Call of the Mermaid, 247-256
carved stencil project, 288-292
chiseled text project, 292-296
Destination Saturn, 240-247
drop shadow and punchout project, 284-288
Fish on Holiday, 225-231
Panoramas, 256-263
Through the Looking Glass (reflective tin can), 231-240
punchouts
carved stencil project, 290-291
creating, 280-283
drop shadow and punchout project, 284-288

Q-R

Quick Mask button, converting selections to/from channel masks, 19, 135-136
Quit function, 336

Raise Layer function, 42
raising layers, 42
RAM requirements, 8, 318
Re-show last function, 28, 216, 337
Rectangle Select tool, 7, 70-71, 84-85, 97, 335
Redo function, 26, 337
remapping pixel value ranges, 194
removing
color casts. *See* color casts, removing
geometric distortions, 257-258
parts of images, 210-213, 221
rendering images, 264
Bucket Fill tool, 264-267
Bump map filter, 274-276
carved stencil project, 288-292
chiseled text project, 292-296
drop shadow and punchout project, 284-288
Emboss filter, 271-274
gradients, 267-270
shadows, 276-283
reordering. *See* lowering; raising
Repeat last function, 337
Replace mode (frame animation), 300
requirements
cache, 8-10
RAM, 8
video RAM, 8, 318
resizing
images, 52-55
layers, 51, 56-59
selections, 86
resolution, setting, 25
resources for the GIMP, 332
reversing. *See* inverting

RGB colorspace, 25–26, 148–149, 152–156
RGB function, 26
Rotate function, 60
rotating images/layers, 60–63, 233–236
Rotation Information dialog, 61

S

Sample Merged option (Tool Options dialog), 82
saturation, 150, 154–155
Saturation blending mode, 172
Save As function, 24, 312
Save as GIF options dialog, 303
Save function, 336
Save Image dialog, 24–25, 302
Save Options menu, file formats, 25
Save to Channel function, 87–88, 105, 111
saving
  images, 24–25, 33, 67
  selections to channel masks, 87–88, 104–106
Scale Image dialog, 51–52
Scale Image function, 51
Scale Layer function, 55–56
scaling
  images, 51–52
  layers, 51, 55–56, 63–64, 227–228
Scaling dialog, 63
Scaling Information dialog, 228
Screen blending mode, 123–124, 167–169
Script-Fu, 315
scripts, type effects, 315
scroll bars, 19
Select menu functions, keyboard shortcuts, 336
selecting
  multiple files, 24
  type of color distortion, 323–325
selection tools, masks, 119–120
selections, 68–69. *See also* masks
  adding, 83
  antialiasing, 78–81
  borders, 86–87
  boundaries, moving, 85
  By Color function, 88–89
  Call of the Mermaid project, 247–250
  clip books, 225–226
  combining, 82–85, 98–99
  converting
    to Bezier paths, 89–90
    to channel masks/layer masks/ alpha channels, 131
    to/from channel masks, 135–136
    to layer masks, 117
  cutting/copying/pasting, 91
  deselecting everything, 86
  feathering, 81–82, 86
  floats. *See* floats
  growing, 86
  guidelines, 96–97
  intersecting, 84
  inverting, 85
  Marching Ants, 44
  moving, 47
  positioning, 100
  refining with masks, 132–135
  saving to channel masks, 87–88, 104–106
  selecting everything, 85
  sharpening, 86
  shrinking, 86
  Stroke function, 91
  subtracting, 83–84
  Toggle Selection function, 90
  troubleshooting, 101

types of, 69–78
zoom view, 99–100
Semi-Flatten plug-in, 326–327
semi-transparency and indexed images, 325–327
Set Canvas Size dialog, 52
Settings (ImageMap) dialog, 311
shadows, 276–283
  drop shadows. *See* drop shadows
  finding, 199–200
  punchouts. *See* punchouts
  tonal range, 185–187
  uses for blending modes, 180–182
shapeburst gradients, 268–270
sharefonts collection, 10
Sharpen function, 86, 336
sharpening
  images, 213–219, 223
  selections, 86
Shear Information dialog, 64
shearing layers, 64
shortcuts. *See* keyboard shortcuts
Shrink function, 86
Shrink Wrap function, 31, 336
shrinking selections, 86
Smudge tool, 7, 118, 335
snapping property of guides, 49
Spread filter, 129–130
square selections, 71
status bar, 18–19
stencils, carved stencil project, 288–292
Stroke function, 91
Subtract blending mode, 165–166
Subtract From Selection function, 110
subtracting selections, 83–85
SuperNova filter, 305
Swap Colors tool, 7, 21, 335
switching foreground and background colors, 7, 21, 335
system requirements. *See* requirements

T

text, chiseled text project, 292–296
Text tool, 7, 10, 335
three-dimensional images. *See* rendering images
Threshold option (Tool Options dialog), 82
Threshold tool
  compared to Magic Wand tool, 141–142
  finding natural mask, 136–141
  finding shadows/midtones/highlights, 199–200
  improving contrast, 204–206
Through the Looking Glass project (reflective tin can), 231–240
Tile plug-in, 317
tileable backgrounds in Web pages, 317–318
timing information (animations), 299
titles of Bezier paths, changing, 92
To Path function, 89–90
Toggle Guides function, 50, 336
Toggle Rulers function, 19, 336
Toggle Selection function, 47, 51, 90, 336
Toggle Statusbar function, 19, 336
tonal range, 185
  case study, 219–220
  highlights and shadows, 185–187
  Levels tool, 187–190
Tool Options dialog, 17, 61, 78–82, 264
Toolbox window, 7, 16–17
tools. *See* names of individual tools
touching up photos. *See* photo touchup
Transform tool, 7, 55–56, 60–65, 335
transparency, 174–176. *See also* opacity
  channel masks, setting, 107
  editing layer masks, 125–127

semi-transparency and indexed images, 325–327
troubleshooting, 66
troubleshooting
  blending modes, 183
  colorspaces, 183
  layers, 66–67
  masks, 143–144
  plug-in filters, 33
  saving images, 33
  selections, 101
type effects, 315–317

U–V

Undo function, 26, 337
Undo History function, 26–27
unions, adding selections, 83
Unsharp Mask, 214–219

value (colors), 151
Value blending mode, 172–173
Value Channel
  improving contrast, 204–206
  Sharpening, 218
video RAM, system requirements, 8, 318
View menu functions, keyboard shortcuts, 336
views, New View function, 32
visibility
  layer, 38
  channel masks, 106–107
  image layer, toggling off for layer masks, 116
  layer masks, 116–117
VisiBone2 palette, 322

W–Z

warping images (IWarp filter), 308–309
Waves filter, 129
Web pages
  animations. *See* animations
  clickable image maps, 309–315
  colors, 318–319
    converting to Indexed color, 322–323
    types of distortion, 319–325
    Web-safe color palette, 321–322
  GIF file format, compared to JPEG, 327–328
  semi-transparency of images, 325–327
  tileable backgrounds, 317–318
  type effects, 315–317
Web sites
  digital image sources, 12
  GIMP, 332
  GIMP News, 333
Web-mirroring software, 13
Web-safe color palette, 321–322
Window Info dialog, 19, 199
windows
  help browser, 32–33
  image window, 18–19
  Layers & Channels, 36–37
  Navigation Window, 31, 99
  opening menus as, 19
  panner window, 19
  Toolbox, 16–17
XCF file format, 25, 33
XinputAirbrush tool, 7, 335
Zoom In function, 31, 336
Zoom Out function, 31, 336
Zoom tool, 7, 30–31, 99–100
zoom view, selections, 99–100
zoomed images
  New View function, 32
  panning in, 31